PASTORAL SYMPHONY

PASTORAL SYMPHONY

A Bumpkin's Tribute
to Country Joys

CHAPMAN PINCHER

SWAN·HILL
PRESS

Dedication

To all who have shared their country amenities,
so generously, with me.

Copyright © 1993 by Chapman Pincher

First published in the UK in 1993
by Swan Hill Press
an imprint of Airlife Publishing Ltd

British Library Cataloguing in Publication Data
A catalogue record for this book
is available from the British Library

ISBN 1 85310 434 5

Printed by Livesey Ltd., Shrewsbury

Swan Hill Press

an imprint of Airlife Publishing Ltd.
101 Longden Road, Shrewsbury SY3 9EB, England

Contents

FOREWORD

In early youth I convinced myself that the kind of life likely to give me greatest pleasure and satisfaction was that of a working country squire — not a country gentleman, because my nature and circumstances demanded that I would always need to do some labour. This book is the story of how, though required to earn my living in towns and always with modest resources, I managed to achieve my ambition well enough not to envy anyone.

It happens that almost all the major friendships and professional contacts which have moulded my life were made in the country — mainly through shooting and fishing — while others which had originated in towns were cemented in the country. Should I be accused of name-dropping in this joyful celebration of my country days, and nights, I would make no apology because it is my deliberate wish to put on record some anecdotes, which may interest others, about famous people who happened to be country friends. As I learned from my north-country days, and has been amply confirmed, 'There's nowt so queer as folk', to which I would add, 'And nowt so full of surprises'. So, whenever I have observed or heard anything special, it has been my habit to make a note of it that day and file it. The conversations which I quote are from those files.

True ruralists are those who not only live away from towns but are grateful for it every morning they awaken and for whom any prospect of being permanently transported to an urban environment would be horrendous. For them the countryside is a place for all seasons, where all weathers and landscape conditions contribute their quota of contentment.

In my lifetime the countryside and everything in it have taken a terrible beating from most forms of dubious progress. Much of it remains, but I have been extremely lucky to have experienced it when it was at something like its best. This book is a token of my thanks for that good fortune.

CHAPTER 1

FORGING THE BONDS

A 'bumpkin' is defined by my dictionary as 'an awkward country fellow'. I am certainly a country fellow, having spent most of my life there, and many people have found me awkward and still do. I reckon that I can claim to have been born in the country because I emerged into the world in a tent — in the small military post of Ambala, in the Punjab where, in March 1914, my father was serving His Majesty King George V in the capacity of drum-major in the Northumberland Fusiliers — the famous 'Fighting Fifth'. An event which would establish Ambala's place in the history of villainy had already occurred two years earlier — the birth of Kim Philby, the traitor who would eventually occupy a fair slice of my time.

My mother, who was accompanying my father — camp-following she called it — regaled me many times, in harrowing detail, with the account of how, shortly after my birth, a lizard fell from the top of the tent on to her hospital bed and shed its tail, which continued to writhe. Whether it was that shuddering experience or the sight of me, my mother, though a devout Roman Catholic, firmly decided that she would never have another child, a vow to which she adhered after returning to England when I was a few months old. It could not have been the lizard which sparked off my interest in biology but, in various ways, that endlessly fascinating subject has been a dominating force in my life.

My strange name, too, is redolent of the English countryside as it used to be. A chapman was a pedlar who walked from village to village selling small goods while a pincher was not a horse thief but the man responsible for looking after the village pound, where stray animals were incarcerated until claimed. Hardly a distinguished ancestry but some of the aristocracy are no better placed in that respect.

A child born into a British regiment on foreign soil was simply registered with the Orderly Room, almost as part of the baggage, so I was never issued with a birth certificate and have never been able to acquire one. Save for Army records, which may no longer exist, the only documentary evidence of my birth is a certificate of the baptism of Henry Chapman Pincher signed by Father O'Brien at the Church of the Holy Redeemer in Ambala. It was to save me from becoming stateless when the concept of UK citizenship was introduced after the Second World War.

On our return to England we resided, during my early years, in the then fairly small market town of Darlington, which had easy access by bicycle, bus or 'Shank's pony', as we called our legs, to the magnificent countryside of upper Teesdale, Swaledale and Wensleydale, where I spent as much time as possible. I had the good fortune to have relatives living in the unspoilt, ancient town of Richmond, the original Richmond on the River Swale, where the 'sweet lass' once lived on the hill, and which was an easy cycle ride.

For as long as I can remember the countryside has held joys for me which have never been approached by any city, not even those with which I have fallen in love, like Venice, Rome and Siena. I admire fine architecture but the best is dwarfed in all respects by the grandeur of a rolling landscape. The conflict between town and country, which the latter has always won when conscious choice has been possible, has conditioned my whole life, changing it on many occasions, sometimes crucially, or preventing changes which I could not have withstood without unhappiness.

I have always been conscious of the peculiar beauty of the British countryside in all seasons, the sheer awareness of being in it generating pleasure, and my fierce opposition to any threats to it has not made me popular with some of my developer friends. Unlike most boys, I was never much enamoured of what was then called the 'seaside' with bucket-and-spade holidays holding little appeal, but I have always felt bonded to fields, woods and streams. I dreamed of being a farmer, and though that never happened, I have only ever felt really content and at ease in the country. During the many years I worked in Fleet Street, with a grace-and-favour company flat near Piccadilly, I almost always commuted by train and car to wake up in country air and surroundings, a fact which the taxman found hard to credit when assessing me on my 'beneficial interest' from the flat. It may be my love of the countryside which generated my hatred of traitors, to which I have devoted so much time in research and writing, for by 'my country' I mean the territory — as Sir Walter Scott expressed the sentiment in 'Breathes there the man with soul so dead, Who never to himself hath said "This my own, my native land!"' From early boyhood I have felt an umbilical attachment to the exposed crust of land known as Britain and the few male ancestors I have been able to trace lived mainly as farmers or miners who worked the earth, or as soldiers who protected it. (One of them, far back in time, is believed to have been a Washington, closely related to George of that ilk, whose family came from the small town of Washington in Co. Durham.) I have to confess to being an old-style patriot who prefers his country to any other.

Being attached to the British soil, perhaps to a pathological extent, has its disadvantages because whenever I am abroad I am soon wishing I was home, which tends to infuriate my wife when we are on holiday. Often, when, on foreign assignments for my old newspaper, the *Daily Express*, I found myself in exciting cities with a wad of the office's traveller's cheques, yet I was usually plotting to devise a way of catching the next plane back home. Short of death itself, I can imagine no more dreadful sentence than banishment and how people voluntarily exile themselves from Britain to save paying taxes I will never understand.

As long as I can recall I was interested in natural history and always had some live creatures around me, from slow worms and sticklebacks to white mice, rabbits and a disabled duck called Willie One-wing. There were newts, tadpoles and dragon-fly larvae in every country pond to stock my small aquarium but my prize possession, on a table by my bed, was an old but effective microscope. My bedroom, with a Keep Out! sign, also functioned as my museum with fossils from the River Tees, mineral specimens, pressed flowers, mounted butterflies, birds, eggs, and even nests, which were inclined to make an unpopular mess. With blackbirds and song-thrushes nesting in almost every bush, yellow-hammers in every lane and skylarks in profusion, taking the eggs of wild birds was not a crime and many boys had a collection. I also owned several cases of stuffed birds which my mother had acquired for me, but I eventually dismantled them to use the feathers to make trout flies. A pair of woodcock were especially valuable in providing the hackle wings for a killing wet fly in the fast northern rivers called a woodcock and orange, while a snipe made another favourite, snipe and purple. A delightful old Scotsman taught me how to tie the flies and even made me a pair of hackle pliers out of a bicycle spoke which, I remember, cost me sixpence to buy.

Whether my love of rivers fired my interest in fishing or *vice versa* I cannot recall but by the age of ten I was taking off for the day on my bicycle, whenever I could, to fish the Tees or the Swale. My parents had bought me canvas waders and brogues and though both rivers were dangerous and subject to regular flooding, it never occurred to them to worry about my safety out there alone in fast water. Nor were they ever concerned about my long bicycle rides with my rod and landing net strapped to the crossbar. Motor traffic was light and accosting of children, especially boys, was unheard of. As with terrorism, violence against children is usually perpetrated by what can only be called 'human trash' and there seems to have been much less of that around when I was young. Nevertheless, I suppose that my parents' lack of anxiety would be considered remarkable today and perhaps reprehensible, though the attitude of my friends' parents was similar. Their confidence was complimentary but, perhaps not so soundly based as they imagined, as I had several narrow escapes from drowning, which I was careful never to mention to them. On one very hot August afternoon two friends and I were spearing eels in the Tees, near Gainford, the river being so low that its bouldered and cobbled bed, some seventy yards wide, was almost fully exposed. We retired to the river bank to prepare the eels for cooking and, on looking round, were astonished to see the water lapping less than a yard away from us. The flash flood, caused by some distant storm on the moors, must have come down in a wall of water and had we still been lifting stones looking for eels we would surely have been drowned. Yet we had heard nothing and our emotional response was not relief but annoyance at having missed the opportunity of seeing the wall. It was the first of many narrow escapes, in various circumstances, in what, I suppose, has been something of a charmed life.

I think that, perhaps, in those days, as had been even commoner in previous centuries, parents were less coddling with their children and more inclined to let them take their chances, if they gave much thought to it at all. It may have been a mental hangover from the days when death in childhood was much more commonplace that it is now.

For some inexplicable reason fishing grabbed me so intensely that it became something of an obsession and I was soon extolling its joys in the school magazine. Nobody in my family had been interested in fishing but a slightly older boy who was keen took me with him one day and that was enough. Oddly, he soon gave it up and our friendship ended. How often one owes a deep debt of gratitude to someone who quickly fades out of one's life!

My first rod and reel were fairly crude and bought second-hand for a few shillings. In the window of a tackle shop in Richmond there was a shiny split-cane fishing rod called The Sapper and I never passed the window without looking at it, longingly. It was priced at two guineas, which was a great deal of money in those days, and for me such a rod remained only a dream until a kind great-aunt eventually bought me one. The purchase of a rod today is still an occasion but with much less charm.

The only time my mother complained about my fishing mania was when hordes of bluebottles suddenly emerged out of the tins of maggots which I had hidden in spare rooms. My attachment to maggots, then my favourite bait — their slightly ammoniacal smell is still delightfully nostalgic — frequently caused social problems. I remember sitting in a train on the way to Catterick Bridge, where for the sum of sixpence a month, paid to the Darlington Silver Trout Angling Association, I could fish many miles of the lovely Swale. Maggots from an insecurely tied linen bag in my wickerwork creel, which was on the luggage rack, began to fall into the brim of a black straw hat worn by a lady sitting beneath. Fortunately she alighted at an earlier station without noticing and may later have wondered how she had acquired this wriggling adornment.

Maggots then cost three old pennies for a cocoa-tin full compared with three pounds now but, to save the money to buy hooks, I used to visit slaughter-houses, scrabbling in the entrails for maggots which left me smelling none too sweetly. I also used to breed them myself by hanging up a sheep's head over a tray of bran in an outhouse until the smell betrayed my secret and my mother committed the writhing mass to the bin.

A wickerwork creel, which always had a hole in the lid wide enough to slide a fish through, had an additional advantage for the successful young angler. I remember catching a three-quarter-pound trout in a little stream, call the Cockerbeck, to which I had walked, and then taking a long detour through the centre of Darlington on the way back so that everybody could spot the speckled trout, which I had arranged so that it was easily visible through the hole.

The men in the fishing club were encouraging but ribbed me when I travelled with them to Catterick Bridge on the little train, which we called the Richmond Flyer. One day, on the return journey, when I triumphantly produced a three-pound chub, a notoriously coarse and bony fish, one of them claimed to know the only way to cook it — 'Get two clean wooden boards slightly larger than the fish and smear them with butter. Add salt and pepper, put the fish between the boards and cook in a slow oven. Remove after one hour then throw the fish away and eat the boards.'

What halcyon days they were! I vividly recall sitting as a fourteen-year-old in magical contentment in the local cinema on a Friday evening knowing that I had two days free before school on Monday and that one of them was to be spent on the river. No anticipation of any adult holiday — in the Caribbean, in Kenya, in Italy or anywhere else has ever generated such a frisson of delight. It was a real and very conscious sensation, almost a tingling feeling, an emotional surge, a quiver, affecting the body, especially the skin, as well as the mind.

The prodigious period of my childhood followed my father's decision to take over an inn, called The Comet, in the village of Croft, three miles outside Darlington and close to the bridge where the Tees separates South Durham from Yorkshire. It was named after a famous locally-bred bull which became the progenitor of the widespread Shorthorn breed and was sold in 1810 for the then enormous sum of 1000 guineas. By coincidence, I had caught my very first fish, a quarter-pound roach, off the wall immediately in front of the pub in 1924. The pub was so close to the river that I awoke each morning to the sound of it and during heavy floods, water came into the beer-cellar. On one occasion I donned my waders to recover some barrels which had floated off their stands and irritated my father by being more interested in the possibility that, somehow, fish might have found their way in.

I also awoke to the sound of the blacksmith, a master farrier, who was usually at work, hammering in his forge by 7.30 a.m. From my bed I could even hear the hiss of the hot horseshoes plunged into the well. The smithy, without a crackless window, its floor thick with the dust and iron scale of ages, old nails and the hoof parings of horses long since dead, was anything but cosy but I spent many an odd hour there for, without notice, the old man was capable of a commentary, with accurate dates, of any event which had occurred in the parish in the previous four decades.

Going to live in Croft was a mutation moment in my life. Most of us, probably all, can pinpoint a few moments which have proved decisive in changing the course of our existence — a chance event or meeting which, while perhaps seeming trivial at the time, proves to be crucial with life taking on a new dimension. Mutation moments is an accurate description of them whether they are immediately obvious or pass unnoticed at the time, as is often the case.

While the landlord and his wife, my beloved parents, slaved long hours for scant reward, life as the landlord's son was one long round of pleasure with a continuous flow of invitations — 'Come on, ferreting!', 'Come on, rook-shooting!' There were sudden summonses to harvest shoots when the last quarter of an acre of a cornfield being reaped would be literally shaking with rabbits.

I confess that I followed the local otter hounds which, though shaming now, was quite 'natural' for a country boy when otters were common enough for the male's most peculiar bone to adorn the 'albert' watch-chains of hunting men, the dog-otter being unusual in having a bone in its 'pizzle', as its erectile organ was called. The hounds never killed while I was there and I gave up following them after I watched a pair of otters repeatedly sliding down a mud path while I was fishing.

In the autumn 'Come cub-hunting, tomorrow!' with the offer of a mount was a wonderful treat. Horse-racing dominated the pub conversation, those customers who consulted the bar's newspapers being interested only in the racing pages. Later on, after an interval of about ten years, I re-encountered a close farmer friend, when I happened to be wearing a bow-tie. His opening greeting after this long separation was 'Ah, Dickey-bow! If it had been running tomorrow I would have backed it'.

There was a riding school attached to the pub but my greatest joy arose from an old man who was in charge of three miles of fishing starting almost at the pub doorstep. His master lived abroad and he gave me sole run of the river which was stuffed with trout and coarse fish. I spent so much time there that my father predicted that I would end up with fins but fish were not my only interest. There was a wonderful, quiet road connecting Croft with the next village, Middleton Tyas, which was so rich in wild flowers, birds, butterflies and other insects that I called it Omnology Lane — because everything could be studied there. When it was a ribbon of moonlight I would stride it with my dog listening for owls and vixens. These days it is a qualification to be 'street-wise'. I have always preferred to be 'lane-wise'.

In the evenings I became a dab hand at dominoes and darts and through such activities developed a strong feeling of kinship with farmers, agricultural labourers, gamekeepers and fish-watchers which has remained with me. Perhaps through my long association with such forthright characters I have always been strong in what I call the syfas (sod you for a start) factor though, perhaps, curt impatience with one's fellows is more a feature of life in big cities. I have also remained fairly strong in northern accent. Among the boys I knew it was unacceptable to 'talk posh', almost as though 'posh' was another language, and I have never made a conscious effort to speak like southerners, though most of my life has been spent among them.

Looking back, what was, perhaps, extraordinary was the extent to which I was aware, so young, of the privileges I enjoyed. I recall saying to a friend in 1936 that if we were killed in the war which looked inevitable, and in which we knew we would have to serve, we had enjoyed a great life. He agreed. Happily we both survived to continue our country interests, his as a doctor in the Wensleydale town of Masham, where I shared his hospitality and we fished together, over many years.

Among those interests, as boys, was sex to which I had been introduced at the age of twelve by a sixteen-year-old maid, who was probably rather advanced for her years in those days. When my father had been briefly stationed at Lichfield and I was, perhaps six years old, we had lodged with a family who had a young daughter a couple of years or so older. I vividly recall saying to my mother 'When she stretches up you can see the tops of her stockings', to which my mother replied, sharply, 'But you shouldn't look!' That had been my first experience of one of the major secrets of purely sexual attraction — it is what he is not supposed to see that the human male finds exciting. The girl in a bikini is of scant interest: the girl in her underwear, which may show less, excites. So when an even more thrilling opportunity was presented to me, six years later, by such an exciting mentor as the maid, whom my mother had instructed to address me as 'Master Harry', I was delighted to exploit it, with repeat performances whenever possible. We were not at risk because desire and its pleasurable climax are quite separate from potency, which I had not then acquired.

Indirectly, it was fishing which led to that premature initiation. One winter evening, when my mother and father were both safely out for several hours, being then deeply involved in the Darlington Theatre Royal, she as an actress, he as manager, a boy called, by arrangement, to see some fishing tackle catalogues I had collected. To my surprise, the maid answered the door, told the boy I was out and rushed up to my bedroom, where I found her in an inviting posture. The visit had given her the opportunity to get into Master Harry's thick head a message which, no doubt, she had been trying to intrude by subtler methods. The two 'fs' have been traditionally associated in northern climes, where both are said to be widely enjoyed in the summer while in the winter there is no fishing. It was an engaging experience, as a twelve-year-old, to sit in the back row at school and think about what might happen again that evening if my parents happened to be out, as they usually were at the theatre. I recall grinning inwardly as the Headmaster, who took us for scripture, unexpectedly encountered the word 'fornication' while reading the Bible to us and hastily dismissed it as 'something that was rife at that time.'

I did not tell any of my pals of my good fortune, not even the fishing friend, suspecting, perhaps, that he would want to share it because he was as precocious as I was and just as subject to early teenage sexual fantasies. By some argument, which I cannot recall, he once convinced me that we were both in urgent need of pubic hairs as we had been invited to accompany my mother to a concert in a remote village, called Thornton Rust, where she would be reciting monologues. A supper and dance were to follow and my friend insisted that we could not attend with any degree of panache without the adornment which neither of us possessed. So, over the next fortnight, we anointed ourselves, daily, with Vaseline, which was rumoured to do the trick. It failed but how we expected to capitalize on a successful result, I cannot imagine.

In those days the country probably played a more important role in sexual education than it does today. Most young couples living in towns had to go into the country for sex because most parents would not tolerate frolics in the parlour. Society was much less openly permissive — indeed, the word was unknown — but we still managed because barns, hedgebacks and hay-ricks were always handy in the country. Indeed, there was a rural rhyme, 'Hooray, hooray, the First of May! Hedgeback bucking begins today!' Perhaps it is no coincidence that early sex has long been referred to as 'sowing wild oats' which, after all, can only be done in the countryside. A 'roll in the hay' has also entered the language, though it is not to be recommended if the crop is old and musty.

A more specialized encounter — what might be called 'a roll in the props' — occasionally came my way as a result of theatrical activities when I played the occasional juvenile part, such as Sherlock Holmes's boy assistant, with the Darlington repertory company. It was surprising what there was to be seen, without peeping, backstage in the dressing rooms. I recall being goggle-eyed in the leading lady's dressing room, where I had been sent on some errand, as she lifted her skirts, lowered her knickers and heaved herself on to the wash-basin, the loo being down a flight of steps. During the six months of each year when the repertory company rested and the theatre staged weekly revues and variety shows I continued my backstage visits. Some of the chorus girls were only too happy to promote the education of the manager's son in handy places behind sections of painted scenery, while it amused some of the men, who assumed that I might enter the acting profession, to let me into such arcane secrets as the meaning of the letters LDTD, penned in the visitor's books of actors' digs. While not wishing to make such precious knowledge commonplace I am prepared to reveal that the first two letters stand for 'Landlady's Daughter'.

The child was certainly father of this man in so many respects and my boyhood interests, including sex, have stretched, unbroken through middle into old age. In my maturity I have enjoyed the best of everything but never with quite the magic of childhood.

CHAPTER 2

THE EAGER LEARNER

In 1923 I won a scholarship to the Darlington Grammar School but being almost a year younger than anyone else, I spent most of my time there in a daze until, some two years later, my father received a letter warning that unless I was prepared to work I would be required to vacate my place to someone who would. I was so frightened of the shame of being thrown out that I did begin to work and have never stopped since. In fact, work gradually became such an obsession that I have never been able to relax without some feeling of guilt about wasting time.

The only subject with which I failed to get to grips, because it was so badly taught, was physics and my dislike of it led to a mutation moment which changed my whole life. The headmaster came into the classroom to announce that biology, which had not been taught to any advanced degree, could, in future, be taken instead of physics as a major subject. He was looking for volunteers and I immediately seized the chance of saying goodbye to my dreaded subject for something to which I was already devoted. Further, I greatly liked the biology master, W.W. Allen, known to the boys as 'Toffee' because Allen's toffee was sold in the tuckshop. I have often thought that if I had been absent with a cold that day my whole life might have been completely different.

Allen, to whom I owe an enormous debt, fired my imagination by opening the bud of a wild poppy and unfolding the crinkled petals. I had done this as a child but what Allen pointed out was the extraordinary fact that the petals had developed inside the tightly confined space of the bud in a most intricate and predetermined manner so that they could eventually unfold into flat surfaces. How this was programmed by the plant's genes was mind-boggling and I think that event, which I recollect so colourfully, triggered off the interest in genetics which was to take me to King's College, London. He also interested me in the marvel of symmetry, a mystery which we all take for granted. Why should our two hands, which are fairly remote from each other be almost the same size and shape, as are the other paired parts of the body? The subject has still not been studied much. Neither has the capacity of the twigs of a bush or tree to grow, thickly, into space without touching each other.

He took a selected few of us on nature rambles, on fungus forays, to ponds, on visits to heronries and other bird sanctuaries. One such was a colony of black-headed gulls on a moorland tarn near Low Row in Swaledale. Many years later I would stay with the moor's owner, Earl Peel, to shoot grouse but, delightful though that experience was, it was not as magical as wading out to the gulls' nests.

In those days it was customary to carry a tin satchel called a vasculum so that flowers, ferns and other plants could be collected without crushing them, an activity which may now be illegal. Becoming a biologist, as I called myself then and still do, induced me to examine every experience critically in biological terms and one of them, which happened when I was fourteen or fifteen, has continued to intrigue me ever since.

Round about 1930 I visited the excellent Carnival at Darlington run on behalf of various charities. The large fairground contained a booth in which a woman was subjected to what were claimed, by the barker, to be X-rays. What I witnessed there in the company of perhaps a dozen others, including my mother, for an entrance fee of three old pence, was quite astonishing and remains vivid after sixty years. There was no stage and no mirrors. A fully clothed woman appeared from behind a curtain and stood on the grass no more than ten feet from the audience, which was restrained only by a wooden barrier. No screen or anything else separated the woman from us. There was a loud whirring sound from behind the curtain — from the alleged X-ray machine — and very slowly the woman's clothes, her hair and her skin disappeared into a fuzzy outline while all the bones of her body became clearly visible. This was no optical trick with mirrors because the bones were not like those of a dry skeleton but were living bones, pink, with blood in them. This was especially true of the skull. Also the fact that they appeared so slowly and in three-dimensional depth ruled out any sleight of hand. After perhaps two or three minutes the whirring ceased, the bones faded and the clothing and features reappeared but, again, slowly.

I have described this experience to eminent scientists who assured me that X-rays could not possibly be responsible and, since the performance was being repeated so often, they would have killed the woman. However, I do recall seeing a small paragraph in one of the Darlington newspapers, probably *The Northern Echo*, a few weeks after the Carnival, stating that the performance had been banned — I think in Sunderland — because of danger to the woman and, I believe, to the audience. If it was a trick it was the best I have ever seen. I do not think that it was. Though mass hallucinations have been recorded this was not one of them. It would be quite impossible to turn one on to order many times a day.

Around the same time, my mother was with me on another occasion which I recall equally vividly but with less pleasure. My schoolboy biological training had made me think critically about evolution, our relationship with other creatures and about religion. Having been baptized a Roman Catholic, I had attended several Catholic schools when very young and was required to go to Mass in Darlington, a three-mile bus journey from Croft, but the more I thought about the faith the less I could accept it. I was not popular when, in an essay on photosynthesis, I wrote, bumptiously but with truth — 'A great preacher once expressed the popular fallacy that the lilies of the field toil not neither do they spin but he was a carpenter and had never studied botany.' I could no longer stomach the devoutly-held concept of angels with feathered wings, because the musculature would not permit of six limbs, while flapping flight would be impossible, anyway, where there was no air. (When I told my Catholic grandmother that I thought my biology master was probably an atheist she snapped 'Something ought to happen to him then!' — hardly a Christian observation.)

All my life I had been exhorted about the dangers of wordly sin to my 'immortal soul'. While in a class of seven-year-olds at a convent prep school, a nun had assured us that our souls were like white sheets spattered with ink. But nobody could ever tell me what a soul really was. Some said it was just the force, or spirit, which animates the body and lives on after death. Others equated it with the mind. Priests said that it is something which remains when the body dies and lives on eternally. On any of these counts I couldn't see why apes, dogs and all other creatures shouldn't have souls, which the Catholic faith denied.

I expressed my misgivings by ceasing to go to Mass or to communion and while my mother was dismayed she did not say much, though privately she went on praying for my redemption. Sadly, having been strikingly beautiful, and aware of it, she had contracted the disorder of the thyroid known, in those days, as Grave's Disease, not because of its lethality but after the doctor who first described it. It was distressing enough through its effects on revving up the metabolism but the protrusion of the eyes which ensued was disfiguring, though not so much as my mother believed as she looked into the mirror. When, after two years in which, to use her phrase, she had 'stormed heaven' with prayer, her symptoms were unrelieved, it was inevitable that she would come to believe that she was being punished by God for permitting her son to lose his faith. My riposte that it was a poor sort of God who would take such vengeance on the innocent produced the usual response that God moves in mysterious ways. I could see the crunch coming and it did. She asked me if I would go with her to confession and communion in the hope that the Almighty might thus be appeased.

So, with no reasonable option, off we went at 6 a.m. in the morning mist by the first bus from Croft to St Augustine's Church in Darlington and I was back in the darkness of the confessional box. Through the square of gauze I could see the Irish priest intoning quietly in Latin until, finally, he asked me the dreaded question 'How long is it since your last confession?'

'Three years, father,' I answered.

'How old are you?'

'Seventeen.'

'Why have you committed the mortal sin of failing to do even your Easter duties?'

'Because I no longer accept the faith.'

'Then why have you come to confession?'

'To please my mother who is very ill.'

A brief argument ensued in which the priest endeavoured to convince me that since G.K. Chesterton and others far more intelligent than me accepted the faith then my doubts must be ill-founded. I responded by pointing out that some of the greatest reasoning minds of all time like Aristotle, Plato and Socrates had believed in the immortal existence of Zeus, Mars, Mercury, Vulcan, Artemis, Athena and many more but everybody now thought they had been deluded on that issue. My arguments may have been simplistic but the priest's were even more so. To his credit though, he was adamant that he could not give me absolution while I continued in that frame of mind. He told me that I must go away and return when I could make a genuine act of contrition. My entreaties that my mother would suffer if I did not receive communion were disregarded.

My mother was next into the box and if the priest realized whom she was he kept to the rule of total confidentiality and did not say so. While she was inside I decided that only one course of action was possible. I would commit the mortal sin of taking the communion wafer while not in a state of grace — being, indeed, in a state of dire disgrace in the priest's eyes. Once the confessions were completed and the morning service was under way, I joined the queue to the altar-rail behind my mother. The same priest who had heard my confession was placing the wafers on the outstretched tongues but he gave no hint of recognition. I have often wondered how he would have reacted had he done so.

I never told my mother what had happened. Her illness progressed as before and eventually burned itself out. I never went to confession and communion again. I suppose that searing episode made me a died-again Christian.

Had I been allowed to confess one sin, or series of sins, I would have excluded the practical biological experiences which, as I have confessed here, began at the age of twelve. As with many other boys — and girls — of my acquaintance, Sunday was sin day in that respect though it is difficult for anyone trained in zoology to regard copulation as sinful when it is the only way by which species are able to overcome mortality. I had to be more surreptitious than most about my female friendships because my mother was so scared of looking old that she was always harping on about never wanting to be a grandmother and what her attitude would be if I ever made her one. So I never dared to take a girl home and if I went out on a date it had to be so clandestine that if I was returning with her along some dark road after an evening's foray and a car approached I would hide my face in my hands to avoid being recognized, explaining to my companion, lamely I fear, that being blue-eyed I could not stand the glare of headlights. Then to change the subject and offset my embarrassment I would bore her by explaining how eye-colour was inherited. The result was that at eighteen I knew a great deal about lust but nothing whatever about love.

Credit for my good fortune in not prematurely reproducing my kind rested with a little, round, aluminium container residing, unobtrusively, in the window of a joke shop in Darlington. Surrounded by entertaining objects like 'Dirty Fido' and labelled 'Mystery Tin', it contained three condoms and one could acquire it for ten pence, irrespective of one's age, by answering, in the affirmative, the shop-keeper's question 'Do you know what's in it?' The local branch of the Toc H, whose members, led by a vicar, knew the answer, planned to waylay and beat up the shopkeeper though they never did so. I knew of the plan because the vicar's son told me. He, too, was a regular purchaser of Mystery Tins, which we both needed for activities inside the vicarage on Sunday evenings when his father was safely in the pulpit. Amazingly, neither the vicar nor my parents ever discovered our regular patronage of this public benefactor, though the round outline of the single condom always at the ready in one's wallet was only too observable, however one tried to camouflage it with paper wrapping.

It was my continuing interest in biology, and genetics in particular, which caused me, at that age, to begin studying botany, with subsidiary zoology, at King's College, London because the professor there, Ruggles Gates, was then, in 1932, a genetics pioneer of the highest repute, though, as happens in science, his standing was later to plummet. I loathed London from the moment I arrived there, having travelled from my beloved Croft down the Great North Road on the overnight bus service. Though the capital was then substantially smaller, more pleasant and far less crowded than it is today, I hated it so much that I marked off every day on a calendar as being one less to endure. Dr Samuel Johnson's quip that 'When you are tired of London you are tired of life' is as baseless as his claim that 'Patriotism is the last refuge of the scoundrel'.

The glamour of London proved to be fraudulent, the famous 'lights' being a few blinking advertisements not to be compared with the country radiance of a windy, moonlit night. The Lyons Corner Houses, where a whole evening with supper and music could be spent for 9p in modern money provided some relief from the hateful Bloomsbury bed-sitter, as did the famous Brasserie of the Café Royal, which was still the haunt of Bohemians like Augustus John. With one lager and two sandwiches one could sit for hours at one of the marble-topped tables and feel important. Full of pep, on entering the building one evening, I executed a somersault on the red carpet which someone who knew me must have witnessed and reported back to my parents because, within twenty-four hours, they knew about it. I little thought that, one day, through my friendship with the Café Royal's future owner, Lord Forte, I would write its history in the form of a novel.

Charley's Café, run by a Spaniard round the corner from my digs, offered even better value, with an apple suet pudding and custard costing three old pennies, and where one could sit in the company of the infamous Vicar of Stiffkey who had been, sensationally, unfrocked for consorting with prostitutes. One of his light ladies might be present to enliven the conversation, of which a single snatch remains in my memory. Remarking on a sprig of the flower, love-in-a-mist, in a jug on the table, she said, without smiling, 'I call it fuck-in-a-fog'. The country boy was learning fast.

Under pressure from older left-wing students in the digs, I became interested in Communism and found it fun to sit with others after supper, in our Oxford bags and Fair Isle sweaters, puffing at pipes, while being harangued about the class struggle. I suspect that I was considered as a possible recruit until one of my mentors told me that, in the event of a successful revolution, Britain would first have to be governed by Russians from Moscow. My gut response was 'Bugger that!' and I terminated all connections and have been aggressively anti-Communist ever since, though for rather more soundly-based reasons. I have often wondered what happened to those Bloomsbury friends dedicated to the Soviet cause and how they felt when the star they had followed so slavishly proved false.

There was some relief with botanical excursions into the southern countryside which I would later come to love. The best of these were autumnal fungus forays under the leadership of a racy toadstool expert from the Natural History Museum, called John Ramsbottom, who took us to places like Epping Forest, Burnham Beeches and Knole. Hundreds attended including elderly spinsters who seemed to delight, particularly, in filling their baskets with specimens of *Phallus impudicus*, the aptly named 'stinkhorn' fungus looking incredibly like an erect human penis, and presenting them to Ramsbottom for his comments. 'A specimen of which anyone could be proud', he would say to some old soul, with a twinkle.

Excepting such interludes, I continued to dislike London, especially on hot summer days. For me, living in a London bed-sitter or even in a comfortable flat, is like being a battery hen. I must have free range. Or, to put it another way, though we all live in cages of various sizes, town people live in a zoo while the English countryman lives in a large game reserve. The 'in' word for unfortunates is 'deprived' and that is what I believe town-dwellers to be when a latter-day Blake could justly refer to those 'dark, Satanic concrete blocks'. For me, to wake up in London is still to begin the day with a defeat.

I appreciate that my boyhood attachment to the country was excessive because I had such an unusually full life there but I regard my first arrival in London as the end of the magic of my youth which, I am convinced, is not just a nostalgic myth but a reality, compounded of curiosity, novelty, a sense of wonder and the feeling of time stretching endlessly ahead. Going to London was the beginning of the serious task of earning a living which, as happens to most men, took precedence over everything else.

CHAPTER 3

THE RELUCTANT TEACHER

An academic career seemed to be established for me when, at the age of nineteen and before I took my degree, I published two papers on botanical genetics which were regarded by my professor as being highly original. He was determined that I should join his department in the usual lowly rank of demonstrator and though that would mean further years in London, the holidays were so long — five months annually — that it seemed bearable and my objective was to move on soon to another university or research institute in more salubrious surroundings. Since no demonstratorship would be available for two years, when I secured my degree in 1935, the professor thought it would be useful experience for me to teach biology at sixth-form level at a school. I would have preferred a post at a major school set in the country, such as Marlborough, but the only school which offered me sixth-form teaching at my tender age was in a city, which I came to hate even more than London — Liverpool. The school was the Liverpool Institute which was later to achieve fame, even immortality, by producing two of the Beatles, McCartney and Harrison. However, its best attribute for me was the huge tray of scrumptious Eccles cakes which arrived, oven-warm, each morning, for sale in the tuck-shop. Their golden brown, flaky pastry was filled with sugary currants and I have never encountered their like since. I always consumed three in the mid-morning break and it is sad that they are the only memory of Merseyside which I can recall with real pleasure. The long holidays, which I was able to spend at Croft, made life bearable, though returning for the first day of term was like entering a forbidding tunnel.

It was satisfying to teach the Upper and Lower Sixth biology classes, which never numbered more than four boys, all keen to gain scholarships to universities, and I impressed the Headmaster, who also happened to be a keen fisherman, by plastering the walls of the laboratory with charts and diagrams which I constructed in the evenings. I had always found these helpful for implanting facts into the memory. My tip that the boys should put up *aides-mémoires* in their bathrooms at home, so that they could contemplate them while sitting on the loo, met with some parental disfavour. I also caused distress among the other masters who had to teach some of their lessons in what I regarded as my laboratory by setting up large aquaria and vivaria, populated by creatures collected from the nearest countryside, because these distracted their pupils. Inevitably some wretched boy deliberately left the door of one vivarium open and a large grass-snake escaped. I assumed that it must have gone down some crevice and died there of thirst or starvation but, six weeks later, I was interrupted by the arrival of another boy in a class I was teaching in the chemistry laboratory with the breathless news 'Sir, the snake's back!' I rushed down to my own lab, gown aflow, to see the whole class surrounding the fattest grass-snake I had ever seen and achieved some kudos by picking it up and putting it back in its rightful home. What it had fed on in the interim remained a mystery. Cockroaches, perhaps.

Further denizens of the vivaria were natterjack toads, rare, delightful creatures which inhabited the sand dunes near Southport. I transposed a small colony to marshy ground near Croft but saw no signs that they had established themselves. On the other hand, like the snake, they may have reappeared, leaving my meagre mark on the North Yorkshire environment.

Collecting laboratory material from the Lancashire and Cheshire countryside offered some relief from the city, as did the summer camp which the school had set up in the Duddon Valley on the edge of the Lake District. The log-book there stated that Great Gable was too far for the boys to climb and return but three sixth-formers and I not only accomplished it but climbed Green Gable for extra measure — an extension of the fell-walking which I had shared with my father, though all too rarely.

All my senior students did well, several becoming distinguished doctors or surgeons, with two eventually obtaining chairs at universities, but I quickly realized that I was unlikely to derive any pleasure from my lower school duties. For that, one needs to be keen for each little Willie to go home each day knowing more than when he came and I soon came to the conclusion that I did not really care. The mental crunch came one day when, at the end of a junior physics lesson — my early pet hate had caught up with me — a boy politely asked me 'Please Sir, what have we learned?' I think that was the event which firmed my resolve to quit school-teaching when the right opportunity offered.

One possibility was a teaching post in Trinidad which I was offered by the Colonial Office but declined. There was a further complication,

I had met a Liverpool girl who was strikingly beautiful — she really turned heads in the street — and because so many men were after her I thought I had better marry her quickly before she was snapped up. We were totally unsuited for, though she was only twenty-one, she needed a man of at least thirty and, at twenty-three, I was far too immature. I quickly came to wish that I had been more appreciative of feminine qualities other than physical attributes and sexual attraction, which cut clean across intellect. Nor did I cease to confuse lust with love in spite of that searing experience which, inevitably, ended in separation and divorce. When, in my fifties, I dedicated a book, called *Sex in Our Time*, to my present wife stating that she had 'taught me little I did not know about sex but almost everything I know about love', the learning process had been painfully slow.

My starting schoolmaster's salary, set by a government scale, had been £249 per annum and finding it insufficient I soon cast around for additional income. Balked of my childhood dream of becoming a farmer, for lack of capital if nothing else, I decided to 'moonlight' as a freelance agricultural journalist. As I had been farming vicariously by reading *The Farmer and Stockbreeder* I decided to submit an article to it on how farmers could recognize whether soil was acid or alkaline by the kind of weeds it grew. I was qualified to do that and to illustrate it with my own line drawings. It was accepted, perhaps because I called myself 'Head of the Biology Department of the Liverpool Institute' which did not sound like a schoolmaster. Anyway, I received two guineas and that set me off. Soon I was being published by *Farmer's Weekly*, *The Dairy Farmer*, *Poultry World* and other journals, some now defunct. I fear that I quickly ran out of articles which I was qualified to write and based most of them on books or papers which I read in scientific journals or in the excellent Liverpool library in my lunch break. I recall some of the titles — 'How to take care of your dairy herd'; 'Foaling down a mare'; 'Making the most of ducks'; 'Potatoes in stock-feeding'. Yet I had never kept a cow, a horse, or a duck (except for Willie One-wing) or grown a potato. There is a moral to the episode — if I had really known much about practical farming I would never have had the brass nerve to write any of the articles.

Of course, as I continued to spend my long holidays at Croft, I was able to extend my knowledge, the bar of the Comet being a regular haunt of farmers prepared to demonstrate their husbandry. Some, I fear, left much to be desired by modern standards. One 'great milker', whom I was urged to watch, spat on his hands before ramming his cloth-capped head into the cow's belly and seizing the teats. Nevertheless, it was all much more interesting than modern farming, threshing days being a marvellous experience, with the great steam-driven machine, the pitchforkers loading the sheaves and the terrier men dispatching the rats deserting the diminishing grain-stack.

It was astonishing, with food so cheap, how families made a living out of small farms, with names like 'Starvegoose' and 'Standalone', though they were all mixed, with some arable acres, some meadow and pasture, a few cattle, sheep, pigs and the wives tending the poultry which pecked everywhere. I managed to try my hand at most farm labours, the toughest being 'pluggin' muck' — hand-forking manure onto the fields from a cart.

My literary output soared when the whole school was evacuated to Bangor, in North Wales within sight of magnificent Snowdonia, on the outbreak of war in 1939, teaching being, temporarily, a reserved occupation. It was a happy release from Liverpool and I quickly made friends with local farmers, who increased my knowledge and gave me some rabbit and pigeon shooting but my main source of information was the excellent agricultural library at the University there. At one stage I was churning out two or three articles a week, having expanded into other magazines, and earned far more that way than I did from teaching.

An exciting opportunity to return to the countryside arose when I was short-listed for a post at an agricultural research station at Auchincruive in Scotland. Foolishly, in my application I had listed all my agricultural articles and the head interviewer, a dour Scot called Principal Paterson, remarked sourly 'You've been very prolific with the pen'. He was pretty prolific himself in the agricultural press and, maybe, did not like the competition.

My major writing project, based on some of the lessons I devised for the sixth-formers, was a simple guide to genetics for farmers. I had seen a second-hand motor car priced at £100 and thought that such a booklet, well illustrated by my own line drawings, might earn it and enable me to get out of Liverpool at weekends. Sadly, my writing career at that stage was abruptly ended by the arrival of my call-up papers for the Army. I was never to return to teaching, either in school or university, but a run of good fortune would decide that I would be doing rather a lot of writing.

That run began when I read the call-up papers. I was to report for training to a regiment of the Royal Armoured Corps based at Catterick in North Yorkshire, two miles from Richmond and only eight miles from Croft.

CHAPTER 4

THE LUCKY SOLDIER

I must have been one of the few wartime conscripts to set off for his unit armed with fishing tackle, waders and a shotgun though, I did have the sense to leave these with a relative in Richmond on the way to Cambrai Lines at Catterick Camp. Richmond was the gateway to glorious Swaledale and I knew I would have no difficulty in finding fishing and acquiring the right to rove a few fields which, in those days, were rich in partridges and hares as well as rabbits. At Croft, I could do even better.

For the first six weeks we were told that the training would break us down and that in the second three weeks it would build us up. It certainly did the first. However, it was such a welcome break from Liverpool that I enjoyed it, though I got a different glimpse of the moors around the small town of Leyburn. There is little that is more unpleasant than trying to repair the track of a heavy tank when it has broken on frozen mud miles away from base. I had always enjoyed the crisp cold weather of North Yorkshire but it was not so admirable when sleeping on the cold floor of a World War I barrack-room.

We were assured that the only thing to which a soldier was entitled was eighteen inches in the ranks and that we should treat a rifle like a wife by rubbing it over each night with an oily rag. Many of my squad held honours degrees but we were treated as idiots. While demonstrating how to clean the floor of our ancient barrack-room, one regular NCO sent one of my comrades-in-arms to bring the 'tucked-up scrubbing brush'. When he returned from the central stove area, where such utensils were kept, carrying an ordinary scrubbing brush, the NCO sent him back for another which had hardly any bristles left. 'My God, you people have a lot to learn,' he said, without humour, as he explained the difference.

'If you can't stand still on the square how do you expect to stand still under fire?', the commanding officer shouted at us on one occasion. None of us had much intention of doing that, at least not outside a tank.

Though my teaching experience had been brief it marked me out as a gunnery instructor, of which the regiment was short, and the rabbits which I donated to the sergeants' mess through the company sergeant-major, 'Nobby' Clark, probably helped to secure my quick promotion to full corporal. To facilitate this supply of fresh meat at a time of strict rationing, I was given permission to sleep out in Richmond. This meant walking in through the open countryside early every morning but, being fitter than I had ever been before, I thoroughly enjoyed it. Most of the troops did the walk back at night, after patronizing the pubs in Richmond's medieval square, and one such was Trooper X, an unwilling conscript whose sole ambition in the Army was to get out of it. He dodged fatigues, feigned sickness to avoid route marches and was dumbly insolent to NCOs but his gambits were so obvious that he seemed unlikely ever to 'work his ticket' that way. Then one night, returning from Richmond, he was set upon by two drunken corporals who beat him savagely, leaving him unconscious. He had to be rushed to hospital where, apart from two broken ribs, his most dangerous injury was an eye so damaged that the white looked like red jelly for several weeks.

There was an immediate inquiry and Trooper X could have had his cowardly attackers court-martialled, demoted and imprisoned. This prospect would have been irresistible to most men, including me, but he spotted a greater advantage. He claimed he could not remember anything about them because he had entirely lost his memory as a result of the attack. Nobody, including his doctors, believed him but, though tested and watched for weeks, he never wavered. Eventually his determination brought honourable discharge.

My only vengeful act as an NCO concerned an older recruit who was drafted to my squad for training. I recognized him as a rather sarcastic Welsh driving examiner from Liverpool who had failed me on my first test with the words 'We don't expect people to come to us for the first lesson'. I am afraid that he peeled rather more than his fair share of spuds. I have often wondered what became of him because he was among many whom I was required to assure that the two-pounder gun fitted to the British tanks, a peashooter firing a solid two-pound shot, could penetrate any German tank while their guns could not penetrate ours. Some of these men were soon to be in the desert against Rommel's much more strongly-armoured tanks which had six-pounders.

Sleeping out in Richmond offered plenty of opportunity for fishing at the weekend. War or no war, I was free after midday on Saturday and it was easy to induce a friend to sign me in on Sunday morning so that I did not have to be there. Being listed as a Catholic meant that I did not have to be on church parade as it was assumed that all Catholics would attend church automatically. I had many memorable days on the River Swale, with the company Sergeant-Major benefitting again from the trout and being strongly in favour of keeping the supply going. One such day was unforgettable because of the beautiful young lady, my Liverpudlian wife, whom I was teaching to fish.

In those days I was mainly a bait fisher, trotting maggots down fast streams on very light tackle, and it was the custom to have the maggots in a linen bag slung from the neck so that they were handy when wading. My wife and I were fishing rather unsuccessfully on a hot day when a friend, who had a car, came along the bank and suggested that we should try some miles higher up where he had special permission. We put our rods through his open car windows and my wife climbed into the back seat while I rode in front with the driver. We had not gone far when she nodded off, having failed to take the precaution of removing her maggot bag from her neck. Eventually she awoke and emitted a piercing scream. Hundreds of the maggots had wriggled out of the bag into the interstices of her woollen jumper. I took the only possible course of action — to pull the writhing garment over her head when, inevitably, many of the maggots fell into her hair and cleavage. The episode intensified her dislike of the country and her need to get back to her beloved Liverpool to which, she knew, I was determined never to return.

One of my joys at Catterick was the proximity of Croft. My father had relinquished the Comet, on being recalled to the Army as a major, but most of my friends remained in the village, being involved with agriculture, so I switched my allegiance to the more splendid Croft Spa Hotel, just across the bridge. Many dances and other rather wild festivities were held there to offset the austerity and one of my squad who had a car enabled us to enjoy them as often as we wished. I introduced other Army friends to its pleasures and the Richmond Flyer, the little train to Darlington which stopped at Croft, became known in my unit as the Flying Fornicator.

We patronized the Comet on occasion and I did not sever my last physical link with it until 1987 when I donated a drinking cup made from one of *Comet*'s horns to the Museum of English Rural Life at Reading University. A customer, whose forebears had been involved with the breeders, had given it to me fifty years previously. Scratched on its base, in an ancient script, was the single word 'Comet'.

Along with most of my squad I was listed for eventual posting to cadet school for training as an officer and I was given advance warning that my name was coming up by our squad commander, with whom I had become friendly in the Richmond pubs. As it was the cream of the fishing season and little was happening in the war, outside the western desert, I told him that I was in no hurry to go and he took my name off the list. Had I gone my life would have been very different. About three months later it was taken off again, though in rather dissimilar circumstances.

Future officers were required to learn to ride a motor-cycle and, being a corporal, I was allowed to take-off on my own over the moors. One lovely summer's day I thought I would revisit Wensleydale and, in particular, see if the old wooden stocks were still present on the village green at Bainbridge, which they were. I then rode up to Semer Water, the largest natural lake in Yorkshire and the source of its smallest river, the Bain, which joins the Ure after only two miles. My father had told me the legend of the old wizard who, having been refused food at a village, commanded Semer Water to flood it and how it still lies at the bottom with all its occupants drowned. I practised rough riding via Hawes and the Butter Tubs, some deep holes in the limestone where farmers were said to have lowered their butter to keep it cool, and down the length of Swaledale, enjoying every minute of seeing so many haunts available to me previously only on a push-bike. Reaching Cambrai Lines at about 5 p.m. in time for tea I found that everyone had been looking for me because my posting to cadet school had suddenly arrived and I was missing when, of course, I should have been on parade for lunch. Various NCOs who envied my life-style made the most of it on the charge sheet and I was marched in front of the Commanding Officer and struck off the list. I could hardly tell him that I could not have been more delighted with a further three months, at least, in the North Riding countryside. Again, had I not been indulging my love of wild countryside, my career would not have developed as it did.

Sadly, nobody's luck lasts forever and the cadet school caught up with me in 1942. The training, both as a cadet and a subaltern took me to new and delightful country places in the West Country, Norfolk, Suffolk, Bedfordshire and Scotland. Exercises which involved sleeping in tents and awakening in fields were specially delectable. On one of them I encountered two sergeants from Bulford, where I knew that a boyhood friend, called Douglas Warth, was undergoing tank training in the ranks. His right arm was slightly malformed by polio but he had gained entry to the Army by lifting his medical examiner onto his shoulder with it. I had heard that Warth was the brightest soldier in his squad and the best rifle shot but the sergeants told me that he had been invalided from the Army because he could not salute properly. It greatly upset him, especially as he was later to parachute into France as a war correspondent but, as will be seen, his expulsion from the Army was a highly significant incident in my life.

One of my better postings was to Winthorpe Hall, near Newark, close by some of the RAF's main bomber airfields. The Commanding Officer was extremely social and RAF pilots had free range of our mess, as did several of the county beauties, who attracted them. As a result I did a lot of practice flying, including searchlight operations, with Lancaster bomber pilots who were to become famous as the Dambusters, some of whom were not to survive the war. It was a way of seeing the English countryside in a manner entirely new to me, both by day and by night.

My respect for security classification died on a night of torrential rain when a dispatch rider arrived at Winthorpe Hall, when I was serving as Orderly Officer, with an envelope marked 'Secret'. Opening it I read 'Tinned sausages are now available'. It was not a message in code. It meant what it said and, perhaps, conditioned my rather cavalier attitude later in my journalistic life when faced with publishing information officially regarded as secret.

My first experience with a real code-word was not auspicious. Again I was serving as Orderly Officer while all those senior to me were out enjoying themselves. The telephone rang and a voice simply said 'Caterpillar!' and hung up. Being new and not indoctrinated, I dismissed the call as a joke to find, when it was far too late, that it meant that the company should have been deployed on a mock emergency exercise against imaginary German parachutists. An inquiry ensued but I was away for three days with a convoy when people were questioned and so my luck held out.

That particular convoy was memorable for another country experience of which I still have some tattered evidence. I was required to call at a unit stationed at Staunton Harold Hall, near Ashby-de-la-Zouche. It was the ancestral home of the Earls Ferrers and had been totally requisitioned by the army for the duration of the war. Trying to find someone in authority I was directed to the large library where there were hundreds of shelves of books which had been covered with soft-board for protection. While waiting for someone to arrive I noticed that several of the boards had been breached and there were two ancient tomes on the mantlepiece with pages ripped out, obviously for lighting cigarettes. I was appalled and said so when a Sergeant-Major eventually arrived. It seemed that the other ranks used the library as a recreation room in the evening and efforts to stop them from despoiling it had been abandoned.

'Anyway it's nothing to what the other lot did before us,' the sergeant-major said.

'What did they do?' I asked.

'They raided the vaults in the church and took the jewellery off the bodies.'

Accompanied by my batman driver, whose civilian life occupation seemed dubious, we put our noses in the ancient church and I told him what the vandals had done to the corpses and were doing to the books, many of which were centuries old.

When we reached Winthorpe Hall that evening he staggered into my bedroom with a load of ancient books which he presented to me saying 'It seemed a pity to let them destroy these when you like them so much.'

To have made him return them or to have sent them back myself would have put him into serious trouble — a charge of theft — so I kept them. Some dated from the sixteenth century but, as they were all ecclesiastical works in Latin, they were of no financial value and, sadly, deteriorated to destruction over the years.

To make the most of the educational facilities which the Army offered I always volunteered for courses, which were often held in some commandeered stately home in splendid surroundings. I recall being on one which was attended by several ATS officers and remarking about their plainness to a rather elderly captain. 'I agree, my boy,' he said. 'But they will become more beautiful as the days go by.' He was right. By and large, the ATS officers whom I met were a delightful lot, as were most of the ATS other ranks. I was popular with the latter because whenever I was making a final tour of my parked vehicles at night I would make plenty of noise to give the girls and boys time to get out of the back of them. It was incredible how some well-bred ATS girl would fall for some greasy cook and shed floods of tears when he was posted away. I recall having to negotiate with an angry farmer who was demanding compensation because his wheat had been 'screwed flat'.

I must have left quite an impression myself on the countryside there because, some thirty years later, Nigel Dempster, the gossip columnist reported in *Private Eye* that he had discovered the extent to which I had enjoyed myself with war-lonely ladies in the Winthorpe area and that, unless I behaved myself, he would reveal all. What did he expect a young officer to do in such tempting circumstances?

While I was at Winthorpe the Commanding Officer called me in to say there was a course which seemed right up my street. The Army was desperately short of scientifically-trained officers to serve as intermediaries between the scientists in the laboratories and the users in the field to ensure that new weapons and equipment would work under battle conditions. The Military College of Science was offering a six-months crash course involving advanced physics, chemistry and mathematics to be followed by a posting for the successful candidates. The dreaded physics did not appeal but I applied, was accepted but was not best pleased to find the posting was to the Potteries, where the Advanced Class in Ammunition and Explosives was to be held in a commandeered school. However, it proved to be another mutation moment with crucial consequences for my post-war career.

Of the eighteen who started the course only nine of us finished it. Of those, a few were posted to country defence establishments, some in the wilds of Scotland. I was displeased to find that I was posted to an out-station of Woolwich Arsenal to work on rocket weapons but it was to turn out enormously to my advantage, outweighing the salmon fishing I might have secured in Scotland.

On the first evening of my return to London I was walking down Charing Cross Road, rather despondently, and literally bumped into my old friend, Douglas Warth, the man who had been dismissed from the Army because he could not salute. He told me that he was working as a reporter on the *Daily Express* and offered me accommodation in a room in a house in Chelsea, which he was renting. As the alternative was living in the Woolwich mess and the Tube journey from Sloane Square to my office was easy I leapt at it.

I quickly made friends with my new commanding Colonel, who was a countryman intent on retiring to farm as soon as the war was over, and introduced him to Warth as I felt sure that they would like each other. The war situation was grim, with Churchill desperate from some good news to impart to the people, when he was told about a new high-powered explosive called RDX, which had been developed at Woolwich. The military wanted it kept secret but Churchill insisted on an announcement to the Press, without, however, giving the type of detail to make it into a good newspaper 'story'. Warth telephoned me from the *Daily Express* to ask if I knew anything about it. As I knew all, I secured the Colonel's permission to tell it, anonymously, and the newspaper was able to print a scoop about the inventor whose name, happily, was Dr Rotter, and about experiments involving the explosive with the code-name 'Marmalade'. Warth had ensured that the news editor was listening to our conversation and he was very impressed. As a result, I came to be telephoned by the *Express* news desk whenever there was a problem involving weapons. I should point out that in those days the *Daily Express* was the world's biggest-selling newspaper, a broadsheet selling right across the community and, therefore, taken seriously as a medium by politicians.

The next major Fleet Street problems were posed by the German V1 flying bomb and the V2 rocket. Again luck was with me as a result of routine visits I had made to the Royal Aircraft Establishment at Farnborough, where I had seen both V-weapons being built-up from parts picked up from those which had exploded on British soil or had failed to do so. Under Churchill's instructions the newspapers were told that they would not be given any information but they were free to speculate. With my Colonel's agreement, the *Daily Express* speculated with remarkable accuracy.

By that time the Editor, Arthur Christiansen, had decided that he wanted me on the staff when I was demobbed so, to maintain that option, I began to go into the paper on Sundays to learn the trade. It was a considerable sacrifice to be voluntarily in London on Sundays and my fishing friend, Marshall Hardy, then editor of *Angling*, to which I contributed, urged me to avoid a Fleet Street career. 'You'll be like a lamb among wolves,' he warned. It did not quite work out that way.

My biggest break came in August 1945 when the atomic bomb exploded over Hiroshima. Lord Beaverbrook, the *Daily Express* proprietor who had been involved in the bomb project through his membership of the War Cabinet, appreciated all its political implications and was insisting that the Editor kept the 'story' going on the front page for at least a week, though no information was forthcoming from Whitehall. Through friends I secured advance access to the American 'Smyth Report' which told almost everything and the *Express* secured a run of world scoops which resulted in a formal offer from Christiansen for me to join the paper as Defence and Science Editor, though in fact, I was never to edit anything but only to ferret out information and write about it.

Until Hiroshima, my name had never appeared on any of the newspaper reports I had written because of the danger that I might be court-martialled, especially as some of my contributions had been critical of the Government, but Christiansen insisted that a name had to appear on articles about the atomic bomb, especially those expressing an opinion. I could either use my own name or a pseudonym with which I would be stuck when I formally joined the paper. I chose my own name, Henry Chapman Pincher, and the Editor decided 'I am going to call you just Chapman Pincher. I like pompous names and Henry or Harry does not carry conviction'. I have been stuck with it ever since.

With the end of the war and weapons research at a standstill, I awaited a posting which would disrupt and possibly end my Fleet Street connection because the Army refused to release me until my 'number came up'. When the posting arrived it was to an office in the Mansion House, just up the road from the *Express*! On reporting there each morning there was nothing to do but examine the few documents in my in-tray and what treasures I found there day-after-day! With so many servicemen and civilians about to lose their jobs the Government had decided that they should be given the first chance of posts in the many new defence research stations being established to deal with developments like atomic weapons, missiles and biological warfare, which had become necessary because the Soviet Union was already flexing its muscles. While official public announcements about these stations would eventually be made, they were being delayed to give the existing defence personnel first bite at the cherry. Of necessity, the job offers involved some description of the new research stations, their locations and purposes and scoops on these places therefore fell into my lap for transfer to my newspaper, a brief bus-ride down the road.

One morning the most exciting job offer was for me. My brigadier had selected me for a post at Cuxhaven, in Germany, where some captured V2 rockets were to be test-fired. The immediate promotion to major with quick elevation to half-colonel was tempting but, as the job would last about a year, it could spell the end of any career in Fleet Street where out of sight was out of mind. The prospect of then being driven back to teaching, with its appalling pay, was horrific. For potent reasons I was terrified of poverty and still am, having heard so much about it from both my parents who had been brought up in grinding penury. My mother's father, a miner, was killed when she was two and when my father was nine his, a soldier, had been accidentally shot dead. I managed to convince the brigadier that the job should go to a regular officer and continued my surreptitious journalism without the leaks being traced to me, though they must have raised official eyebrows, until I was duly demobbed in June 1946 at the age of thirty-two and joined the *Daily Express* office next day.

Over the previous months I had realized the particular potential of the exclusive story, not just as a source of merit, but as a means of living in the country. The Editor and other executives did not care where their specialists worked so long as exclusives kept rolling in and they were available on the telephone. Further, the paper did not expect more than one contribution a day so, if two exclusives could be obtained from a source, one could be held over and filed by telephone the next day, which could be spent in the quiet of the countryside instead of in London. It was a device which I was to refine to give me three or four full days in the country out of every seven, for the next thirty-three years.

CHAPTER 5

THE LUCKY JOURNALIST

During my last year in the Army I had completed my farmer's guide to genetics, illustrated with numerous line drawings, and in 1946 it was published as a Penguin Handbook under the title *The Breeding of Farm Animals*. As it cost only one shilling, the author's revenue was modest but it brought an enormous and quite unforseeable bonus. On one of my first visits to a government establishment as the official *Daily Express* defence correspondent I was approached by a man who had read the book and liked it. Though a civil servant by profession, operating at the highest levels of secrecy in Whitehall, he was a farmer and countryman at heart and ran a herd of Redpoll cattle along with huge flocks of turkeys and chickens at Emsworth, in Hampshire. His name was Sir Frederick Brundrett and he was shortly to become Deputy Chief Scientist and then Chief Scientist in the Defence Ministry. He invited me down to see his farming ventures and we became close friends, meeting regularly for lunch in London, at restaurants or at his club. He also became my main source of information, often so sensitive that it confounded Ministers and MI5, right until his retirement in 1960. Fred was intimately involved with every major defence development and decision at a time of fundamental changes and attended Cabinet committee meetings as an adviser. He took the view that, in an age when nuclear weapons threatened the civilian population as never before, the public should be accurately informed about defence issues by at least one journalist and I was the one whom he selected, thanks to my interest in agriculture which had first brought us together. From then on there was little concerning defence issues and weapons developments that was kept from me and I was able to publish most of it. He introduced me to other senior civil servants in the charmed circle so that when he retired I remained in it.

My friendship with Fred quickly taught me another valuable journalistic lesson — try to secure sources who are so eminent that they cannot be censured without causing a major scandal. I have recently been told that some of my conversations with Brundrett were monitored by the security authorities. A London restaurant much used by foreign diplomats during the war had been fitted up with microphones which remained in continuing use. The microphones were inserted in panelling behind some of the banquette seats and linked with listening equipment in an upstairs room. Every day a security man arrived to see who had booked in for lunch or dinner and, if they were of interest, he would be in the room to record the conversations. It seems that when I began to use the restaurant — always having a banquette seat — I was a regular target. The authorities must have been horrified by some of the things Brundrett told me but could do nothing about it. He was chairman of a most secret MI5 committee and various senior politicians, including Duncan Sandys, the Defence Minister, and Harold Macmillan, when he was Prime Minister, were shooting friends of mine and condoned what he did, agreeing with him that I should be kept informed, especially on nuclear issues.

Occasionally I was able to repay his confidences, as I did early in 1957 when Fred summoned me to his country home on a matter of great urgency and secrecy. I was further in his debt because he had provided me with a notable scoop by telling me that the tests of Britain's first H-bomb were to be carried out on Christmas Island, in the Pacific. He took me into his garden and told me that the Japanese, who were understandably agitated by the dangers of radioactive fall-out, were planning to make the tests impossible by sailing a thousand small ships into the test area. If they forced the tests to be abandoned, Britain's entire defence policy would be ruined and huge sums already spent would have been wasted. Fred explained that the Government had decided to fool the Japs with a dirty tricks deception operation and it needed my help. The object was to convince the Japs that the tests, which were scheduled for May, had been postponed for several weeks because of technical problems. This might be achieved if I could induce my Editor to print a front-page article implying that there had been a delay and this was duly done. The tests went ahead, successfully, without any interference. Though our readers may have been deceived, to a modest extent and for a short time, I have no regrets regarding my part in helping to maintain the nuclear deterrent which, I am convinced, was instrumental in preventing the march of Soviet Communism with all the consequent horrors which everyone can now see. In fact, few endeavours in my journalistic career gave me more delight. Inevitably, I was rewarded with further exclusive leaks and facilities, making my visit to that English country garden even more memorable. One I recall, with relish, enabled me to visit the RAF bomber station deep in the Suffolk countryside, at

Honington, to be photographed leaning against a huge 'Blue Danube' H-bomb, which the public had never seen.

In addition to allowing me to operate to a considerable extent from home in the country, my concentration on the exclusive story carried a further virtue — it allowed me to maintain the initiative with the newspaper executives. Apart from Press conferences, I cannot remember ever being sent on any assignment. I took steps to ensure that I always suggested what I should cover and that was, usually, where I wanted to go. That way I could govern my life to a large degree and, by maintaining a steady stream of news, I was soon left to my own devices. My enthusiasm almost encompassed my early death — appropriately in a cornfield.

Early in my career, the Editor engaged the services of the Flying Car, an odd-looking four-wheeled vehicle to which portable wings and a propeller could be fitted. We were all asked to think of ways in which it could be used on assignments and, as a few doses of the then rare drug, streptomycin, had come my way I suggested that we should rush them to a child patient, whose doctors had appealed for some. The American inventor and pilot of the machine, Bob Fulton, took me by road to Croydon Airport where the car was converted to a plane. Flying low, Fulton found his way to Wolverhampton Airport by reading a road map as the compass was out of order. We eventually reached the hospital by road without mishap, save for a small fire in the heating system which had to be doused with an extinguisher. By the time we had returned to the airport and I had telephoned my story to Fleet Street only two daylight hours remained and when Fulton told the authorities that his radio would not work on British frequencies we were urged to wait until the morning. Instead, he telephoned Croydon Airport, where it was agreed that searchlights would be put up to guide us down. Stupidly, I agreed to accompany him.

As dusk gathered it was clear to me that, because of the faulty compass and no radio, the pilot was unsure of his exact position. He explained that in America there was so much traffic on the roads and railways that it was as easy to map-read by night as by day. Unfortunately, petrol rationing was still in force and the railway signals still had their wartime hoods on. Nevertheless, Fulton was all for pressing on, insisting that the glare of London and the searchlights would guide us safely to Croydon.

With less than half an hour of dim light left I was sure that we were lost and convinced the pilot that we should find the nearest flat field and make an emergency landing. He agreed and I picked the field, which could not have been flatter because, when it was too late, we saw that it was standing corn. The plane turned over, landing upside down, its four wheels in the air. As we tried to unfasten the single seat strap, with the petrol tank leaking down my neck, I remembered the fire in the heating system but we managed to extricate ourselves and walk to the nearest farmhouse, where we spent the night. The machine remained in the wheat like some gigantic stricken insect for most of the next day until recovered, and, as the local Press never spotted it, the disaster was kept secret, though our readers may have wondered why they never heard of the Flying Car again.

It was fortunate that many defence establishments which I had to visit were in the country — Porton, on Salisbury Plain, Harwell, in rural Berkshire, Sellafield, in Cumbria, and some as remote as Thule in Greenland, and Woomera, the rocket station in the Australian outback. Rum Jungle, the uranium mine not far from Darwin, in tropical Australia, even gave me an excuse for going 'down the bitumen' all the way to Alice Springs.

I particularly remember Dounreay, the atomic establishment in wild Caithness, for my meeting there with an impressive-looking young journalist attached to the *Express* Scottish office. He had blonde hair and a yellow beard and flowing moustache which made him look like a Viking, from which stock, he claimed, he was descended. Thanks to my friendship with the Dounreay management, I secured a little scoop which rather stole the Viking's thunder but he was to do rather well later. His name was Magnus Magnusson and when we occasionally meet he kindly recalls the episode.

The country sometimes impinged on my office work in an unusual way. At about 4 p.m., the Features Editor would sometimes put a worried face round my door and say 'Do you have a feature you could let me have in a hurry?'

'How big?' I would ask.

'The size of a Giles cartoon.'

Carl Giles, the immensely popular cartoonist of the *Daily Express*, lived near Ipswich and refused to work from the office, visiting London rarely. His cartoons were sent by rail to Liverpool Street station to be picked up by a dispatch rider. As can be imagined, the system occasionally failed and the space reserved for his effort had to be filled at short notice.

In partnership with an *Express* writer called Bernard Wicksteed, I was able to put my biological knowledge to journalistic use in a long-lasting series called 'It's Fun Finding Out' which took us all over the countryside. Our most memorable trip was to the Welsh island of Skokholm, where we ringed puffins and Manx shearwaters, which made the whole island reverberate as they cooed and crowed in their burrows at night. The series, and the eventual books which they created, established my reputation as a mine of trivial information. So much so that when I gave a lift to a hiker on my way to Scotland and he learned that I worked in Fleet Street he asked 'Have you come across that chap who's a bloody walking Whittaker's Almanack?'

By keeping in touch with the scientific literature I was able to get some newspaper 'firsts' on new discoveries which also took me to distant country locations. One, for example, concerned a vaccine against foot-and mouth-disease which was being mass-produced in a French laboratory, near Tours. Lord Beaverbrook, who had a large herd of milking cows on his country estate at Cricket Malherbie, in Somerset — 'He storms down and counts every teat', his farm manager averred — was in favour of using the vaccine in Britain where it was, and still is, prohibited. So, he was keen that I should make a full inquiry at Tours which meant that I could also take in the chateaux of the Loire valley and look at the river where the splendid Rabelais had dangled a worm. It was always advantageous for the office executives to know that the Beaver had a personal interest in a story, for they did not then exert pressure for a quick return to base. The old man's intense interest in the scientific quest for a pill or potion that would extend life-span obtained some memorable foreign trips for me — some of them, I fear, to interview dreadful phonies. Though gerontology, the study of the ageing process, has been a serious science for forty years now, the absolute human life-span, about 115 years, has not been extended, though more people are living longer than they did.

There was always a demand, on all national dailies, for a major exclusive every Sunday for Monday morning's paper, preferably something that would make a front-page splash, and I endeavoured to fulfil it as frequently as possible. Often, I was able to secure the story during the week, in addition to those I submitted then, and by putting it over on the telephone on Sunday it counted as a day's work. This meant that I could take Friday off at home or some other weekday if someone asked me to fish or shoot. Occasionally, I would be seen at a shoot by the *Express* managing director, Jocelyn Stevens, who had also been invited but, as he was in the same position as myself, there was little he could do. Sometimes the chairman, Max Aitken, Lord Beaverbrook's son, would be there but as he occasionally invited me to weekday shoots that did not matter either.

As most people do, I began serious shooting in a modest way — in a roughish syndicate shoot, near Midhurst in Sussex, where fifty pheasants for nine guns was a good day. The birds were mainly driven but there were not many of them. Through a social occasion at the home of Hugh and Antonia Fraser, at which I managed to express my interest in field sports — there is some skill in doing this without making it too obvious — I was invited by one of the other guests, Peter Adam, who ran a syndicate shoot at Brimpton in Berkshire which was part-owned by the late Lord Sieff, one of the founders of Marks and Spencer. Lord Sieff became such a friend that he sent my present wife and me on a honeymoon trip to Israel and — came with us! On a later occasion at the same shoot I met Charles Forte (now Lord) and that was my moment of entry into the charmed circle of the shooting world. Apart from having his own shoot at Ripley, in Surrey, Charles, who became an intimate friend, rented the major part of the Ickworth shoot in Suffolk and while enjoying myself there as his guest I met the legendary shot, Joe Nickerson (later Sir Joseph), who then regularly asked me to shoot pheasants on his Rothwell estate in the Lincolnshire wolds, grouse at Wemmergill, South Durham, which he made into the finest of all moors and, later, his exciting wild partridges in Spain.

It is surely no coincidence that a random check in *Who's Who* reveals that shooting is the recreation listed repeatedly by leaders of industry, commerce, and the professions. A simplistic explanation is that game-shooting is expensive and that only the successful can afford to engage in it, but the real reasons are more deep-seated. Perhaps the major reason why shooting is so suitable for the busy executive is that it brings him into the open air for a full day and is the perfect sport for taking the mind off business anxieties. It is also essentially non-competitive and for anyone embroiled in competition all week that is what is needed.

In the shooting world, since there are usually about eight men in the line, one introduction leads to more. Though I was to be based in Fleet Street for thirty-three years, almost all my major friendships and most of my professional connections were to be forged through the countryside and mainly through shooting. Fishing is not so social, as a rule, but it was through that first country love of mine that I had the great fortune to meet Sir Thomas Sopwith, the aircraft pioneer and yachtsman who died only recently aged 101. Sir Thomas had eight miles of the River Test, the angler's Mecca, and his only son, Tommy, whom I had met shooting, hated fishing because he had been made to do it when a boy. He once told me that when he was very young and his father owned a salmon river on the Island of Harris, he had been required to fish before breakfast and caught so many that he never wanted to do it again. So knowing my fanaticism, he introduced me to his father at their country home, Compton, near King's Somborne in Hampshire. That turned out to be another mutation moment. Compton was also a famous pheasant shoot and, from then on, I stood, regularly, in the line there with the people whom I had met professionally but not socially — Lord Mountbatten, Prince Charles, Harold Macmillan, Lord Dilhorne, the Lord Chancellor, Duncan Sandys, Marshal of the RAF Lord Portal and others, some from the aircraft building world, who became helpful to me in my work.

It is extraordinary how a day's shooting together can break down barriers of reserve. I had met Lord Mountbatten, for example, through interviews and parties at the Defence Ministry when he was First Sea Lord. He was always affable but also grand, generating the aura that he was of a different breed, but after only one day together at Sir Thomas's shoot in Hampshire we were on first name terms. The shooting lunch is the occasion when the barriers disappear and on that day, the formidable Lady Sopwith, a fine shot herself, and who, for some reason, approved of me, said 'Dickie, sit next to Harry and don't mumble!'

'Mumble? Mumble? Yes, I suppose I do mumble,' the noble Earl admitted.

As I had already discerned, great men do not obey the laws of optics — the nearer you get to them the *smaller* they become — and from then on Mountbatten was just another human being. I could not have done badly in the conversation because 'Dickie' invited me to shoot at Broadlands and always insisted on having me with him in the front seat of his Land-Rover. He was keen to develop his own views about defence so that they would colour my reporting in the newspaper but even more keen to know what might be going on behind his back.

On one such trip he told me how the Queen had been made Lord High Admiral of England — several older admirals had been squabbling about who should have the ancient title when it became vacant so he offered it to the Queen, who accepted it. On another he talked about his claim to being King of the Isle of Wight. In 1965 the Queen was to install him as Governor of the Isle of Wight in a ceremony at Carisbrooke Castle and, typically, he had the situation thoroughly researched. He discovered that in 1444 the island had reverted to being a separate kingdom and in that year Henry, Duke of Warwick, is believed to have been crowned king of the island by Henry VI. Then, about forty years later, Henry VII had put it under the command of captains who later took the title of Governors. Mountbatten believed that the title of king had never been legally revoked. 'The Queen may find that she has made me King of the island,' he said.

I discussed the Northern Ireland situation with him on several occasions. He admitted that he could see no solution, believing that in the end North and South would have to be united. He greatly regretted the fact that British troops had ever been sent to Ulster in such numbers and blamed Harold Wilson for it. He also confessed that, in the interest of future peace, he would like to see Germany split up into a lot of small principalities again.

Surprisingly perhaps, on such occasions, I was trusted not to reveal anything I saw or heard. Discretion is absolutely essential when in the day-long company of distinguished people who might want to let their hair down among close friends. This, of course, is especially true when Royalty are involved. I arrived at the Sopwiths' once to learn that Prince Charles, who was on his way there, had been involved in a car accident in the fog. It was disconcerting to see the story in a rival paper a week later but my discretion did not go unnoticed. With terrorism such a real threat, it is essential not to mention that VIPs who might be targets are in the habit of attending a particular shoot. However, after a decent interval, and with careful wording to cover the source, I was able to make use of almost everything I learned without offending anyone. Indeed, so productive did my days in the shooting field become that I tried to induce Lord Beaverbrook into agreeing that the *Daily Express* should finance my entry into various exclusive syndicates but all he said was 'A nice try but, from what I hear, I think you are shooting enough.' Nevertheless, he never declined a brace of pheasants or a salmon.

It was at a shoot where I became privy to what had been the best kept official secret of recent times — that the late Sir Maurice Oldfield, the Chief of the Secret Service (MI6) had been a secret homosexual and that when this had been discovered, very late in his career, he had suffered the appalling disgrace of having his security clearance withdrawn. I had heard of it from a Scotland Yard source but Sir Michael Havers, then Attorney-General and later Lord Chancellor, confirmed it in detail while we were walking to our shooting stands, describing how the Prime Minister, Mrs Thatcher, had been so devastated that she had put her head in her hands.

When I eventually revealed this in a book about the motivations for treachery, few Whitehall officials, save those in the know, would believe it. However when questioned in the House, Mrs Thatcher confirmed the truth of it in all essentials, also revealing that Sir Maurice had confessed to his problem. She pointed out, as I had already done, that Sir Maurice, who had been a personal friend of mine, had not been subjected to blackmail by the KGB or anyone else but, nevertheless, had been a security risk. Had his habits been known he would never have been appointed Chief of the nation's most secret organization.

No spy was less likely ever to have been seen in the shooting field than the late Sir Anthony Blunt, the long-term KGB agent inside MI5 who became Surveyor of the Queen's Pictures. Country sports were not the scene of this detestable aesthete, former MI5 officer and habitual homosexual. Nevertheless, it was through shooting that, soon after his public exposure in 1979, I learned the answer to the question that so many were asking — when Blunt was forced into confessing that he was a traitor, secretly to MI5 in 1964, was Her Majesty told that her art adviser was a Russian spy? The answer was that she had indeed been told, by her Private Secretary, then Sir Michael Adeane, and she had behaved as might be expected. While angry, the Queen asked Adeane 'What is the professional advice regarding what we should do?' Adeane replied that the advice — mainly from MI5, but also from the Home Office — was that the Palace should leave things as they were while Blunt was interrogated over many months. The Queen agreed and Blunt remained in his position without public censure, meeting Her Majesty on occasion and knowing that she was aware of his treachery.

Peter Wright, the renegade MI5 officer who interrogated Blunt, has confirmed this in his book *Spycatcher*, as Lord Jenkins has in his autobiography. However I may not reveal exactly how I heard such a prime secret and published it twelve years ago in my book, *Their Trade is Treachery*, save to say that it was told to me between drives at a pheasant shoot by someone who had heard the Queen admit to it, quite openly, while she was picking up birds at a shoot elsewhere.

An even more surprising disclosure to pick up at a shoot, especially on a grouse moor, was the astonishing fact that Blunt's homosexual friend, the unspeakable Guy Burgess, who eventually defected to the Soviet Union, had been under deep suspicion before the Foreign Office made the blunder of posting him to the British Embassy in Washington. While I was shooting in North Yorkshire, one of the guns, whom I had never met before, described how, as a young Army officer, he had been transferred, against his will, to a post specially created for the purpose so that he could keep Burgess under surveillance, which he did for several months.

The savage laws of libel frequently prevented me from revealing intriguing information I picked up from shooting friends. When the retired diplomat, Sir Peter Hayman, was convicted of homosexual indecency in 1984 after having previously been involved in a child sex ring, a former Service Chief gave me information I would dearly have liked to publish. Following his retirement in 1974 Hayman was secretly involved in the selection of recruits for MI5 from which all sexual deviants were supposed to be barred. An even more bizarre appointment of a homosexual in the security world came my way, but no reputable publisher would print it because of the libel risk.

I was deeply involved in inquiries into the Profumo affair, with its security overtones, in the early 1960s and, again through shooting, was able to hear Harold Macmillan's views at first hand. He was poorly informed of the true circumstances concerning the part played by a Russian intelligence officer — a situation which, I believe, hastened his own resignation. In the further context of shooting, I would like to put on record an example of the resilience and sense of humour which helped Jack Profumo to ride the appalling results of his indiscretions. Not long after his departure from Parliament, I was a fellow guest at a partridge shoot and before Jack arrived our host urged us to avoid any lunch-time conversation which might embarrass him. We were succeeding until I asked him about the work he had undertaken at Grendon Prison, where he was a Governor. He then told us about his first day there when he had the duty of 'welcoming' a dangerous criminal with the usual helpful advice.

'Who the 'ell do you think you're talkin' too?' the prisoner responded angrily. 'You should be in 'ere your bleedin' self for what you done to the country.' We were all amazed as Jack told the tale with great amusement.

Perhaps the most sensational security incident involving shooting concerned a Government Minister who happened to be an outstanding shot at high pheasants — Lord Lambton, who resigned as Minister for the Royal Air Force in 1973 following an unfortunate sex scandal. The call-girl who brought about his downfall was called Norma Levy and her husband had managed to take photographs of his wife with the Minister in compromising situations.

On occasion, Norma Levy worked as a hostess in a London night-club and she confided her fears to the lady who ran it that her husband might try to blackmail Lord Lambton or, worse still, perhaps sell the pictures to a foreign power. Aware that one of her regular patrons, a prominent shooting man, moved in political circles, she told him of her concern, suggesting that the Government should be informed of the possible danger threatening Lord Lambton and his position in the Defence Ministry. After careful thought, the gentleman, a shooting colleague of mine, decided to approach Jim Prior (now Lord), whom he also met regularly in the shooting field. Because of the possible security implications, which happily never materialized, Prior informed the Prime Minister, Ted Heath, who was so appalled that Lambton was required to resign. The shooting connection was the immediate cause of the official interest but Lambton's fate was sealed, anyway, because the photographs and the story behind them had been sold to a Sunday newspaper. Lord Prior, who told me the background while we were shooting together,

47

referred to this sad incident, which deprived the RAF of an excellent Minister, in his memoirs.

The *Spycatcher* affair, which occupied so much media space, led to some embarrassing and, on occasion, farcical, situations in the shooting field. I had been in conversation, mainly at shoots, with Sir Michael Havers, the Attorney-General, concerning various sensitive matters. While committed not to reveal their source publicly in his lifetime I had mentioned certain relevant details to Peter Wright in letters under conditions of absolute confidentiality. Unfortunately, to pursue his bid to publish *Spycatcher* in the Australian court, he released all my confidential letters to the media to embarrass Havers, and the Government generally, and much was made in Parliament and the media of my association with the Attorney-General. As I was continuing to meet Havers at shoots, I offered to withdraw from them lest the fact that we had been together again should leak and lead to further mischief from Labour backbenchers and the newspapers supporting them. Manfully, he advised me to do no such thing. 'Life must go on, especially shooting life,' he declared. All that happened was that when we found ourselves at the same shoot we tried to keep as far away as possible but, inevitably, there were occasions when we were drawn next to each other in the shooting line or had to travel in close confinement in a vehicle. When Havers wished to say anything he would loudly preface his remarks with 'Addressing nobody in particular . . .'. He had a good sense of humour and needed it.

There can be little doubt that, for most journalists responsible for high-level political affairs, it would pay to live in London. Valuable friendships can be forged by joining the right clubs, by accepting invitations to embassy cocktail parties and by having a London home to which contacts can be invited. My intimate interviewing in London had to be restricted to three or four lunches a week, as I was prepared to dine there so rarely. I justified the flat which the office provided by using it for interviews with people who felt it unsafe to be seen lunching with me. These included Ministers as well as civil servants and intelligence officers. On the positive side, however, by living out of London and getting the first train home I dodged the major hazards, such as booze and time wasted with the 'great champagning journalists' in El Vino's and their other Fleet Street haunts. It would seem self-evident that a news-gatherer should waste no time in the company of his rivals because they are never going to tell him anything of value. No doubt I carried this antipathy to extremes and was considered eccentric. So much so that, once, on being introduced to the manageress of a Scottish fishing hotel in the wilds of Deeside she immediately said, 'I've heard about you. You are the Lone Wolf of

Fleet Street.' I used that hotel, the Raemoir, near Banchory, many times and she always called me 'Wolf'. Recently, after many years, I returned again and though the lady was dead her sister, who was running the hotel, greeted me as 'Wolf'!

My commuting train journeys rarely wasted time because I could work during them and sometimes had influential companions who used the same country station, one of these being Harold Watkinson (now Lord), then the Defence Minister, with whom I established what journalists call a good working relationship. He kindly kept my thinking 'on the right lines' and enabled me to score an ace with Beaverbrook by being able to assure him that de Gaulle would veto Britain's entry into the Common Market long before he did so. Beaverbrook was so impressed that I was able to bring them together, which did me no harm at all.

I used the return journey to whip through the large pile of magazines and learned journals which arrived each day at the office for me. Having torn out the few pages containing likely 'stories' I left the rest on the rack and was told on several occasions how, when I had alighted, there was a scramble for them by my fellow passengers. My strange habit had an extraordinary consequence which distressed me for several years until I realized what was happening. For no apparent reason I was smitten with bouts of severe allergic rhinitis, an inflammation of the membranes of the nose and eyes which was sometimes incapacitating. Allergy clinic tests for every conceivable cause failed. As it often hit me on train journeys I suspected it might be dust in the carriage. It was, but of my own making. Eventually, it dawned on me that the culprit was the dust created when I tore the pages out of some of the magazines. Cutting them out with a razor-blade solved the problem.

Working from the country was possible only because of the telephone but, as other journalists have also found, there are dangers in operating by that device. One Sunday, while sitting in my study near Ewhurst in Surrey, I decided to file a report about a crisis in the Navy's dockyards and dialled the Guildford operator to make a transfer charge call to 01-353-8000, the *Daily Express* number. A voice I did not recognize answered and I asked to be put through to the News Editor. As even his voice was unfamiliar I asked who he was and then found that the operator had mistakenly connected me to 01-353-6000, which was the *Daily Mail*. The conversation ended in laughter and I eventually filed my copy to my paper.

A few days later a paragraph appeared in *Private Eye*, indicating that I was selling stories to the *Daily Mail* on the side and urging my proprietor, Sir Max Aitken, to do something about it. I was prepared to ignore the libel but Sir Max insisted that I sue, with the office bearing the costs. In the result I was awarded £1000 damages, a reasonable sum in those days, with which my wife bought herself an ankle-length mink coat. Technology has since solved this communications problem with the fax-machine.

A further necessity for the Fleet Street journalist stealing a march in the country is a loyal secretary who can head off problems until her boss can be contacted. I was magnificently served in this respect by Miss Yolande Brook, a Suffolk girl, who could be guaranteed to track me down in any emergency while suppressing any office curiosity as to my whereabouts.

Her unfailing kindness expressed itself late one afternoon when I was racing to finish an article to get home early. I asked her to deal summarily with a Mr Freddie Forsyth who had arrived, unsolicited, in the Fleet Street lobby to sell me a story I did not want. Instead, she brought him into my office along with three cups of tea. Stuck with this rather ascetic-looking stranger, I asked him what he was doing and he said that he was finishing a novel about the attempted assassination of General de Gaulle. As the French leader had been dead three years I did not think much of the idea and when my visitor had gone I told Yolande that the poor chap's novel was bound to fail. It proved to be *The Day of the Jackal* but I had not been alone in my judgement. Several publishers turned it down.

My country way of life was seriously endangered when Lord Beaverbrook suddenly took a deep dislike to overweight journalists. I feared, particularly, for my News Editor, Morley Richards, when the Beaver leaned forwards during a discussion about him and said, emphatically, 'He's too fat,' going on to argue that a fat body meant a lazy mind. He then named other fat ones, including Sefton Delmer, our most prestigious foreign correspondent. Sure enough, both Richards and Delmer were dismissed and, to my horror, the Beaver decided that I should be made News Editor of the *Daily Express* in the misguided belief that, as I was successful in finding stories in my fields, I would be good at directing others in theirs. When the Editor offered me the post I immediately declined it but, in deference to the Beaver, agreed to consider it for twenty-four hours. The longer I thought, the less I wanted it. I would be desk-bound in London and spending nights there. Instead of living life I would only be reading about it on bits of paper written by others. Worst of all, my country days, established with much subtlety as well as craft, would be devastatingly eroded.

As nobody had ever refused the News Editorship of the *Express*, I was called to the Beaver's presence at his country house at Cherkley, near Leatherhead, to be told that I was running away from promotion. To my surprise, I had little difficulty in convincing him that I would be quite unable to pass on my high-level contacts to anyone else and that they would no longer by available as sources to the newspaper. As I had introduced him to several of them he saw the wisdom of my stand and gave me a salary rise. As I drove home I was in no doubt that I had got my priorities right.

Later in my career I was offered a substantial increase by Vere Harmsworth (now Lord Rothermere) to switch to the *Daily Mail* and, again, I saw my good life in danger. I avoided it by inducing Sir Max Aitken to give me the same money and, as an extra incentive to remain, he put me on the Management Board of the newspaper. Regrettably, the board met every Wednesday, a day when I was often asked by Harry Hyams to shoot on his Ramsbury Estate in Wiltshire. So, before the season opened, I made an excuse to quit the board. Each time I lined up at Ramsbury's famous Plantation pheasant drive I knew I had got my priorities right yet again.

Since I retired from daily journalism people have often asked me if I miss Fleet Street. One reason that I do not is because I was never there that much.

CHAPTER 6

SEEING THINGS

It used to be possible for the payment of one shilling (5p) to secure a permit to fish many miles of the River Tees belonging to Lord Barnard. One of my favourite stretches was Winston, near the village of Gainford, where access by bicycle was easy and the river ran in a swift stream over an easily-wadeable bottom of flat boulders and pebbles. There were trout to be caught by means of fly, worms or, in the early summer, aquatic larvae called 'creepers'. When the river was low it was easy to spear eels with a kitchen fork for there were few flat boulders that did not hide one, anything up to eighteen inches in length. There was a belief that the skin of an eel wrapped round the wrist would strengthen it but the main purpose in spearing them was to fry them, along with chips made from potatoes usually brought from home but sometimes purloined from a field on the way. For this purpose, my friends and I kept an old frying pan, along with other utensils, hidden in the crotch of a big ivy-covered elm on the river bank.

One hot summer's afternoon, I was preparing a fire while a friend climbed to the crotch, about twenty feet up. There was a tremendous crack as the main limb of the tree crashed down a few yards in front of me. I saw the boy fall, clinging desperately to the limb. I saw him smashed between the weight of the limb and the hard, cobbly ground. The sight of his 'pepper and salt' Norfolk jacket, caught in the wind as he fell, is vivid after more than sixty years. I suppose that I blinked with horror, for I felt sure that the boy must be dead or gravely injured. Then I heard him shout from the still-standing trunk. He was still up there. The limb had fallen but not the boy. The vision I had seen of the boy falling looked every bit as real and solid as the branch which actually fell. Had I run away to get help I would have sworn on oath that he had fallen and nobody would have convinced me that he had not. After all, I had 'seen it with my own eyes'.

That experience, and later ones, led me to take a special interest in the relationship between the brain and the eyes in producing such realistic visions. What I realized at the time, and which still seems extraordinary, is that, under certain conditions, the brain has the capacity to project an imagined scene on to a real scene so that it is impossible to distinguish between what is real and what is not. Had I imagined the whole episode, the falling tree, the boy and the river-bank, it would have been more easily explicable because it would have been just like a dream, which is totally imaginary. Instead, the falling boy had been inserted by my brain into the actual surrounding circumstances and behaved just as he would have done if his fall had been real.

The similarity between that vivid hallucination and most people's alleged experience of a ghost struck me at the time. The sentry on duty in the Tower of London at midnight does not imagine the whole execution scene of Anne Boleyn. He sees the ghost of Anne Boleyn walking across the real Tower Green just as Hamlet saw his father's ghost on the real battlements of Elsinore. It is the same with hallucinations seen by those suffering from alcoholism. They see pink elephants dancing on a real bed. The hallucinations of schizophrenics and those suffering from senile dementia are also a mixture of the real and the imagined, so ingeniously intertwined by the brain that the two cannot be separated.

As I progressed with my biological studies it seemed obvious that, in all such visual hallucinations, the eyes as well as the brain must be deeply involved and a possible explanation, which now satisfies me fully, presented itself. When we say that we see an object, such as a tree, what we really see is the light reflected by that object to our eyes. This light passes through the lens in each eye on to the retina where if forms an image. This is converted to nervous impulses which pass along the optic nerves to a certain area of the brain which reconstitutes them to the three-dimensional picture of what we say we 'see'. We see the tree with the brain rather than with the eyes, which are just the collecting instruments.

Normally, the nervous impulses can pass in only one direction along the nerve fibres — from the two retinas of the eyes to that part of the brain which does the seeing. That is so because there are structures in the nerve fibres, called synapses, which act as valves, ensuring that the impulses travel only in the one direction. However, it is my belief that, under certain conditions, such as severe emotional stress, the influence of drugs or illness, the valves may not function properly. If that happens, the nervous impulses can then also pass, briefly, in the wrong direction — from the brain to the retinas. In such a circumstance, the retinas would record a mixed picture made up of what was actually coming into the eyes from reality and what was coming in backwards from imagination by the brain. This mixed image would then travel back as nervous impulses to the brain which would be unable to distinguish what was real from what was imaginary and would build up a picture composed of both. In other words, it would be an hallucination, such as I 'saw' on the river-bank during a moment of horror. I had never experienced anything comparable before and I was not, I believe, the type of child likely to do so. Nor have I had such a vivid experience since though, for a few moments some years ago, it seemed that I was doing so. Driving across heathland near my home near Ewhurst, I came across a gallows at a crossroads with a man about to be hanged and a priest intoning his last rites before a crowd of onlookers. On closer inspection, however, it turned out to be a film set.

Many of us have convinced ourselves that an object was something which it was not, due, I suspect to this type of eye-brain phenomenon. When stalking a rabbit which eventually turned out to be a tuft of grass I have frequently convinced myself that I could see its eye and its whiskers and have even fired at it. Recently, I lost £1 to my wife over what I was sure was a dead hedgehog lying on the road but which turned out to be a clod of turf. I was certain that I had seen the prickles.

Full-blown hallucinations are not uncommon, especially among young children and old people. The most usual times for such experiences are during the process of going to sleep and waking up. For example, my mother was convinced that she had seen a vision of Jesus in a half-asleep condition while under the influence of a sleeping pill. An hallucination caused by the process I have described is a likelier explanation especially as her description of the figure matched the image of Jesus projected by European painters and sculptors, which, in all probability, bears no relation to what Jesus really looked like as a member of the Jewish race. The same applies, I believe, to the many alleged visions of the Virgin Mary.

When my children were small we lived in an ancient cottage in Ewhurst village, in Surrey, and they heard how, before it was modernized, an old woman who inhabited it alone died and was not found for several days, by which time rats had mutilated her face. Each, on different occasions, claimed that the old woman had entered their rooms while they were not quite asleep. I have experienced such a half-waking hallucination long enough to experiment with it. I was sleeping in the attic bedroom of a country hotel and on opening my eyes, round about midnight, I was astonished to see a huge wooden chest on the floor beside the bed, its intricate carvings glowing with green fluorescent light. I knew that I was at least partially awake because I could see the dim outline of the other furniture and was conscious enough to try a couple of quick tests. I shut my eyes and the chest disappeared but it was still there when I opened them again. The phantom therefore had to be something more than just a dream. I then turned over and looked into the darkness on the other side of the bed. The chest suddenly materialized there, as before, satisfying me that it was a product of my mind and had no separate existence. Then it vanished and I could not conjure it up again.

More significantly I have recently found that — on occasion, though not regularly to order — I can imagine something like a square or diamond while I am lying down with my eyes shut and then see a definite after-image of it. I have done this many times and can see no explanation other than that the mental image which I conjure up in the brain is projected to the retinas. Sometimes I can do it with an imagined human face and feel that, with practice, it might become much easier.

Perhaps visionaries and mystics, especially those who indulge in long bouts of fasting, experience this phenomenon more often and to a more vivid extent. Some may be able to do it to order. This may also apply to some fortune-tellers who gaze into crystal balls. What they believe they see may be half-way between thoughts and hallucinations and it is not surprising that their ability to 'see' pictures there is enhanced by drugs like LSD and mescalin. Scientific tests have shown that they see such visions in colour and in three dimensions. This same general explanation could apply to auditory hallucinations — the hearing of things which are demonstrably not there. Like sight, hearing happens in the brain, the ears being simply the collectors of air vibrations which are translated into sounds.

This explanation, then, should suffice to explain every kind of vision, including ghosts, except for those seen by more than one person at once. I have questioned several people who claim to have seen a ghost but have never met two people who saw the same ghost at the same time.

Strange noises, often attributed to ghosts, have, of course, frequently been heard by two or more people at the same time. My school friend, who eventually became the family doctor in the village of Masham, in Wensleydale, told me how he had visited a remote cottage to comfort an aged man whose wife had died and was lying 'laid out' upstairs. The old man told him 'You know she's not dead, doctor. Listen!' The doctor heard what sounded like footsteps and the sound of drawers being opened and closed. He rushed upstairs thinking he might have made some terrible error when he had previously certified her death but found the corpse exactly as he had left it on the previous day. He could offer no explanation but accepted that there probably was some physical cause of the noises, which the old man had obviously heard several times.

Shortly after the end of the Second World War I encounted the most famous ghost-hunter of his day — Harry Price, who had inherited a fortune and spent it on psychical research. His fame rested largely on the evidence he had collected 'proving' that the old rectory in the village of Borley, near Long Melford, in Suffolk, was haunted by the ghost of a nun who had been violated and murdered by some aristocrat — most hauntings being usually associated with violent deaths. (In a fair world it should be the murderer, not the victim, who has to do the haunting, injustice apparently being perpetuated beyond the grave.) Price admitted that he had never seen the nun but, while he was watching one night in the company of Charlie Sutton, a Fleet Street journalist, Sutton had suddenly rushed forwards crying 'There she is!' and wrote a newspaper report saying how he had seen the apparition, which Price believed.

The rectory had burned down when I visited it but the ruins were said still to be haunted by the nun and I spent fruitless hours at night looking for her. Former servants of the rectory assured me that it had never been haunted and that all the strange noises recorded by Harry Price had been caused by jackdaws in the chimney. Shortly before he died, Charlie Sutton told me that he had not seen anything but was determined to take back a 'story' for his newspaper.

In 1954 the Society for Psychical Research branded Harry Price, who had been dead for six years, as a man whose word could not be trusted after an investigation into the alleged haunting of Borley Rectory. They concluded that there was no convincing evidence that the nun had ever existed in real life, much less as a ghost. All my other investigations into alleged ghosts have ended in similarly disappointing fashion.

While I suppose some ghosts are reported in towns the great majority are attached to old country houses, often in remote places. Of course, the older a property is the more inhabitants it has had, and the more have died there, some, perhaps, violently. Now that more people die in hospital than at home perhaps there will be a reduction in allegedly haunted houses.

There is obviously a close association between hallucinations and dreams which have always been vivid in my life and, except for rare occasions, have been an added joy. If only I could visualize in imagination as vividly as I can dream, how much better would I be endowed for writing! As an occasional author of fiction it would be of enormous benefit to me if my imagination could function during consciousness with the clarity and virtuosity it displays when dreaming. I have dreamt every time I have slept, even when dozing in a chair, and the countryside has dominated my dream life as much as it has influenced my real existence.

On waking I can always remember the dream, which is invariably in colour and often includes sounds as well as sights, and sometimes it affects my morning mood. So, 'getting out of the wrong side of the bed' may really mean 'getting out after the wrong dream'. In general, I suppose, dreams are a mixture of past experiences, present anxieties and future hopes and, sometimes it is possible to recall the real-life event which appeared to have triggered off the dream. However, it is my view that far too little research has been undertaken into the capacity of the brain to imagine situations which are entirely new and project them into a sequence which is as vivid as watching a colour film and, perhaps more so, because, usually, the dreamer is aware of his participation in the scenario. On nearly every occasion in my dreams, while many of the people involved may be real people whom I have met, the venues are almost always entirely imaginary. Somehow, in ways which I regard as quite astonishing, the brain creates images of places and buildings which I have certainly never seen and do not really exist. They are often highly innovative, architecturally, both inside and out. Perhaps most of us are more creative in our dreams than when awake.

Sometimes, I am fishing pools on rivers which I have never visited or, so far as I can recall, have never read about. Yet they are there in all colourful details — the banks, the trees, the rocks, the currents, even the fishing huts. Sometimes the river will run through a town or village which is totally fictitious. It is the same with shooting dreams. I rarely, if ever, dream about a real-life shoot but the fields, woods, the birds and the other guns are all there in as much detail as they would be in reality.

I wonder to what extent painters of invented landscapes or country scenes where imagination has obviously impinged on reality have been affected by dreams or fantasies. With artists like Turner mental fantasy overrode reality, while some, like William Blake, seemed unable to distinguish between them or did not see any point in doing so when committing their messages to canvas. Indeed, the whole Romantic movement in painting, poetry and music seems to have been based on a deliberate rejection of reality in favour of fantasy, visions and dreams which offered a more pleasant and more satisfying interpretation of the world.

None of my dreams has ever been prophetic in the sense that I dreamt in accurate detail of a new place or river which I eventually visited. I can only remember one instance of a prophetic dream which, though it had national impact, could, I believe, be attributed to coincidence. While I was salmon fishing in Scotland in 1974, not long after Harold Wilson had become Prime Minister again, I dreamt that the government had tested a much improved nuclear warhead for the Navy's Polaris submarine missile. I made a note to check the situation on my return to Fleet Street, when evasive replies from the Defence Ministry convinced me that a test was imminent. When questioned in Parliament, Wilson admitted that a test had already taken place in secrecy, causing international outrage because Labour MPs had been loudly objecting to nuclear tests by the French.

It would be reasonable to assume that the brain assembles imaginary places from little bits of environments which have been experienced and then forgotten but I do not think that is correct. I believe that most of my dreams are novel in their entirety. My brain is quite unable to imagine such scenes in consciousness with anything remotely like the same capability, yet in dreaming it appears to do it effortlessly and immediately. Most of us day-dream and fantasize more than we would care to admit and do so in the form of mental pictures but these are rarely, if ever, as vivid as those which the brain produces during sleep. The power of imagination, which is probably unique to the human mind, has been central to civilization and sleeping dreams offer a means of studying it which has been neglected.

Usually, the people I dream about are those whom I know or have known in the past but sometimes the faces and personalities which I dream up in great detail are of people whom I cannot remember having ever seen and, again, I think that the brain has the capacity to construct such human forms which are entirely imaginary. They do not seem to be jumbled compositions of the features of several real people but are entirely new to me and I believe that they have never existed. Occasionally such imagined people can be quite frightening. While sleeping in a country hotel I experienced a nightmare in which I was tied to a bed by a most evil-looking character who threatened to slit my throat with a knife. Mustering some courage I shouted, 'If only I could get my hands free . . .' Then I felt his hot, horrible breath as he yelled, mockingly, 'If, if, if . . .' I awoke in a sweat and could hear a guttural voice in the darkness intoning 'If, if, if . . .' It took some time for me to realize that the source of the sound was the landlord's aged dog breathing huskily in its sleep outside my bedroom door.

The speed with which such realities are sometimes incorporated into a dream is also a tribute to the brain's extraordinary capacity during sleep. Many have had the experience of dreaming that they hear some loud noise such as a pistol shot and immediately awaken to find the postman knocking on the door. In 1940, while I was a trooper in the

Royal Armoured Corps sleeping on the floor of an old barrack-room at Catterick Camp, along with about thirty others, one of our squad was late for early morning parade. When asked why by the Sergeant-Major he claimed that he had not heard the reveille trumpet, which was sounded on the barrack square about 200 yards away. Nothing more was said but, precisely at 6 a.m. next morning we were all rudely awakened as the trumpeter, with the Sergeant-Major standing by, blew reveille in the exposed ear of the offending soldier. In the iron-roofed barrack-room the din was deafening and I must have awakened immediately. Yet I remembered details of a dream in which I was heroically leading a cavalry charge to the spurring sound of trumpets. I watched myself doing it for, while some dreamers habitually take an active part in their dreams as they would in real life, others, like me, tend to witness the events as detached observers, seeing themselves in action as though in a film.

Some people may believe that they never dream about anything but they would be wrong. Dreaming is an essential part of the restorative sleep process and everybody does it, though its purpose remains a mystery. When any person is dreaming the eyeballs oscillate gently under the lids as though scanning the imagined scene. During dreamless sleep they remain still. These oscillations can be recorded by means of small electrodes taped near the eyes so that charts of the dreaming pattern can be recorded throughout the night. This phenomenon suggests that the eyes are involved in dreaming. So, perhaps, my theory that feedback from the brain to the retinas is involved in hallucinations may also apply to dreams. Experiments involving many hundreds of people have shown that every normal person dreams — and for about the same length of time — roughly ninety minutes, usually broken into three or four sequences separated by dreamless slumber. Those who insist that they never dream can remember their dreams if awakened during a period of rapid eye-movement and questioned immediately.

Dreaming has provided such a pleasurable annexe to my life that I feel sorry for those who believe that they do not dream. But there is one most unpleasant aspect of dreaming, half-dreaming, which I could have done without. For some sixty years I have experienced, intermittently, a curious disorder known as sleep paralysis. I seem to be going to sleep normally when, suddenly, I become aware that, while being awake, I am completely paralysed. While all my senses are working I am unable to move or speak. Worse, I feel that I am sliding into deep unconsciousness from which there might be no return. My brain urges me to act quickly and I know, from instinct as well as experience, that I must make a tremendous effort to get some part of me moving. I also try to shout for assistance but nothing emerges apart from guttural sounds. And all the time I seem to be drifting down into coma. When all seems lost I manage to get a finger moving, then a hand and with a shudder I am out of the vortex. The ordeal lasts perhaps no more than a couple of minutes but has never ceased to be less terrifying. If I try to go to sleep immediately afterwards the odds are that the paralysis will recur but, being ready for it I can usually defeat it.

I have had attacks while sitting dozing in a chair and even in a train. Little is known about sleep paralysis except that it is not a symptom of any disease and occurs because the body is asleep while the mind remains awake. I have been assured that if I let myself go I would simply sleep and wake up normally but I have never been prepared to try and remain unconvinced, wondering how many people who expired in their sleep from 'heart failure' really died from sleep paralysis.

Scientists comparing the brain to a super-computer have suggested that, in dreaming, it is rifling through the store of memories and eliminating those of no value. This cannot be true of the dreams I experience because the village, imaginary river or a piece of countryside which my brain has conjured up may reappear in another dream on another night, perhaps weeks later, meaning that it has gone firmly into the memory store. I can also deliberately recall it while I am awake.

The recurrent dream is of particular interest to the psychologist, who believes it may tell him something about the nature of the dreamer, and for almost all my adult life I have been subjected to recurrent dreams which, while they vary in detail, have the same central theme. I have arrived at a shoot but I have mislaid my gun, or its parts won't fit together, or the cartridges won't fire. Quite often night falls before I get started. Sometimes, when I arrive at my shooting peg I am inside a closed room. Alternatively, I am about to fish an inviting river but never get started because I have forgotten the rod or some other item of tackle or I am held up for various reasons until darkness falls.

The Freudian interpretation of these dreams, which I experience at least once a month, is obvious, both the gun and the rod being phallic symbols — my brain is giving visual expression to my fear of becoming impotent. The only thing doubtful about this theory is that I have never had reason to feel threatened in that respect, though it may be a deep-seated fear that affects all men subconsciously. It would be illuminating, in this context, to know whether women who fish or shoot ever have similar dream experiences. My wife does not.

As the central component of my recurrent dreams is frustration, they may be no more than an expression of frustration in my professional life, or even in my real-life sport. I certainly experience plenty of frustration due to ineptitude in shooting. In fishing, where I could claim some competence, frustration is common enough in pursuit of the salmon, which is the usual subject of my fishing dreams.

There can be little doubt that dreams provide insight into human character because, whatever other purpose they may have, they are clearly an extension of the fantasies which occupy a large part of everybody's conscious thinking, and certainly of mine. Perhaps my problem is that I devote too much time to thinking about shooting or fishing while I am awake. While some people who cannot get to sleep count sheep jumping over a fence I have a different ploy. I count salmon leaping a fall. Though that may sound eccentric I am in good company. That super-sportsman, the late Sir Thomas Sopwith, sadly became blind in his later years and spent much time alone in his study with little to do but day-dream. I asked him once what he thought about most, expecting that the reply would be about his exciting days as a pioneer aviator or his international yacht-racing experiences. He thought for a while then said 'I think mainly about days spent shooting and fishing'.

CHAPTER 7

SOME DREAMS COME TRUE

M y boyhood dream was to own a country estate with an ancient house of character, with its own fishing and shooting and a large home farm. It needed to be tucked away, peacefully, yet not too far from the civilization which would be essential for me to earn enough money to support it and enjoy it. This dream arose from an experience I had, at the age of sixteen or so, in fields belonging to Kiplin Mill, a then functioning flour mill on a tributary of the River Swale near the village of Langton and just a cycle ride from Croft, where I was then living. Before entering the mill sluice, the little brook expanded into a large lake in front of a Jacobean mansion called Kiplin Hall. The lake was teeming with roach and pike and I had permission to fish it because it was rented by the fishing club of which I was a junior member.

Late one summer's evening, while I was camping there with several school friends, I met the gentleman in residence, who was a tenant, and he suggested that I would catch bigger fish if I used the boat which I had often noticed tied up in front of the house. He then took me into the Hall for a sherry and piloted me through all the rooms, putting on the lights so that I could see the panelling and the pictures. It was my first sight of the inside of a stately home and I was so impressed by the contribution to the atmosphere made by the panelling that a panelled house became an ambition, which I eventually achieved, though on a minor scale.

The idea of an ancestral home with family roots, deeply down, has remained most attractive to me but, failing the right forebears, one can savour that satisfaction, vicariously, to some degree, by being invited to such homes as a guest and the considerable extent to which I have experienced this has been almost entirely thanks to shooting and fishing.

I was fortunate, in some establishments, to be just in time to experience the remnants of Edwardian-style hospitality with butlers and valets, who were clearly displeased if one unpacked or packed one's own bags, but now, even in the largest houses, financial restrictions necessitate a growing degree of DIY. Nevertheless, the experience of staying in a stately home remains uniquely pleasurable. Of those I have visited, my prime choice, as a building, would be Ramsbury Manor, in Wiltshire, because, though grand in every sense and set, magnificently, in rising parkland on an expanded arm of the River Kennet, it is small enough to be homely. The home of Harry Hyams, the property developer, who has lavished love and resources on the Carolingian building and its surroundings with faultless taste, it is a heartwarming example of money made out of concrete blocks being ploughed into the countryside to its long-lasting benefit.

The outstanding room there is the saloon, panelled in walnut. Above each of the four corner doors there was a plain rectangular panel and on one occasion while my wife and I were there I noticed that one of the panels was missing. Harry explained that an art expert had been inspecting his paintings one late afternoon when the sun's rays had slanted on to the panel. His eye had spotted markings caused by a concealed painting which had been covered over at some time. A few weeks later the panel was back in place bearing a beautiful landscape of the type painted by Claude Lorrain in the mid-seventeenth century, when Ramsbury Manor was built. Eventually, each of the four panels was found to bear such a landscape and examination of the huge brown walnut panel over the fireplace revealed signs of an even grander painting hidden beneath. Cleaning produced a splendid portrait of a small boy, probably an early scion, garbed in classic style with a ruin in the background, which almost certainly represents the previous house on the site.

The immediate question centred on the identity of the person who could have been guilty of such vandalism in having them painted over and it was confidently assumed that some tasteless 'Victorian' or other was to blame. If Harry knew the answer he did not say but, a few years later, at a dinner in the district, I sat next to a gentleman who knew it because he had overseen the dreadful act, much to his own disgust. The culprit had been the wife of a relatively recent owner of the house who preferred the panelling to look bare and to match.

To the sorrow of many friends, Harry gave up shooting and gunfire is no longer heard at Ramsbury, which is now a sanctuary for wildfowl, some of them exotic, even including flamingos. His last shooting day, though we did not appreciate it then, was marked by the biggest bottle of champagne I have ever seen. It took two of us to lift the table-high bottle, which had been brought as a Christmas present, and little of it remained when we all departed.

The largest stately home I have stayed in is Woburn Abbey, the enormous abode of the Marquis and Marchioness of Tavistock in

Bedfordshire. The excellent family pheasant shoot is enlivened when the beaters put up some of the strange creatures living wild and safely in the park. The first sight of a wallaby hopping in front of the shooting line, for example, is highly entertaining. Dining there, in distinguished company, surrounded by a splendid collection of Canalettos, ingeniously illuminated as though by the Venetian sun, can never be forgotten. Nevertheless, my wife and I felt sorry for our hosts. Deeply happy in a much smaller home which they had loved, they had unexpectedly been loaded with the huge responsibility of Woburn and its upkeep far too soon because the Marquis's father, the Duke of Bedford, was determined to live abroad. This burden may have been a factor in causing the massive brain haemorrhage, from which Robin Tavistock has made such a miraculous recovery, largely thanks to the love and determination of his wife and children.

Sandbeck Park, home of the Earl of Scarbrough near Maltby in Yorkshire, is the most impressive 'shooting-box' in which I have stayed. A large establishment, it really was a place used only occasionally for shooting when Lord Scarbrough's ancestors, the Lumleys of Lumley Castle, in Durham, were vastly wealthy. A small portion of that wealth can be seen in some of the family portraits collected by the Elizabethan Lord Lumley and sporting the Lumley 'cartellino', a painted-on addition giving information about the sitter's identity and other details. Had that vast collection not been dispersed its value would be incalculable. While gesticulating rather wildly in conversation with Field Marshal Lord Harding during breakfast there, I shattered the antique chair which was supporting me but Lord Scarbrough seemed unconcerned 'Not to worry,' he said, buttering his toast. 'There are twenty-four more of that set upstairs.'

The grounds at Sandbeck are surrounded by coal mines and there are streams where, should a pheasant fall in them, a dog sent to retrieve returns black with coal dust. On one occasion when I was there a major pheasant drive failed because poachers had been busy the night before. Looking at the beaters, who were mostly local miners, I had little doubt that the culprits were among them.

In Scotland, shooting-boxes usually look like what they are supposed to be and a typical one is Kinveachie, near Grantown-on-Spey, where I have stayed for grouse-shooting and salmon fishing. The main sitting room is panelled with half-sawn trunks of pine trees embellished with the heads of stags shot on the estate, which belongs to the Earl of Seafield. The surroundings are spectacular but my favourite Scottish estate, incomparably, is Kinnaird, close by Dunkeld, owned for many years by the Ward family whose main seat, Chilton, is close to my home in Berkshire. Kinnaird, which covers 9000 acres

SOME DREAMS COME TRUE

of particularly beautiful Perthshire, is not large for Scotland but has everything — a beautiful salmon stretch of the Tay, trout lochs, a pheasant and partridge shoot and a small grouse moor in process of being regenerated. The main house has been converted to a luxury hotel and whenever I am there I always visit the billiard room to see the array of salmon on the walls — all 40 pounds or more and one 50-pounder taken from the beat or nearby. While staying at Kinnaird as a guest of the late laird, Reggie Ward, I met the lady who had caught the monster when she had been a slip of a girl. She had arrived back from the river to find the owner standing, proudly, over a 43-pounder laid on the steps. A very experienced fisherman, he was none too pleased to have his ace so decisively trumped by a girl beginner. Happily, we continue to be asked to the Kinnaird estate, now run and much embellished by Reggie's widow, Connie.

Over the years, the splendid ambience of Highclere Castle near Newbury, has given my wife and me great pleasure through friendship with the last two Earls of Carnarvon, whose seat it is. My association with Highclere began, rather inauspiciously, shortly after the war when I rented the pike fishing in Milford Lake there. During each of the three years I had it, someone caught a pike weighing more than 30 pounds but, sadly, I never had that good fortune. I was in with a chance, though, when quite a large pike I was playing from a boat, was seized by a monster which made off into the water-lilies. It hung on for a few exciting minutes but then let go.

I lost the fishing rights when the Earl of Carnarvon's heir, Lord Porchester, decided to live in the delightful small house built on the lakeside by William Kent in the eighteenth century. It was Lord Porchester whom I was to meet socially first, while shooting at Sir Thomas Sopwith's estate. He kindly invited me to fish the lake again which I did with some success. When I came to live near Newbury our wives became friendly through their mutual interest in the Newbury Musical Festival and we have remained closely in touch through shooting, music and socially. Through that relationship I became friendly with the late Lord Carnarvon who asked me to his family Christmas pheasant shoots. He was a rare character who had lived life the way he wanted to and had an outstanding capacity to bring laughter into the lives of his friends, all too rare a talent in a now too-serious world. He was superstitious about the number thirteen and, should that chance to be the total at one of his delicious shoot lunches, he pacified the evil spirits by sitting at a table set one inch from the top of the main one.

Compton Manor, near King's Somborne, the medium-sized country home of the late Sir Thomas Sopwith and his wife, could hardly be described as stately in that it was not 'grand, lofty or imposing' as the dictionary definition requires, but no friend's house, has given me more pleasure. Tommy's greeting on arrival was invariably 'Welcome home!' and that is how one felt throughout the experience. Being a regular guest at such a place gives added joy, not just through established friendship with the hosts and other guests, but through the house staff, the shoot and river-keepers and even the beaters. The easy, comfortable atmosphere of the manor house attracted many distinguished guests and it was a privilege to see them humanized when behaving like ordinary mortals. On several nights when the young Prince Charles was able to attend dinner at Compton, I was much impressed by how well he managed to fit in to a group all so much older and to contribute constructively to any conversation. As a consequence, I wrote to Lord Mountbatten saying that he had so much confidence that he would do well in his public relations when he came to make speeches. Mountbatten replied that he had shown my letter to the Queen who had remarked — as any mother might — 'He must be better than we thought.' When discussing the youthful Charles with Mountbatten, later, he remarked, 'He has inherited the best qualities of both parents' — rather implying that he had been spared the worst, whatever they might be.

My experience of the Prince, then and later, does not square with the image of him conjured up by journalists regarding the severe problems of his marriage. He was caring, warm and sensitive and, I believe, still is. To his credit, he has forbidden close friends to tell his side of the extraordinary story which would engender widespread sympathy for him while his staff, who regularly witness the sad truth, are sworn to secrecy. In Royal life especially, circumstances and people are rarely what they seem.

When he was Prime Minister, Harold Macmillan held his distance from journalists, though my wife and I had been to dine at Birch Grove, his country home. Round the Sopwith dinner table, however, he could hardly have been more forthcoming. He shook with laughter as he told how, when visiting the White House, accompanied by Sir William Penney (later Lord), to discuss the East-West balance of nuclear weapons, Penney had been asked by the US President 'How many Russian H-bombs would be needed to knock out Britain?' In his deceptively lackadaisical drawl Penney had replied, 'I think five would finish us, but shall we say eight to be on the safe side.'

Another regular at the Sopwith table was Reggie Dilhorne, the Lord Chancellor who, when the mood took him, would take us into his confidence about fascinating cases, like the trial of the KGB agent, George Blake — 'If he had retracted his confession in the box we

SOME DREAMS COME TRUE

couldn't have touched him'. Or that of John Stonehouse, the Labour Minister — 'He was in it up to the neck', referring to his doubtful contacts with Czech intelligence agents. His *bête noire* was Dr Bodkin Adams, whose trial for ending the life of a patient for gain collapsed while Dilhorne, then Attorney-General, had been prosecuting. I attended the trial which was the only one in my experience to rival a Hollywood court drama with last minute evidence totally undermining the Crown's main witnesses.

Such indiscreet dissertations continued at Scarr House, the Sopwiths' Yorkshire establishment in Langthwaite village, in Arkengarthdale, at the centre of a 20,000-acre grouse moor. Looking from the windows there had been no change in the view during the last two hundred years. I remember coming in from the moor with Dilhorne when the butler told him that it had just been announced on the radio that Edward Heath had dropped him from his shadow cabinet. It was the end of Dilhorne's long political career and he was near to tears. Such are the pleasures of power.

Over the hill, in the next valley, another close shooting friend, Sir Joseph Nickerson, had his shooting-box in Middleton-in-Teesdale on the edge of the greatest grouse moor of all — Wemmergill. To stay in Middleton House was to revert to the days of the early nineteenth-century squires with the best food and wines in profusion. It was the same at Joe's main base, his farmhouse at Rothwell in Lincolnshire, which he had acquired in 1939 to find sheep in what is now a most elegant dining room and chickens in the palatial bedrooms now adorned with his collection of sporting paintings. Whatever Joe, and his wife Eugenie did, they did it in style.

While the Edwardian game of musical beds may still go on in some great houses I have never encountered it. I have, however, stayed at a grouse moor where my wife was warned about the bedroom movements of a certain guest, which, it so happened, did not surprise us.

Unlike Mr Jorrocks, I have dined in many stately homes where I did not sleep, being a near neighbour. One of my favourites is Faccombe Manor, owned by Brigadier Tim Landon and set in a superb estate on the high ground of North Hampshire. Mrs Landon is an Esterhazy so many of the guests there are of the European aristocracy, now mainly of historic interest only. It is, nevertheless, fascinating to break bread with an Austrian Archduke who is the grand-nephew of the Emperor Franz Joseph, and whose father was the last of the Habsburgs to rule over vast areas of the Danube Basin.

These delightful experiences, and many more, have induced my fantasy of the perfect estate which would be one entirely cut off from public access by high cliffs, with woods providing challenging pheasants and partridges and with a salmon river and a trout stream running through it. The nearest I got was a Tudor farmhouse, off any well-beaten track, with a bit of rough shooting and only a pond filled with coarse fish. Nevertheless, for twenty-three years Lowerhouse Farm, near Ewhurst in Surrey, was heaven for me and mine, as it had been, for exactly that period of time for its previous owners. When I put the nose of my car up its long drive, every pot-hole was a pleasure. Once I reached the old, oak front door I could see no other form of human habitation. I was surrounded by woods and fields, with sheep and cattle, happily not my responsibility. The only lane wound over a hill with nothing visible beyond. My little patch of water housed waterfowl and plants of various kinds. At dawn I could shoot rabbits out of the bedroom window, though the resulting smell of gunpowder did not endear me to my wife.

Further away, but in view, were two hills of almost 1000 feet — high for the South. The house was only 32 miles from London yet so remote that, one night when all hell was let loose in the *Daily Express* office because I was urgently needed and had deliberately put my telephones off the hook, a dispatch rider sent to rouse me failed to find it.

Inside the house, which dated from 1525, was a wealth of beams, massive inglenook fireplaces and old panelling which I had acquired and installed with my own hands. Over the years, again with my hands, I embellished the place with stone walls, pillars, fountains and other structures which looked ancient but, as may have since been discovered, were strengthened inside with hundreds of wine bottles in lieu of rubble.

Doing anything constructive has always been a joy and I much prefer to do something, even badly, than watch anybody else doing it well. Seeing a stone wall grow provides a special sense of achievement though, while it looks so solid and permanent, one is always aware of the poet's observation that there is something that doesn't like a wall.

Alternating stints of writing with bouts of panelling and stonemasonry, I reckon I wrote my signature with loving care all over that house and its grounds — the first where I really felt I belonged since my days at the Comet pub in Croft. I set about the neglected garden but made the error of trying to do too much, the wisdom being to keep it small to avoid being imprisoned by its demands.

As I have always experienced in the country, there was so much to do that there was no time to worry about what life is all about. That pointless exercise is for people with time on their hands in bed-sitters or cafés while indigenous rustics, as opposed to the urban invaders, are too busy with constructive work or challenging play. There may be less frantic rushing about than in the towns but time always seems to be short perhaps because, with no traffic jams and journeys to and from work being so much shorter, effort can be sustained for longer. It used to be said that country living was slow because the pace of agriculture could not be hurried but with modern farming techniques that is no longer true. It is hustled along all the time, with turnover being king, and perhaps the attitude has spread.

Fortunately, my daughter, Pat, and son, Michael, loved the ancient house and, though they both now work in London, their married homes are in country villages close to mine. Sadly, their mother, like my brief wartime wife, was not a country woman, hated fishing and shooting and pined for brighter lights, for which she eventually opted with somebody else. Seeing no form of human habitation from Lowerhouse Farm was a tremendous plus for me. For her it was staring into nothingness and she, too, was aware that under no circumstances would I be prepared to base myself in London, whatever the consequences. In general, concerning this sour section of my pastoral symphony, I believe that technology has seriously impinged on country marriage, which used to be more stable than its urban counterpart for lack of opportunity, if for no other reason. In particular, I blame what I call 'the three Ts' now available — time, the telephone and transport.

The replacement lady in my life, a Norfolk girl, was altogether more compatible with the country and my country activities and friends. One of the latter was Beaverbrook's daughter, the late Janet Kidd, who lived a mile away. She regularly visited us in her pony and trap but occasionally dropped in by helicopter, which used to annoy me because she chose to land by the outdoor swimming-pool which was surrounded, except on the sunny side, by cypress trees and climbing roses. The wind created by the rotor blades showered the pool with rose petals and other botanical debris. When I complained she rightly commented, 'If all you have to worry about is rose petals in your swimming pool . . . .!'

Lowerhouse Farm continually paid for its rather heavy upkeep by being a marvellous venue for entertaining contacts and it was particularly intriguing to have members of both MI5 and the KGB present at the same time. It was at such a party, with a senior KGB officer, Anatoli Strelnikov, present that the gregarious Defence Ministry official, Colonel Sammy Lohan, first met the rather mysterious, Russian-speaking Tory MP, Henry Kerby. They took to each other but both were too devious for each other's good. The meeting led to the sensational 1967 incident call the D Notice Affair, which was to end in the sacking of Lohan, amid outcries from all the media.

What I did not know was that, even when I had deliberately avoided having guests from British intelligence departments, there was usually one present who reported fully on the occasion to MI5. That was Lohan, himself — something I did not discover until researching a book in 1990. The records of the Civil Service Tribunal which had engineered Lohan's dismissal showed that he functioned as an MI5 informer with an expense account. They included a detailed report of a private party at my house.

Most of the time though, Lowerhouse Farm was a place of quiet for, while increasingly polluted by noise, the country still offers peaceful space for clearer thinking. It was no coincidence that Plato's Academy, the original of all think-tanks, academies and universities was located in a quiet grove in the country outside Athens. If cast away on a desert island, the record I would play on rising would be the most raucous made by the Rolling Stones to remind me of the worst horrors of the civilization which I was being spared and to underline the preciousness of the silence with which I was blessed.

It is my opinion, too, that life is more real in the country than in the towns, for in spite of its invasion by television, less time is spent there in the fantasy world than in towns, with their cinemas, theatres and other places of entertainment involved in diverting attention from reality. The 'theatre' is commonly given as a major advantage for living in London but, while sitting there, I have rarely thought my time well spent, a feeling I have never experienced about an evening on the river or a matinée in the field. The theatre is an escape from reality and the essence of country living lies in being occupied in ways which are not escapist.

As happens to most owners of any substantial property, my wife and I became too old for Lowerhouse Farm and my income too small to maintain it after my retirement from Fleet Street in 1979. I suppose that I had hoped to end my days there but there comes a time when the ageing process makes the occupation of an over-size establishment, with the children gone, too exacting. The large garden and grounds were beyond my resources, both physical and financial, and I could no longer view, with equanimity, my pennies going up to heaven in steam from the electrically-heated swimming-pool. Nor could I stomach the cost or the irritations of living-in staff, who were essential there and who tended to depart at such short notice.

It was after the last housekeeper had given notice on Christmas Eve and the expected replacement withdrew when she heard that we had gundogs, because she could never work where there were bloodsports, that I made my decision while driving back from a shoot. When I, rather diffidently, declared it to my wife, believing she would be upset, she was delighted. We both felt the need to move into a village where we could walk to the shops, feel more secure and exist when, perhaps, we could no longer drive a motor car. Our choice was conditioned entirely by country sports. We both wanted to move near some good trout river, which does not exist in Surrey, and some good shooting. We chose the village of Kintbury, in Berkshire, because the Kennet flowed through it and I was already in an excellent shoot there. It was an emotional break as we sold Lowerhouse Farm within a week, without having to put it on the market, through a friend whom we met at a shoot. My wife found the marvellous Kintbury replacement within two hours of beginning a search, while I was shooting nearby. My debts to shooting seem to be endless.

Shortly after we had moved, a knock on our new front door revealed the presence of an old journalistic colleague, called Ralph Hewins, who happened to be passing by. When I told him that I intended to continue with some measure of investigative journalism he remarked, incredulously, 'In Kintbury?'

Kintbury has done me rather proud and it is not over yet.

CHAPTER 8

A COUNTRYMAN CALLED BEAVERBROOK

It was purely coincidental but my Surrey home was only a short journey from Cherkley Court, Lord Beaverbrook's country seat, near Leatherhead. This meant that I was called to the presence there more often and, while this was always enjoyable, there were times early on Saturday, as I would be preparing to go off shooting, when the phone would ring and a voice would say, 'Ah got'cha! I want you come to lunch.' Before any explanation could be attempted the line would go dead. It was irritating but, in retrospect, I wish the telephone had rung more often for the Beaver's lunches were always memorable, often educational and sometimes hilarious.

I think that most people would think of Beaverbrook as a metropolitan politician and Fleet Street baron but all the time I knew him he was essentially a countryman pulling the strings mainly by the telephone, dictaphone or summonses to the presence. (How he would have loved the instant fax machine!) He could be very awkward indeed and therefore fits my dictionary definition of a country bumpkin. As his friend, Winston Churchill, would have commented 'Some bumpkin!'

Though he did not indulge in country sports any more — he had given up riding and had made Cherkley into a bird sanctuary — he had been a keen fisherman in his Canadian youth in New Brunswick and explained to me how a bad day's fishing had been a mutation moment in his career. On his twenty-first birthday, in 1900, he had been alone in a boat with nothing biting and, beset by an overwhelming feeling of futility, barked 'Ah, to Hell with it!', packed up and left to make his fortune. He decided to make money quickly and to do it by selling bonds. Canada was booming and people had savings to invest. He was a millionaire by the time he was thirty, after effectively cornering the cement market.

In his day, the east-coast Canadian rivers had been packed with Atlantic salmon and I cherish some of his thank-you notes for those I sent him from Scotland, especially one in which he thought that only a salmon caught by a Fourteenth Earl — meaning Lord Home — could be better than the one I had supplied. He never tired of poking fun at aristocrats, whom he affected to dislike. One of the long-term problems of having a humble background, as we both did, is that members of the so-called aristocracy tend to make one feel inferior. One such man with whom I used to fish in Scotland had never done a day's work, was not bright, certainly not courteous and mean to such a degree that, on one occasion, after dining with him, I had to stop at the fish and chip shop on my way back to my hotel. Yet when he walked down the river bank in his deerstalker I almost felt the necessity to touch my forelock. I never felt subservient to Beaverbrook or to anyone else who had made it through effort.

He enjoyed walking me round the grounds trying to catch me out, as a former botanist, on the names of wild flowers, one of his chuckling successes, I recall, being Ploughman's Spikenard, which did not grow in the North, where I learned the native flora. Throughout our long relationship, conducted mainly at Cherkley, Lord Beaverbrook treated me with kindness and warm consideration, even when I disagreed with him, as I frequently did on technical issues. When worsted in an argument he was wont to say 'You mustn't be hard on a poor old man', a remark which, according to Duncan Sandys, he had also made in a wartime Cabinet meeting, where the preposterous image had brought raucous laughter.

Some of my colleagues were not so fortunate. A few were treated to what became known as ordeal by lavatory. A senior writer or executive would be summoned at a certain time and when he arrived the butler would announce that his Lordship was in the bathroom and awaiting him there. The Beaver would be on the throne and would continue his function while engaging his visitor in conversation.

While grouse shooting with the present Lord Swinton, on his marvellous moor near Masham, in Wensleydale, he told me how, in the lavatory context, his grandfather, Lord Swinton, the Conservative politician, had turned the tables on Beaverbrook. While working at the wartime Ministry of Supply, Swinton was wont to have rather long sessions in the lavatory each morning and was thus engaged when Beaverbrook sent a male secretary to knock on the door to ask him to attend a meeting. Swinton said that he would not be long. A few minutes later the secretary returned with the message that it was imperative for Beaverbrook to see him right away. Swinton responded with 'My compliments to Lord Beaverbrook and tell him I can only deal with one shit at a time.'

While Beaverbrook's lunches were always of the highest quality, trying to eat them as the solitary guest, was an ordeal because he expected me to talk all the time and there was always some danger of my plate being whipped away as he took notes in his little red book. In everything he did he had a style of his own. He always wore a black tie with an enormous loose knot (which certain members of the *Express* staff copied). When he ate a pear he put the fat end down on his plate, cut the fruit across and then scooped out both halves with a small spoon as though eating an egg. Even the way he poured wine for his guests — he tended to drink whisky himself — was highly individual. Though he was rather small, he was able to grasp a champagne bottle by the base and refill his guests' glasses by pointing the bottle at them and pouring from a distance.

His dinners, when he always seated himself in the middle of the long table whence he could command all the conversations, were more relaxed because more people were present. Nevertheless, one had to remain alert as he had a habit of calling on anybody for a sudden opinion. On occasion this would be from someone I had suggested as a guest and it was rather essential that he should sing well for his supper. In that respect I was rather anxious about George Brown, later the Labour Foreign Secretary, who had a habit of becoming aggressive after a few drinks. Fortunately, his account of his Cockney youth in Peabody Buildings amused his host while the permanent guest, Lady Dunn, the rich widow of a Canadian financier, warmed to Brown's heart-of-gold wife, Sophie, whom he eventually deserted. After Lady Dunn had explained to Sophie her difficulties in coping with the huge interest flowing from the nine million dollars which her husband had left her, George's comment was 'To us five hundred quid would be a godsend'.

Beaverbrook's taste in the after-dinner films which he showed in his private cinema at Cherkley was also odd for such a man. His favourite star was Betty Grable whose only notable feature was her legs. Fortunately, he wanted to talk politics throughout the film and that was always interesting.

Like many men who owe their success to relentless drive, Beaverbrook had a full sex life. Not only did he have a succession of mistresses, some young, some middle-aged, but was prepared to take casual intimacy when it was on offer or could be arranged without too much trouble. When an attractive girl from one of his newspapers was invited to Cherkley for the night he would place her in the bedroom next to his and when she went upstairs to retire she would find the connecting door open. If the girl shut the door, the Beaver made no move but if it was left open he regarded it as an invitation. Very civilized!

He also enjoyed talking about sex with his intimates, though never about his conquests. Once, when I was discussing the intellectual merits of a woman well-known in the newspaper world, and with whom he suspected I might be involved, I asked him his opinion of her. He did not answer my question but puckered his face into a leery smile and said 'I bet she's got a big bush!' Later, I told the lady in question what he had said, expecting her to be furious, but her only comment was 'But isn't that a good thing?'

One of Beaverbrook's best kept secrets came my way while I was salmon fishing far away on Royal Deeside in the spring of 1962. On returning to the Raemoir Hotel I drifted into the bar before changing and was introduced to a famous radiologist who was drowning his sorrows after a blank day. After asking me how Lord Beaverbrook was and hearing my response that he seemed fine he remarked, 'He'll be dead in six months. He's got inoperable cancer of the prostate.' When I doubted it he assured me that he had been called in and had seen the X-ray plates.

On my return I managed to see Lady Dunn, who had been Beaverbrook's companion for several years, and told her what I knew. She was horrified and insisted that nobody else should know because of a quite extraordinary event. In view of his many financial interests Beaverbrook had instructed his doctors that he must always be told the truth about his health, believing that he could face death with equanimity. When told that he had an incurable malignancy he had been so devastated that Lady Dunn called in Sir Daniel Davies, the physician who had made the pronouncement, and demanded that he should reverse it. He declined but agreed to go through the motions of calling in a second opinion which would attribute his pain to lumbago. His Lordship was then told the good news and appeared to become his cheerful self again though I doubt that he really believed it. His assurance to me that the cobalt bomb treatment he was receiving was very good for lumbago did not carry conviction.

It so happened that, on being bidden to Cherkley at a later date, I also became the first person outside Beaverbrook's family to learn of his second marriage at the age of eighty-four. He was not downstairs when I arrived and the hostess I knew as Lady Dunn, by then dubbed by him 'My nine-million dollar nurse', said he was not well but would appear later.

'I don't know what he would do without you,' I remarked, sincerely, as she was not sparing herself in her constant concern.

'Oh, I do no more than any woman would do for her husband,' she replied.

'Sorry, I don't understand.'

'We were married yesterday at the Epsom Registry Office.'

After subduing my astonishment I asked her if the wedding was to be kept secret. She made it clear that she would prefer the world to know but insisted that I should get 'the Lord's' permission. He refused, saying 'Ah, you don't want to be writing about things like that.'

When I pointed out that the story might break in the rival *Daily Mail* he replied, 'If any young journalist gets a scoop on it good luck to him.'

In fact it was an old journalist who broke the story — Mike Wardell, one of Beaverbrook's close friends who printed the news in a small Canadian magazine which he ran. I was in the *Daily Express* office with the Editor, then Robert Edwards, when the item came over the news-tapes. He immediately called Lord Beaverbrook to tell him and ask what should be done.

'Ah, you don't want to be writing about that now,' was all he got out of him. So far as the national newspapers were concerned the first report of the marriage did appear in the *Daily Mail*.

Though fiercely critical of any *Express* journalist who was badly scooped, he often told me things and then instructed me to keep them secret. One such was the result of an inquiry which he had initiated into the true parentage of the politician, Brendan Bracken, who was widely believed to be the illegitimate son of Winston Churchill. The Beaver sent the outstanding crime reporter, Percy Hoskins, to Ireland, where witnesses convinced him that Bracken was only the son of a stonemason. As a connoisseur of mischief, it suited the Beaver's sense of humour to let the rumour run.

As early as 1959 I was given a clear lead to the most major secret of the war which did not become public until 1974 — that the British had been able to decipher the Germans' most secret codes by a system code-named 'Ultra'. The Beaver, who had been in on the secret, induced me not to pursue it. Later he informed me that President Kennedy was suffering from the dangerous defect of the adrenal glands called Addison's disease, when few knew this, but again swore me to secrecy because he had been told it in confidence.

My dearest memory of the 'Chief Reader' is of a visit I paid to Cherkley shortly before his eighty-fifth birthday in 1964 when we were all pushed to find some present that he would really relish. Again my luck had held. While visiting the country home of Colonel Sammy Lohan I had spotted the original visitors book belonging to Cherkley, with signatures like Cobden and Bright in it. The parents of Lohan's wife had originally built Cherkley and had eventually sold it to Beaverbrook. I persuaded Sammy to part with the book and both Beaverbrook and his wife rated it the present which had pleased him most. Lady Beaverbrook's present had involved much more thought and effort but had fallen flat, perhaps because the old man, whose remaining days were to be brief, was not feeling too good that morning. She had bought an old Italian barrel-organ and, at much cost and effort, had it restored. The glass panels were repainted with scenes from the Beaver's Canadian childhood. She had smuggled the machine into the house and planned to be playing it as her husband descended on his birthday. To heighten the authenticity she had hired a donkey and an organ-grinder's monkey and was turning away merrily in expectation of a mirthful reception. Instead the Beaver's first remark was 'Get rid of that donkey! It'll do its business on my Bokhara carpet'. Then on spotting the monkey he cried, with greater alarm, 'And get that ape outta here. It'll give me asthma'.

Lady Beaverbrook turned the handle of the instrument for me as she told me the sad story — surely the first and only multi-million dollar barrel-organist. Presumably, it is still at Cherkley along with my visitors' book.

On my next attendance, a day or two later, Lady Beaverbrook told me that the end was so near that she was sure that the big birthday dinner arranged in his honour by Lord (Roy) Thomson at the Dorchester would have to be cancelled. For that reason, she explained, she had withdrawn all the invitations to women because, otherwise, they would go out and spend a lot of money on dresses to no purpose. When, in fact, Beaverbrook, by a colossal effort of will, summoned up enough energy not only to attend the dinner but to make a most memorable speech, the ladies took a less than charitable view, especially as Lady Beaverbrook was there herself. He even joined some of us for an hour's talk after the dinner before going back to the bed in which he died a few days later.

I know that, in spite of his apparent religious beliefs, he was so much in love with life that he was loath to leave it. A couple of years before his death I had been lunching alone with Beaverbrook and Lady Dunn, as she then was, and we were holding him on either side as he shuffled along to the lounge. He started to sing a hymn, which was his common practice, but stopped as he reached the last line. Lady Dunn asked him to finish it but he declined. 'I don't like that line and I'm not gonna sing it.'

'Please sing it, dear,' she insisted.

'Until I come to Thee,' he sang, then added 'Who the hell wants to got to Him? I don't. At least, not yet.'

He died eleven days after the birthday dinner. Later, his son, Max, described to me how his dying father had instructed him to burn all his secret papers in the garden at Cherkley. He had thought twice about it as he built the sizable heap but had then put the match to it which, historically, was a pity.

My saddest memory of Cherkley was my last visit to say farewell to my old friend and master as he lay, embalmed, in his coffin, with a hint of a mischievous smile and looking even smaller than in life. I paid my respects in the company of a lady, who kissed the corpse, and Michael Foot who, though a left-wing socialist, had long been admired by the old man and had a cottage on the estate. About eight of us then stayed on for an early evening wake, at which I was instructed by Lady Beaverbrook to try to make them laugh. The gathering was hilarious in itself in a half-grim way. I had injured my right leg and was limping badly with the aid of a knobbly blackthorn stick. Michael Foot and his wife had been in a serious car crash and had various obvious injuries. Another guest, Mike Wardell, had a permanent black patch over one eye. As this motley gathering sat down a violent thunderstorm broke over the estate.

Someone had presented Lord Beaverbrook with an enormous, square birthday cake, which he had been unable to deal with, and his widow had put it on the lawn outside the French windows. A fluttering crowd of black birds, mainly starlings and jackdaws, were hard at work on it, assisted by the torrential rain. At the end of a path leading from the lawn was a huge wooden cross which Beaverbrook had erected early in his tenure of Cherkley as a symbol of his belief and was being dramatically illuminated by lightning flashes followed by crashes of thunder. Inevitably, in such an atmosphere, my jokes fell flat.

An even closer neighbour was Beaverbrook's daughter, Janet, who had a large house, called Slythehurst, and a stud-farm on the edge of Ewhurst village, about a mile away from our home. The eldest of Beaverbrook's three children, she should have been heir to the newspaper empire, which might then still have been under family control. Though her brother, Sir Max, had a splendid wartime record in the RAF, he lacked the drive, determination and, eventually, the health essential for a successful business life in a competitive world like Fleet Street. Janet was assertive and tough to a degree I have never seen in any other woman. In her sixties she learned to fly a helicopter and won championships. After being grounded for medical reasons she took up two-in-hand horse-driving and won championships.

I was with her at Slythehurst when A.J.P. Taylor, the historian and television celebrity, was discussing the proofs of the huge official biography of Lord Beaverbrook which he had written. Janet upbraided him for failing to show the dark side of his subject's nature, giving instances of what she called his 'cruelty' to his children, grandchildren and his mistresses. She recalled 'I never liked my father after the incident when, at the age of eleven, I went with my mother to see him when he was staying at the Hyde Park Hotel. We found him in bed with Josie Collins, the music-hall star, and the effect on my mother was shattering.'

Nevertheless, Janet said, her father had been heart-broken when his wife, Gladys, had died of a brain tumour in 1927, at the age of thirty-nine — the only time she could remember when he had been really upset emotionally.

She related, with some bitterness, that she had inherited a fine pearl necklace from her mother but had been forced to sell it to live. At some stage, when she had been short of money, Beaverbrook had ordered her to move in with him in Stornaway House, his town residence near St James's Palace, and when, understandably, she declined, he cut off her allowance.

Later, when Janet, aged eighteen, had married Ian Campbell, who later became Duke of Argyll, she had been given a splendid emerald and diamond tiara as a wedding present, by Princess Louise, a daughter of Queen Victoria and the widow of the ninth Duke of Argyll, Campbell's uncle. Campbell, an inveterate gambler, had married Janet believing she was rich which she was not. Pressed for money, he soon got his hands on the tiara and pawned it for £1000. Janet managed to steal the pawn ticket from her husband's trousers and then induced her father to redeem the tiara, expecting that he would give it back to her. Instead, he hung on to it, and having found that it came apart to make a necklace and brooches, he eventually gave them away to women friends.

Taylor listened to the stories with obvious interest but his sole response was 'I just couldn't put any of that in my book. I loved the old man too much.' In fact, he had not know him very long and I suspected that his real reason was his determination not to offend Lady Beaverbrook.

In front of him, Janet made me promise that if ever I wrote any reminiscences about her father I would do it 'warts and all'. To that end, she told me a great deal more. One evening, while we were both visiting the home of Beaverbrook's grandson, Timothy, she took me into a room to look at an oil painting of her brother, Peter, who had been killed in a sailing incident soon after the war. She said that he had been a very sensitive person, like her mother, and, as a result, had never been able to get on with his father. In fact, she said, they hated one another and Beaverbrook showed no emotion or apparent concern when he heard the news of his son's death. 'But then he didn't give a damn about any of us,' she commented.

Certainly his attitude to his son and heir, Max, was hardly fatherly. Though he was eventually proud of Max's fine war record, he kept him very short of money both before and after the war. Once when Max and I were dining with Uffa Fox, the yacht designer, at Cowes, they both recalled how they had shared a flat there and sometimes had to go to bed early because it was so cold and they could not afford any coal.

I witnessed a weird aspect of this attitude to his son when I was staying with Beaverbrook at his seaside villa on Cap D'Ail, (Cape Garlic) near Monte Carlo. He called me into his study early one morning, sat me down next to him and telephoned Max, in London. He then proceeded to criticize his handling of the paper, tearing strips off him in a most offensive way and it seemed that, somehow, he was deriving extra satisfaction from my presence. On paper, Max was my boss as well as being a shooting companion and I was embarrassed. As soon as the conversation was finished, Beaverbrook said that he would not be needing my company until lunch.

This sadistic streak was confirmed by Lord Sieff, now my country neighbour and fishing companion in Berkshire, who told me how he had been immensely embarrassed when visiting Beaverbrook in his penthouse at Arlington House in London. A meeting of top newspaper executives, including the editors and managers was in progress and, instead of asking Lord Sieff to wait, he called him in and proceeded to dress them all down.

Beaverbrook left most of his money to a Foundation in Canada so, when Sir Max succeeded to the newspaper empire, it was hopelessly under-financed. Some suspect that this unplayable hand was dealt deliberately to ensure Max's failure. If so, it achieved its objective, along with the severe financial problems of his son, Maxwell, the present Lord Beaverbrook, fulfilling the 'riches to rags in three generations' portent.

What rankled most with Janet was her father's treatment of Jean Norton, an intimate friend of Edwina Mountbatten who, though married with a family, was Beaverbrook's mistress for many years and loved him deeply. She was so liked and admired by Janet and the other children that they hoped, after their mother had died, that her father would marry her. Instead, while retaining his attachment to Mrs Norton, Beaverbrook took up with a ballet dancer, called Lily Ernst, whom he had met in Vienna. According to Janet, for appearances' sake, Mrs Norton was living in Wellbottom Cottage, a 'grace and favour' house on the Cherkley estate and when, in 1945, he decided to give a party to which she had not been invited, he asked her to move out for one night to provide extra accommodation for his guests. She did so but was greatly distressed to find that her home was being occupied by Lily Ernst. She returned to the cottage and died of a heart

With Lord Beaverbrook at Cherkley 1963.

Janet Kidd – Beaverbrook's daughter –
by her pool in Barbados.

Shooting at Beaulieu with Sir Max Aitken, Graham Hill, Keith Showering,
Jack Wynne-Williams, Sir Richard Levinge and Ernest Bigland, all since
deceased (Sir Max, second from right). (Author on the left, front row).

Jointly signing books with fishing friend and country neighbour, Lord Sieff.

Three generations of Springer Spaniels. Scat, Scoop and Scamp at Lowerhouse Farm. *(John Wolstenholme)*

The 'A-Team' Relaxing with Dido after a big pheasant shoot. *(Daily Mail)*

Has he got it right? The ghost-writer at work with the authoress. *(Daily Mail)*

Have we got the right fly? Dido on the Kennet at Littlecote. *(Solo Syndication)*

In Norway with Bruce McKenzie and my 31-pound salmon.

With my wife, Billee, Dido and three 'sea-licers' at Little Blackhall, September 1991.

The author's favourite fishing companion – his wife Billee on the home pool, Inchmarlo on the Dee.

Nealry 80 and still trying! *(Eric Thorburn)*.

attack. Beaverbrook went through her papers and found some passionate letters from Mountbatten, written when he had been young, but that was not the cause of their fall-out, which had a more devious origin.

While shooting at Broadlands, Mountbatten told me how Jean Norton had brought him and his wife into contact with Beaverbrook and, for several years they had been firm friends. Then, at the dinner table one evening, Beaverbrook had barked 'Between you and me, Dickie, from now on it's war! It's war!' Mountbatten claimed he had never discovered the reason for what became Beaverbrook's long feud against him but Janet was sure that it stemmed from the wartime raid on Dieppe which cost many Canadian lives and had been master-minded by Mountbatten. She said that when her father met Mountbatten after the raid he held out his hand and said 'Shake hands with one of the few Canadians you haven't murdered.'

I asked Mountbatten, who had been the Chief of Combined Operations, what the purpose of the raid on Dieppe had been and have a note of his reply: 'To liberate France we needed to land several divisions quickly from the sea. In 1942 nobody knew how to land one division on enemy-held territory. So to find out we had to try it against a defended port of the kind we would need. That was what Dieppe was about — to enable us to plan the invasion with confidence. It showed us that we had no hope of taking a port well defended by the Germans without bombing it so hard that the facilities would be destroyed. That was how we realized that we would have to invade across an open beach bringing a prefabricated port with us — what became the Mulberry harbour. The Germans wrongly assumed that it was a rehearsal for a later attack on a port, so when we found that they were concentrating on port defences we encouraged them by deception techniques to believe that we were going to invade near Calais. But that was an unexpected bonus.

'We intended to hold Dieppe until we got our equipment ashore and then reload it, taking with us any enemy material and prisoners we could lay our hands on. Churchill demurred when told that the casualties would be heavy but the chiefs insisted "No raid, no invasion".'

However, Beaverbrook's animosity became so great that there must have been some additional motive. As an Empire crusader, he despised the role which Mountbatten had played as Viceroy during the partition and hand-over of India, but his dislike seems to have been intensified by the closeness of the Mountbattens to Nehru, the Indian leader. Beaverbrook loathed Nehru for his long struggle to take India out of the Empire, but a prime informant told me that it was Nehru's success in a different direction which was responsible for the extravagance of his feelings. Sir Archibald Rowlands, a senior civil servant and wartime friend of Beaverbrook, who had been loaned to Delhi to assist with the division of the subcontinent, became very close to the Mountbattens in the process. He was also a friend of mine and when I asked him about the relationship between Nehru and Lady Mountbatten he described it as 'frankly adulterous'. He suspected that Beaverbrook detested Nehru because the Indian had succeeded where he had failed and that he despised Mountbatten for condoning it.

While Mountbatten was First Sea Lord, Beaverbrook urged me to attack him in print on various pretexts but, apart from my sporting relationship with the earl, it would have been professionally stupid to do so. With the connivance of the editor (who was eventually removed) I ignored the order.

In 1975, Sir Max Aitken began to record the true story of his father because Taylor had failed to do it but illness supervened. Eventually, his sister Janet resolved to write a book revealing her father's true nature as she had experienced it but, when *The Beaverbrook Girl* eventually appeared, she, too, omitted most of the stories of her father's excesses, as I predicted to her she would. Though she was the toughest lady I ever met she had a broad streak of kindness, as did her father. One day she telephoned me in some distress about her old friend, Anthony Eden, then Lord Avon, with whom I had renewed my acquaintance while staying with Janet in Barbados, where the Avons had a beautiful, old plantation house. He had just told her that he had incurable cancer and wished to talk with Margaret Thatcher, whom he had never met. As a former Prime Minister himself, he felt he could not make a direct approach and Janet asked me to try and arrange it. The following day, Mrs Thatcher, so often portrayed as cold and uncaring, was helicoptered down to the Avon's Wiltshire home.

CHAPTER 9

THE JOY OF COUNTRY FRIENDSHIPS

In my experience country people have a greater share of happiness and it is no coincidence that in pictorial art down the centuries, and in much poetry and music, the countryside is the location for fun and games — the pastoral image. Happiness is not an entity but a lot of components which need to go on happening and country people seem to devote more conscious effort into making them do so. In that respect few local friends gave us greater pleasure than Edward 'Jimmy' James, a permanently overweight prankster whose main objective in life was to laugh and induce others to join in. He was an ardent admirer of the exuberant Squire Mytton, whose peculiarities, such as setting fire to his nightshirt to cure his hiccups, were so extraordinary as to make him certifiable, had he been of lesser estate. Jimmy's determination to 'liven things up' dominated his behaviour to such an extent that I was often scared that he would be driven to emulate Mytton even more outrageously than he actually did. Accompanying him to Scotland for salmon-fishing in his new E-type Jaguar, I watched him rolling in his seat as he told me how Mytton, while driving a friend in his gig, was astonished to learn that he had never been upset in such a vehicle. 'Never been upset in a gig?', Mytton cried and immediately proceeded to put that right by forcing the horse to attempt a five-barred gate. I carefully avoided indicating that I had never been upset in an E-type, which feat Jimmy eventually accomplished for himself while scorching across a ploughed field to escape the police, pursuing him for speeding.

Jimmy's eccentricities were mainly directed at deviously constructed practical jokes often involving considerable effort and expense. He bought and surreptitiously introduced into my smallish duck-pond a huge carp, which he had bought, in the hope that I would eventually spot it and be duly amazed. One evening, while I was feeding the golden orfe with bread, a duck was swimming towards a piece of crust when the carp, with the same idea, surfaced beneath the bird and upskittled it. I rushed into the house crying 'I always told you there could be a monster carp in there!' My wife, who was in on the secret, suggested that I might have been seeing things and when she told Jimmy he laughed as heartily as if he had witnessed the event. 'What a coup!', he cried. 'What a coup! Don't tell him.'

Being brilliant at dialects he telephoned me at home one Saturday morning posing as the enraged Mayor of Blackpool and threatened proceedings after I had reported in a newspaper that Blackpool topped the seaside resorts in the number of illegitimate conceptions by girl visitors. He was also the alleged Pakistani community leader threatening to sue me under the race relations act. He even rang me as Lord Beaverbrook, though I did detect that imposture. Eventually I reached a stage of wondering when anyone rang me, 'Is it Jimmy?'

Another extrovert friend, who specialized in propelling his gigantic frame through the windscreen of overdriven cars, was Sir David Stirling, the founder of the SAS, who, like Jimmy, is no longer with us. He and his elder brother, Bill, had been brought up on the Scottish family estate at Keir to be so tough that, whatever the weather, neither wore an overcoat. I shot with Bill, one of the finest marksmen of his generation, and when quite old he would stride the moor in cold, driving rain wearing nothing above his waist but a threadbare, grey shirt. He was notorious for arriving late at night and, at one country house, when everyone else had retired, a stone was always left on the doorstep with a long string attached. Bill then traced the string upstairs to find the room allotted to him.

David had his own rules for snooker, at which I partnered him at Knowle, the home of Bruce McKenzie, close by in Cranleigh. They included the privilege of kneeling on the table for certain shots and when doing that at White's Club, in London, he brought down all the lamps, plunging the building into darkness with a loud bang and causing its evacuation in the belief that the IRA had struck. I have also heard it alleged that while staying at the country seat of a certain Duke, who required each of his November shooting guests to plant a sack of daffodils, David was allotted the area beneath a window of one of the main rooms. In the spring his flowers spelled an unmistakable two-word message to the Duke.

My country home was even closer to the estate owned by Charles Forte, since most rightfully ennobled, if only for the enormous number of jobs he has created. It was only about twenty minutes to the Forte shoot at Ripley, near Guildford and he and his son Rocco were most generous with their invitations. They are among very few hosts who provide one large vehicle, affectionately known to some as the 'Green Maria', for transporting all the participants. This makes for closer cameraderie and much badinage, the only penalty being that items like over-trousers and shooting-sticks tend to get left behind by a few offenders like myself.

Charles Forte frequently makes fun of his own lack of inches with such remarks as that, when he received his first honour, he was the shortest knight of the year. But his best story is his account of how, in his younger, more athletic, life he set the Scottish record, still unbroken, for the long jump. As he explains it — 'Actually, I was not competing in that event. I was throwing the hammer and forgot to let go.'

Watching this man, in the shooting field, on the river bank and at his homes I still find it incredible that from a milk and sandwich bar near Piccadilly Circus he has built up the world's biggest catering and hotel empire, creating careers for so many thousands in the process. Further, having acquired great wealth he has enjoyed it, sharing it with his friends, without being spoiled by it.

Comparisons are always invidious but there is something unique in my experience about the Boxing Day shoots staged by Lord and Lady Forte which I have been privileged to attend for many years — the intimate atmosphere of a really close Italian family who all set great store by friendship. As at so many festive season shoots there are lots of young, including grandchildren and their friends, who are such an essential component of Christmas. As Lord Forte is fond of saying, the lunch, prepared by his wife for about thirty people, and with a table worthy of a still-life painting, is the most reliable drive of the day but the rest are pretty memorable too. For my wife and me that shoot has long been one of the major occasions of our calendar.

For several years Charles also rented a big shoot at Ickworth, near Bury St Edmunds and often asked me there. The centre of the shoot was reserved for the owner, the late Marquis of Bristol, who seemed to rely mainly on straying pheasants put down by Charles. I recall meeting there the late John Brazil, who had made his fortune out of sausages and pork pies. Whenever he saw any pigs whilst out shooting or hunting he always raised his hat because, 'But for them I wouldn't be here'.

Close by the Forte shoot, at Ripley, was Dunsborough Park the beautiful seventeenth-century home of Charles Hughesdon and his wife, formerly Florence Desmond, the hilarious cabaret star known to all as Dessie. There was a partridge and pheasant shoot close by, providing not only good sport but the opportunity to meet new people. It was there I first met Lord Cowdray, the Sussex landowner and sportsman who lost the whole of his left arm in the battle at Dunkirk. I knew that he was a fine shot but to stand next to him in a partridge drive was a revelation. Using his gun like a pistol, he appeared to sight the birds down the barrel. He had the advantage of a leather gun-rest, to take the weight of the weapon during waits, and the service of a fine loader. Still, determination was chiefly responsible for Cowdray's success, as I witnessed when salmon fishing with him on his Lower Crathes beat of the Dee. By the time my wife and I were tired, the total catch for the beat that year had reached 499. His Lordship was determined to make it 500 and we left him manipulating his heavy split cane fly rod while waist-deep in the river. Not only did he catch the 500th fish but the 501st.

Even more gutsy was his behaviour during a winter duck shoot on the Dee, according to the late Jock Leslie, who assured me that he had witnessed it. The river was low and half frozen across in places when Lord Cowdray sent his Labrador into the water to retrieve a duck. The dog had no difficulty until, with its paws on the edge of the ice and the dead duck in its mouth, it could not haul itself out. When the dog was becoming dangerously exhausted and everyone was wondering what to do, Cowdray took off his jacket went into the river and rescued it.

It was also at the Hughesdons' table that I met the extraordinary Paul Getty, the extremely wealthy and unsmiling oil tycoon who lived at the nearby Tudor mansion, Sutton Place. When explaining to my wife why he avoided air travel because of the frequent airport delays, he made what was alleged to be his only recorded joke. 'If you've time to spare go be air,' he quipped with an attempt at a smile. He seemed out of place in the country where people, generally, are more at ease with themselves and with others, and quit it soon afterwards.

Even closer than the Hughesdon and Forte shoots was one of few estates which have approximated to my ideal. Wintershall, near Bramley, has all the basic requirements — a medieval manor-house, dating from at least 1227, set in fields, woods and gardens of outstanding beauty, with copious wildlife and flora. It is free from the hum of traffic and aircraft roar — so rare these days and unlikely to change because of Wintershall's peculiar geography. Yet it is little more than than an hour's drive from the centre of London. Surrey is still full of surprises and none is more remarkable than Wintershall with its hills, ravines and dells which enhance the sense of remoteness. At all times of the year the views are quite splendid, for it is truly a house for all seasons. By their nature, many ancient houses are cold and grim but Wintershall exudes friendliness and echoes to the cries of children and grandchildren and the laughter of good fellowship, for the owners, Peter and Ann Hutley, have always derived a great deal of their pleasure from sharing it. When the Christmas tree in the old hall reaches high above the minstrels' gallery, almost to touch the fourteenth-century beams, the Christmas cards from the

Hutleys' many friends hang in festoons. Even the inevitable Wintershall ghost — the wraith of a lady in a dark green habit — appears to be gentle and well disposed as she, allegedly, sweeps out of one of the rooms off the hall.

Wintershall also enjoys an unusual compactness. The best pheasant drives and the fishing, in a succession of ancient ponds, are so immediately round the house that they are reached without transport. Since he became the squire at the age of thirty-six, Peter Hutley has added steadily to its acreage, with the estate gradually recovering its old grandeur, which has proved most satisfying not only for him and his family but for all those who love the old place. Since nobody, however fortunate, is much more than a short-term tenant of any property, it is most heartening for those who care about the countryside to see the house, grounds, lakes and land made fit to withstand the rigours of yet more centuries.

Closer still to my old home was Baynard's Park, the shoot still owned by Alan Bristow, the forceful founder of Bristow Helicopters, the largest such operation in the world. Most of his guests used to be oilmen and many were the days when the telephone would ring with news that some airport or other, usually Aberdeen, was fogged-in so that there were gaps in the shooting line which I could help to fill. I rarely failed to oblidge, though the shoot was always on Mondays.

Bristow took great pains with the presents he gave to his Christmas guests. One year, mine was a beautifully bound volume with gold lettering entitled 'Highlights in the Sex Life of Chapman Pincher', and which I still treasure. It was filled with blank pages! In those days, the Christmas shoot ended in a rather wild party in the Great Hall of the mansion, since demolished after a fire. Alan even arranged for a headless rider to materialize for the young. Sadly, Baynards was among many Surrey shoots to be devastated in the great hurricane but is recovering.

Closest of all to my old Surrey home was a shoot in Cranleigh called Knowle and when its owner sold the estate he introduced me to the purchaser, Bruce McKenzie, who was perhaps the most remarkable man I have ever met. Big in every way, his main base was Nairobi where, as a settler after gallant war service in the RAF, he had entered Kenyan politics, becoming a Minister and eventually the chief confidant of Jomo Kenyatta, who realized that a white man could never succeed him and therefore trusted him. For several years he was Kenyatta's roving representative and had become friendly with many of the world's political leaders. In this pursuit he had developed close personal relations with British, American, Canadian, Iranian and Israeli intelligence and at the lunches he frequently staged at Knowle, where he spent part of the year, I met many intelligence chiefs who would otherwise have been inaccessible and, certainly, would not have wished to be seen with me in London.

I had my own contacts with Mossad, the Israeli secret service, but it was through Bruce that, sitting in the country quiet of my study, I was able to play a modest part in the famous Entebbe raid to rescue Jewish hostages being held there by Palestinian terrorists abetted by Idi Amin, the Ugandan dictator, in 1976. The Israelis had decided to rescue the 110 hostages, and kill the terrorists, by a most courageous and risky air assault for which Bruce had secretly arranged Kenyan logistic support. They realized that they might face international criticism for attacking a sovereign state, especially if Ugandan soldiers were killed, as seemed inevitable. To forestall this they needed to show that Amin and his soldiers were assisting the terrorists, so I was telephoned by a Mossad agent and given the full facts about their behaviour which, until then, had been deliberately suppressed. My report, which was picked up by other papers world-wide, appeared as the front-page *Daily Express* 'splash' and I received another call from my Mossad friend full of gratitude. That night the raid was staged with complete success and no diplomatic repercussions of consequence. Once again, I had been in the country at the right time because I doubt that Mossad would have telephoned me in Fleet Street, where the conversation could have been overheard.

I shared in the jubilation in the McKenzie household but it was to have tragic repercussions for Bruce. Two years later while he was trying to repair Kenyan relations with Amin, and do business with him, a bomb was placed on his small aircraft while it was parked at Entebbe airport. It exploded as the plane was over the Ngong hills in Kenya killing the three passengers, all friends of mine, and the pilot. Recently, while dining at the Berkshire home of General Hashim, an Arab shooting friend, a table companion who ran a chain of dental clinics in Saudi Arabia told me that one of his regular patients was Idi Amin. I envied him his opportunity.

As a member of the 'Marks and Spencer' shoot at Brimpton, near Newbury, I became friendly not only with the Sieff family but with several of their relations including the late Michael Sacher, who had a country property near the village of Greywell, in Hampshire. It was while attending a large Sunday lunch there in May 1974 that, unwittingly, I triggered off the totally unfounded rumour that MI5 had been plotting to overthrow Harold Wilson and his government. After lunch, a group of us moved to the music room for coffee and I was asked for the latest Fleet Street gossip about the Wilson regime and, in particular, about the peerage which had been awarded to Marcia

Williams, Wilson's personal secretary. Spurred on by other questions, I referred to various other matters in a light-hearted way, unaware that a member of the audience was a friend of Wilson and duly reported a garbled version of what I had said to him. There is no doubt, whatever, as Lord Wilson eventually agreed, that this report, which he took seriously, was the origin of his delusions about an MI5 plot against him and the prime source of all the Parliamentary and media allegations about it which followed and still persist in some quarters. I fear that my country activities have a lot to answer for!

Another of our Surrey neighbours, a self-made tycoon who once staged a two-gun pheasant shoot at which only one bird appeared all day, said to me 'I know that you don't have much money but I've noticed that there's nothing a millionaire does that you don't do.' He was almost right and it was due to the kindness of many friends who happened to be rich. None was kinder than Janet Kidd, whose house became almost a second home, as did her old plantation house in Barbados, where she trained six young black boys as 'mini-butlers' to wait at table in smart trousers, shirts and red bow-ties.

We repaid such friendships, as best we could, with hospitality at our home where for several years we could stage outstanding Chinese meals, thanks to Kim, a Malaysian Chinese cook, and her several friends in the area who all assisted in the lengthy preparation and presentation. They were special enough even to attract Harry Hyams from his Ramsbury lair. He was hard to get but invariably made some memorable comment. When seeing him out with his wife and her lady friend I saw that, instead of the Ferrari, he had come in a two-seater estate car. As he opened the back hatch to accommodate the other lady, who clambered in, Harry remarked, 'Always carry a spare!'

Kim was involved in another evening which was not so memorable for the guests but was unforgettable for us. After I had visited the Shah of Iran at his Teheran Palace in 1972 it was his welcome habit to send me a Christmas gift of three bottles of champagne and a large can of the best caviare, delivered to my office by his London Embassy. One year my secretary took a call from the front hall and told me that the present had arrived. I asked her to put the caviare in the office fridge, which she did. Later that evening, when it was time to go home, she recovered the can which I put in my brief-case. I handed it to my wife who, joyfully, put it the fridge at home.

The following day she rang a few country friends, including Janet Kidd, to come round that evening for champagne and a caviare feast. The chopped egg, the onions and the melba toast were duly prepared and as the first guests arrived Kim was instructed to open the caviare.

She rushed into the living room, ashen-faced, with the news 'Madam! Not caviare! Pistachio nuts!'

What was extraordinary was the fact that the tin of nuts was less than half the weight of a tin of caviare yet, because we had all assumed that it was caviare, we had never noticed it. Such are the sad delusions to which the mind is subject.

When saying farewell to Lowerhouse Farm I felt like the mandragora plant, which is said to scream if pulled up by the roots. I kissed the oak front door and as I motored down the drive without stopping for a backward glance I vowed never to submit myself to the trauma of returning. However, my wife and I breached it a few years later by being photographed there for a newspaper feature. The whole place was in spanking order, the borders weedless and filled with flowers and the black-and-white house looking very pleased with itself, especially as the new owner had bought back all the land around it. Memories flooded back but we have had no real regrets. It was a massive relief for us to be able to dispense with living-in staff and, in modern circumstances, it is surprising how many owners of lovely homes would prefer to dispense with them on that score alone. In Kintbury, next to the Norman church, we are closer to a few old friends and have made many new ones so the move has been rich in its compensations and opened a new chapter in our lives. Lord Sieff and his family live close by and welcomed us to 'the kibbutz'. The Wards of Chilton and the Carnarvons of Highclere went out of their way to make us feel at home as did many others. The MI6 officer, Nicholas Elliott, whose memoirs *Never Judge a Man by his Umbrella* (It may not be his) epitomized his off-beat sense of humour, proved to be a neighbour and our evenings have been regularly enlivened by the historian, Nikolai Tolstoy, whose charm has been enhanced, rather than diminished, by the enormous damages awarded against him in a libel action.

The trout fishing on the lovely estate of Littlecote, ten minutes from the house, has turned out to be quite superb and mornings and evenings spent there with my wife and our dogs have made up for what we left behind in Surrey. We became friendly with its owner, Sir Seton Wills, and his wife, Gillian, through the activities of a rabbit which had burrowed under a long-lost Roman mosaic and thrown up some of the coloured cubes composing it. After attending the official opening when the mosaic had been restored we all holidayed together in Rome, where my professional knowledge of political 'dirty tricks' was extended in an evilly memorable way. We were invited to the private 'cell' of the Pope's confessor, Father Flavian, who had kindly conducted us round the Vatican gardens. Above his fireplace was a crucifix which the priest took down from the wall. The cross was black, of ebony, about eighteen inches long and eight inches wide, while the carved Christ was of ivory, yellowed with age. The priest explained that it was English and had been used when Roman Catholics were being hunted down by the Protestant authorities. He asked me to kneel and go through the motions of kissing the cross and, as I did so, he smartly pulled away the section above the Saviour's head. It was the handle of a long, razor-edged dagger for which the lower part of the cross was a scabbard. What was most extraordinary was that some authority had ordered it and a craftsman had spent hours employing his skill to make it, aware of its terrible purpose.

Friendship is an attachment which can consume much time and effort and I have noticed that older people tend to be increasingly selective with those whom they wish to socialize, preferring the few with whom they feel really comfortable. As a consequence, especially as friends die, my wife and I spend more and more time alone together but, fortunately, as an old country couple used to put it, 'We like we-selves.' No man is an island but a man, a woman and a dog can be.

CHAPTER 10

THE JOY OF DOGS

The continuous company of dogs has always been a major joy of country living for me. One is never alone with a dog and at any time of day there is little that is more welcome than an intruding snout. People and dogs have shared the same circumstances in a uniquely intimate relationship for many centuries and no animal more closely resembles man in temperament. The degree of communication between dog and man is far more definite than with any other creature, as anyone watching a sheep-dog trial, a gun-dog working to orders in the heather or a guide-dog conducting its sightless charge through city streets can appreciate. For me, a whole day without dogs is a day without sunshine and those who do not experience the dog/man relationship miss one of the most rewarding joys that life has to offer. Dogs help to unify human relationships, especially for married couples whose children have grown up and left home.

London or any other big town is no place for the lively breeds I have preferred. When Lord Beaverbrook set me up with a 'grace and favour' flat just off Piccadilly, one of the reasons I spent so few nights there was because I missed the dogs so much. Whenever I was abroad they were one of the most pressing causes of my urge to return with all haste.

For almost all the first forty years of my shooting life I was served by only three Springer spaniels, Honey, Scat and Scoop, who all remained active until they keeled over with kidney failure at the age of almost fourteen. I have always preferred bitches, which tend to be more affectionate and more biddable than dogs. They are also likely to live longer, females, as with humans, being born with a longer expectation of life than male puppies.

My dogs and I have always revelled in each other's company whenever I have been in the country, our walks and activities in the shooting field and on the river and our quiet association in my study cementing the common bond.

Dogs are not usually associated with fishing but, as it is essentially a lonely sport, a dog by one's side provides active companionship without the vocal intrusion which one is anxious to avoid on the river, where all should be quiet and peaceful. Scoop loved fishing, being totally absorbed by what went on. Without any training on my part, she learned to position herself where she could watch the fly and the moment a fish was hooked she moved downstream to the point where, in her judgement, which was rarely wrong, I would be most likely to net it. However fishing dogs can have their faults if they become too keen, as a ghillie friend of mine experienced. The owner of a large English Springer, called Duke, was fishing for salmon on the Inchmarlo beat of the Aberdeenshire Dee, when he foul-hooked a huge fish which ran him downstream half a mile in heavy water, with the faithful Duke in pursuit. They all ended up on the final pool of the beat, the Roe Pot, which has several casting jetties built out into the stream. Having reached the last one with the salmon almost beaten, the angler shouted to the ghillie, 'I'll have to bring it in now if we are going to get it.' Sadly, 'Get it!' was the command on which Duke had been trained to retrieve a pheasant. He leapt on the salmon from the jetty as it was being drawn in, broke the nylon cast and the fish flapped away.

When Scoop died I acquired a chocolate-coloured Labrador, called Dido, and, until I learned about the origin of the breed, was quite astonished at the even greater interest she took in fishing. Labradors were developed in Newfoundland by the commercial fishermen there to assist them in their work. The dogs, which have a thick coat enabling them to swim in cold conditions, would retrieve cod and other fish which fell off the hooks when the long lines were being hauled onto the small boats. They would also swim between boats carrying ropes attached to nets and pull out live salmon struggling through the shallow waters of rivers.

My first spaniel, Honey, whom I bought on sight on a grouse moor, started my love affair with Springers which are so-called because they were widely used to spring birds trying to conceal themselves and have such boundless energy that it would be worth a metabolic investigation. When any of them disappeared after a pheasant drive, the question, 'Where's that bloody dog?' would be quickly answered by the spaniel returning with a bird in its mouth. Honey would occasionally bring in a hen's egg which she had found 'laid away' in the orchard and there would never be a mark on it. Such is the determination of the Springer that, on one occasion, Scoop, climbed an ivy-coloured tree to retrieve a dead bird lodged in its branches. Nor, in my experience, can the spaniel's sharp intelligence be doubted. I would take Honey with me to the shooting school and she would retrieve a clay pigeon which had fallen without being hit but she would never bring back a broken one. Her eyes seemed to say, 'I thought you could use this one again.'

I did not breed from Honey but Scat, also bought on a grouse moor, begat Scoop and the way this happened could only be described as romantic. Lord Forte's dog, Shaun, took such a fancy to Scat that he made persistent passes wherever they met. The ultimate was reached when Scat emerged from a wood carrying both a cock pheasant and Shaun. It was decided that they should be allowed to get the attraction out of their systems and the eventual encounter gave me the lovable Scoop.

My wife fell in love with Rhodesian ridgebacks, superbly handsome and valiant animals designed for lion-hunting, as a result of a country disaster. I had arrived at a local shoot to be asked if I would like a Rhodesian ridgeback bitch which had to be disposed of without delay. That morning, the dog in question had found her way into a pen containing pheasants and had killed a hundred of them. The keeper had threatened to leave unless the dog was off the premises or shot within twenty-four hours. I declined the offer but, casually, told my wife about it on my return that afternoon. She said nothing but, early the following morning, collected the dog, called Gemma, and there she was by my fireside with the spaniels when I returned from the office. While somewhat perturbed, as we had chickens and ornamental ducks, there was nothing I could do and she quickly became such a much-loved member of the pack that my wife bred several litters from her, the deal being that she would feed the pups and I would clean up their quarters. They grew so quickly that it was like mucking out nine small ponies. In fact, I became convinced that, like geese, more comes out from a ridgeback than goes in.

No bird was safe from Gemma — she never really forgot her fun morning in the pheasant pen — but we kept her strain going until 1989 when the last of the line, my beloved Sheika, died suddenly of a twisted stomach, a complaint which I thought was peculiar to horses but which is not uncommon among breeds of large dogs. We toyed with the idea of a ridgeback replacement but the whole situation was irrevocably changed by the arrival of a bombshell called Dido, as the next chapter will explain.

While dogs of an individual breed are broadly similar in conformation, their personalities (perhaps we should say 'dogalities') may be very different and mine were. Some dogs are rumbustiously extrovert while others are timid and introvert. For a happy and productive relationship they need to be matched up with similar kinds of owner and ours were.

Some owners, especially of gun-dogs, are convinced that it is healthier to keep them outside but this is probably a myth invented and promoted by house-proud women. The idea that the high temperature of a centrally-heated house must be bad for a dog is surely misguided. The dog's body temperature, averaging 101 degrees Fahrenheit, is about three degrees higher than man's and dogs have shared the fireside with human families since the dawn of their association many thousands of years ago. Somehow a dog by the fireside looks right and no fireside of mine has ever looked complete without a dog, preferably several. At Lowerhouse Farm, where fireplaces were huge, there were always four, including two lolloping ridgebacks, and that was never too many.

I am in no doubt that, given the option, most dogs would prefer to be allowed in the house and to sleep there in an allotted place — for a simple inherited reason. In the wild state it was dangerous for any pack animal to be alone and dogs still tend to feel insecure when they are, just as many humans do. Being gregarious creatures by nature, they instinctively prefer to be in the house with the human pack than to be alone in a kennel. It is because the dog and man are pack species, with similar emotional needs, that the close relationship was possible and became so successful. We both require regular companionship, with physical contact and a show of affection. This basic need, which must be constantly reinforced, is probably underestimated by most dog owners. It is the reason why a dog makes such a delightful fuss when welcoming its human companions returning to any empty house. It feels safer, as well as happier, as it also does when the human members of the pack re-enter its world in the morning.

Many dogs express their need for repeated physical contact by 'wuffling' their owner's hand — touching it with the nose and lips or even taking it gently into the mouth. It is a quest for reassurance as well as a sign of affection, expressing the bond on which the dog feels it is dependent. Dogs which are kept alone in kennels for long periods are denied this regular reassurance and their feeling of being deprived is likely to affect their natures, making them taciturn and withdrawn. It may even make them savage because of the undue attachment they acquire for their restricted territory. Having so little they can call their own they defend it against all comers — sometimes including their owners.

It is often argued that keeping a dog inside a house will make it 'soft' and lazy. But do ordinary creature comforts make us 'soft'? Or to put it as a dog might, would we improve the prospects for our health, our longevity and our natures by living, throughout the year, in unheated wooden huts? I doubt it. We heat our houses to avoid the danger of hypothermia as well as for comfort and dogs, especially the silky-coated breeds, can be subject to it. Many sheepdogs which work in harsh climatic conditions in hill country, including some which become trials champions, sleep in the warm farmhouse without effect on the performance of their duties.

With the exception of working dogs, most get far too little exercise for their need to expend their pent-up energy and that is especially true of those kept in kennels. An owner may ensure that his dog has a concreted run attached to his kennel but how often does it exert itself there? Without the stimulus of companionship, the lone dog is usually to be seen staring hopefully — and forlornly — through the railings or wire mesh. Being gregarious, a dog rarely plays for long on its own, either in a kennel or in a house though the dog with free range of a house and garden may cover a lot of ground in the course of a day.

Some owners, of working breeds especially, believe that dogs are inherently too 'unclean' to be given the run of the home. My much missed friend, Joe Nickerson, who was famed for the quality and discipline of his Labrador and spaniel gun-dogs, was one of them, but I always felt that he was over-hygienic on that score. He also believed that exposure to too many strangers was bad for a gun-dog, which should respond only to its handler though I always suspected that he just did not like dogs mooching around his house, which was so often full of guests who might be annoyed by them. One undoubted disadvantage to having a gun-dog in the house lies in the danger that it becomes overfed through getting too many titbits if there are children and servants, though that can be controlled.

There can be no doubt that the dog/human relationship can be cemented more firmly when the dog is regularly on hand. The life-span allotted to dogs — surely one of Nature's major errors — is so short and slips away so rapidly that we should both make the most of it. There are some, mainly in the world of working breeds, who put down their dogs when they begin to show signs of decline. 'You can't be doing with old dogs', was how one shooting acquaintance of mine put it. I disagree. My old spaniel, Scoop, became purblind and deaf but she had been my close friend and helper for fourteen years and she had an honoured place in my home until she became terminally ill, as any dog of mine always will.

There is a growing need, these days, especially in the country, for an alert house-dog capable of giving early warning of an intruder or vandal and, if necessary, able to stand him off without attacking him. Some dogs belonging to friends have slept through robberies while living in the house — three of them in one instance — but the dog inside the house must be better able to fulfil its function as a sentry than one remote in a kennel.

When a dog barks at an intruder who appears to threaten it or its human owners it is really defending what it regards as its own property, the house and all its contents forming its den with the garden and area around it being its rightful territory. We may think that the dog belongs to us but it regards the family as belonging to it, as part of the pack and resents any outside interference with its possessions, whether they be living persons or dead bones. Dogs include a car in which they are used to travelling as part of their territory and, being of nomadic origin, will also include any area taken over temporarily by its pack-leader. Scoop always defended the pheasants collected at my peg, attacking marauding dogs much bigger than herself.

There is a further reason for having one's dog readily to hand — it is healthier for *us* to have them indoors. An increasing body of research has shown that the act of stroking and fondling a dog lowers human blood pressure to a degree that could be therapeutic. So much so that dogs are being taken into some hospitals and old people's homes. A dog's companionship reduces the mental impact of depression, loneliness and boredom, thereby enhancing the quality of life. The mere presence of a dog is said to reduce the stress imposed by an onerous task, and I know that the sight and occasional feel of my dog, in my study, helps when I am working against the clock.

Many men, of whom I am one, are inhibited in displaying their emotions to another human being but not to a dog. It is not that they do not want to show their love or sorrow to another person but find it difficult and even unmanly to do so, while they have no such problem with a dog and this outlet can be therapeutic. And, of course, by inducing their owners to take regular exercise, dogs reduce the risk of heart ailments and improve fitness generally.

My dogs have always paid for their keep as founts of laughter, for others, if not always for ourselves. I rate that as a major therapeutic contribution in itself. I am not in favour of teaching dogs tricks but each of mine has developed her own party piece. Honey's was to bring her water-bowl when it was empty. My Labrador's is to lie on her back and juggle with a large ball, rather like a seal. She also finds it fun to seek me out and shake herself all over me when she has been in the water, though, after the third time it stretches my sense of humour.

All my dogs have been smilers, able to grin when they are particularly happy, a pleasure-giving characteristic in itself. Smiling seems to be something dogs have copied from us because wolves do not smile in the wild, though they learn to do so in captivity. It is fun just watching a dog chasing dream rabbits, for numerous experiments have satisfied scientists that dogs definitely dream, probably mainly in smells because their nostrils quiver while dreaming. Most of them occasionally 'talk' in their sleep but in an unusual voice because they are making their sounds through a closed mouth.

Pet dogs at shoots, usually brought by wives or girl friends, can be fun — I remember one peke that diligently found pheasants and then sat on them until its owner arrived to pick them up — but not if they habitually get lost, as some do. A black Labrador owned by a member of a shooting syndicate to which I belonged had the extraordinary habit of patronizing wellington boots. It would sidle up to whoever happened to be handy and direct a stream into the boot so accurately that the hot trickle was the first that the garrulous owner knew of it, always, of course, to the hilarity of any witnesses. It was never stimulated by leather and was the only dog I have ever encountered with a rubber fetish.

With my one-time zoologist's hat on I have collected scientific information about dog behaviour over many years and am in no doubt that to derive the maximum advantage out of the dog/man relationship it is important to devote some time to trying to think like a dog. By making a sustained effort to put myself inside the skin of my dogs, with a dog's-eye view of the world, I have learned a great deal, becoming much more understanding of their behaviour and limitations and more aware of my previous inadequacies in the man/dog relationship. To do this one must appreciate that the environment of a dog, even one that lives in a household, is very dissimilar from ours. It lives with its sense organs a few inches from the ground where the world looks and smells very different, as you can quickly appreciate if you get down on your knees to that level on a carpet, in a field or on a pavement, as I have done to the quizzical astonishment of onlookers. A dog's environment is a world swimming in odours which are hardly discernible to our noses, five feet higher. The pavements, roads, and walls give off a variety of smells which make a walk so much more meaningful for a dog.

Apart from being beset by human legs for most of the time the dog's horizon is so much shorter than ours, especially on rocky ground or where there are hummocks so that it has to rely on its sense of smell to tell it what is round the corner. Because of the domination of its sense of smell, a dog's brain does not see us as we see ourselves in a mirror. Its concept of us is a mixture of sight and smell, which is why sniffing is part of the rapturous welcome we receive on returning home.

A dog's vision is not nearly as acute as ours and it seems to be generally agreed that a dog sees colours only as shades of grey. The brown rabbit or hare in a field is difficult enough for us to see if it remains still, but imagine what it is like to a dog — a grey creature on grey ground. So we should not be surprised — as shooters often are — when a dog cannot see a cock pheasant visible to us. Apart from the height disadvantage the bird is a grey on grey background, its camouflage being much more effective to a colour-blind predator than it appears to us in all its colourful glory. Tests also show that, in general, a dog is poor at distinguishing pattern and form.

One thing a dog can always distinguish is another dog, sometimes in ways which strike me as astonishing. Over the centuries man has modified the original wolf-like dog to produce scores of dissimilar breeds, some huge, others tiny and many frankly misshapen. Yet a huge wolfhound will immediately recognize a tiny Yorkshire terrier as another dog and will do this from a long distance and from inside a closed car when smell cannot be involved.

Whereas man is a diurnal creature, with body-rhythms conditioned to being actively awake by day and sleeping mainly at night, the dog, being less dependent on its eyes, is a twenty-four-hour animal, capable of being as active by night as by day, sleeping in naps like wolves. It does its best to accommodate to our timetable but we need to be understanding when a dog is restless at night.

Through the close bond my dogs and I have established, they have heightened my perception of canine capabilities. It is because dogs are alert to some smells to which we are totally oblivious that we fail to understand some of the things they do, like barking when we can hear nothing or becoming restless for no obvious reason.

Dogs can also detect minute differences in sounds such as footsteps, even through double glazing, which pre-empts scent. Mine have been able to distinguish the noise of our car from anybody else's when it pulls up outside the house. The sound of other people's cars means nothing to them.

Joe Nickerson probably owed his life to the extraordinary canine capability to sense direction. When he was young he was out wildfowling on some marshes with three men when fog came down. As the tide began to flow in they were totally lost in a maze of muddy creeks. The men had a springer spaniel with them and the master shouted 'Go Home! Go Home!' The dog immediately knew the direction to take and Joe and the men followed it to safely. Scent may have played some part in that episode for the nose of a good dog is literally a million times more sensitive than ours. It can detect the odour of meat through seven layers of paper. While we can see what is there a dog can also detect what has been there.

Experiments show that breeds vary in intelligence and so do different individuals within the breeds. Dogs have little facility for overcoming a problem by reasoning but memory is a facet of intelligence and dogs are strong on that feature, which is why they are so good at learning. Scientists doubt that dogs benefit much in training by watching other more advanced dogs going through their paces. Nevertheless, when I acquired my two-year-old Labrador recently and it was faced with going through two swinging dog-doors to the garden it learned in a few minutes, having watched another dog do it a couple of times.

I have been assured that there was a country house which accommodated a large family and many dogs, some gun-dogs, others simply pets, all of which were allowed in the dining room. After dinner, when the ladies quit the dining room to leave the men with their port and stories, all the bitches went with them and the dogs stayed behind.

There are stories of dogs howling at the moment when their masters died, as though there was some telepathy between them. Perhaps the most remarkable case was described to me by the late Lord Carnarvon whose father was involved in the discovery of Tutankhamen's tomb. The father died from pneumonia in Cairo at 1.55 on the morning of 5 April 1923 and, at that precise moment, his dog, which had been left at Highclere Castle, near Newbury, howled inconsolably and expired.

There seems to have been no chance that the two would be reunited in Paradise because, according to my old Church, which claims to be the authority on such matters, neither dogs nor any other animals — even the lambs, donkeys and doves featured in so many religious paintings — qualify for entry because they do not possess souls. Recently, the Pope suggested that animals might have souls after all, giving delight to Catholic dog-lovers, but when I consulted the Vatican for further enlightenment the solemn reply, from the Secretariat, stated that while dogs and other animals do indeed have souls these are not immortal souls. Without an immortal soul dogs could not possibly experience any after-life which is a potent reason for making their one-off sojourn in this world as enjoyable as possible.

The Vatican's edict also implies that there can be no fish, game-birds or song-birds in Paradise, which would make eternity there boring for me. With nothing but virtuous human beings in view I suggest that it would be boring for most of us.

CHAPTER 11

A DOG CALLED DIDO

The death of Scoop, my last springer, was not unexpected but still, distressed me very much and when Sheika, our last ridgeback, died prematurely, in harrowing circumstances from a twisted stomach, I was quite shattered, as was my wife. The news that we were grieving and contemplating a replacement reached a young lady, of whom we had never heard, on the inter-village bush telegraph and she duly knocked on my door in Kintbury. As I was recording a television interview about spies it had to be interrupted while the lady and the chocolate Labrador, named Dido, which she had brought with her, were put in my wife's study to wait. When the interview was completed, the TV men wanted an introductory shot of me walking through the churchyard, preferably with my dog. As I was explaining that my last remaining dog had died I realized that there happened to be one handy. So Dido was able to act as a stand-in and, two hours later, we appeared together on the main evening television news. Clearly, we were destined for each other, as Dido's mistress had already surmised. She also thought that there must be something prophetic about the doormat, which I had recently bought from a sports shop. It had the silhouette of a large dog woven into it and the only dog likeness which the shop had been able to provide was that of a Labrador. So, before Dido even set paw in the house, there on the mat was 'Welcome' in the form of a dog which looked just like her. (The mat which warns 'Beware of the Wife' had not been available.)

I had insisted, to my wife, that we must have any new dog for forty-eight hours before buying her so that we could spot any behaviour problems and have her thoroughly examined by a vet. Instead, the moment my eyes met Dido's, I realized that there was something magical about her and had decided to acquire her before her owner changed her mind in a fit of remorse. I did so, cash on the nail, after an exchange of delighted looks with my wife. It had been love at first sight and in Dido's case at first sniff. I do not think it an exaggeration to use the word 'love' in connection with a dog. When we love somebody we feel happiness in their company and sadness in separation and that has been the situation with all my dogs. 'I wonder how the dogs are,' I have often remarked, plaintively, to my wife when in some enchanting situation such as breakfasting on the Grand Canal in Venice, or on the beach in Barbados.

Dido, who epitomizes the spirit of dogliness more than any other I have encountered, was the right dog in the right place at the right time. Her pedigree certificate showed that her registered name was Keneven Fantasy, so, needing a shorter name, her young mistress, who had bought her as a puppy, browsed through a classical dictionary and came upon Dido, the beautiful princess who founded the ancient city of Carthage in North Africa. It has turned out to be as rare a name as Fido and ideally suited to the star which Dido has become.

As a spaniel fan I had often been told 'Ah, but Labradors are special.' Dido certainly is. In the first place she is what I call a properly proportioned dog with the same shape as her wolf ancestors. That was the result of thousands of years of natural selection to produce the best machine for the environment and the rough conditions it imposed. In the last few centuries man has changed the truly dog-shaped dog by selection into more than 150 different breeds. They all have their qualities but the dog 'fancy', and so-called 'cosmetic breeding', have led to the production of some types which, nice though they are, are certainly not proportioned as Nature intended. In fact, some of them are freaks — the canine counterparts of those large-headed human circus dwarfs.

Dido's skull is wide to accommodate a large brain. Her almond-shaped eyes are dark amber and properly set in their sockets with no danger of popping out, as those of some pekes often do. They are set at a slight angle on her head to give her a wide range of vision so it is very difficult to creep up on her unobserved. Her muzzle is broad, not snipey, like some Labradors. Because smell is easily her main sense she needs a big nose set well in front of the rest of her body so that it is the first thing to confront any situation. Inherited from the past, when she needed them to hunt and kill large prey, she also has large and powerful jaws. Her water-repellent coat is short but dense and glossy, with a soft undercoat, which moults in the spring, and an overcoat of longer hairs, moulted in the autumn. It keeps her warm in the coldest weather and she can stand in freezing snow without discomfort.

Her ancestors were imported to Britain by Labrador fisherman bringing shiploads of salt cod. The dogs were a normal part of the crew and, when in foreign ports, the sailors would demonstrate their unusual retrieving ability by throwing objects overboard. In 1823 some of them were seen doing this in Poole Harbour, in Dorset, by the

Earl of Malmesbury who realized that they might be equally good at retrieving wildfowl. They were, in fact, so good at retrieving game-birds of any kind that these immigrants are an established part of the British country scene. Dido, herself, was not trained to retrieve birds and dislikes feathers but she is, by nature, a great fishing dog. She gets so excited when I hook a fish that I know she would love to try to land it herself though, so far, I have lacked the courage to let her in case she became hooked. Instead, to repay her for her companionship, I am trying to immortalize her name in a salmon fly. There is a well-known yellow fly called a Garry Dog which was originally made from a dog's hair. I sent off some of the chocolate hair from Dido's fat tail to a fly-tier and had our first success on the Dee, in the last week of the 1991 season. The mainly yellow fly containing a few of Dido's hairs accounted for five fresh-run salmon averaging nine pounds, but I have yet to catch one on the fly made entirely from her fur. However, I will persevere for it would give me intense satisfaction to say 'I got it on a Dido!'

When we are trout fishing Dido never barks when I hook a fish but when we are salmon fishing and happen to be on our own she invariably barks when I hook one. Whether her intention is to let the ghillie or my wife know that we might need some help I do not know, but it has had that effect more than once.

She certainly displays a measure of intelligence. When Dido was allowed into the dining room of dog-loving friends, where a swing door leads to the kitchen, she pushed it open within a few minutes whereas the Labrador living there, though always keen to get into the kitchen, had never done so. Dido is highly perceptive in other ways. She watches carefully what clothes I put on in the morning. Suits are bad news for her while the ropey old clothes I usually wear are an excellent sign, signifying that I am not going to London and will probably take her down to the river fishing for a couple of hours or so.

The clackety-clack of the printer attached to my word-processor sends her off looking for my wife because she realizes that I shall be busy for quite a while. When we have guests to dinner she is shut in my study and when I let her out any time after 11 p.m. she knows exactly what is expected of her. She rushes into the living room, giving me the chance to explain that she is creating a fuss because she needs to be taken out which, of course, is rightly interpreted by the guests as a signal for them to leave.

Dido can detect familiar bumps and turnings on roads when we are in the car. Without looking, she knows when we are nearing home or getting close to the river or a shoot, even a strange one. Main roads are of such small interest to her that she curls up and sleeps but as soon as we turn into a lane she becomes excitedly alert.

I have heard it said that there are three kinds of gun-dogs — gentlemen's dogs, keepers' dogs and beaters' dogs. In fact there is a fourth kind. Dido is very much her own dog! While she has a mind of her own — if I am a bumpkin, an awkward country fellow, then Dido can be a dumpkin — an awkward country dog — she has charm, which gets her out of all sorts of difficulties. She also has more than her fair share of feminine wiles. Much of her behaviour is most endearing. She does a lot of touching with her nose and lips — what I call a wuffle, the softest of soft bites, reserved for the highly privileged.

Sometimes at night, if she feels lonely, she finds the odd shoe or an item of washing off the clothes-horse or something else belonging to the other pack members to remind her that she is not really alone and, come the morning, will be back in the bosom of the pack. It has to be in contact with her to serve as a comforter, like a child needs to be in touch with its teddy bear or favourite blanket. This behaviour may be paralleled by the fact that when my wife and I go away we always take some small pillows which, we believe, help us to sleep better in a strange bed perhaps because they are a symbolic link with home.

It was an incident on the river which triggered off the joint venture which was to change all our lives. One summer evening in 1989 I was standing with Dido by my side, on a high bank of the River Kennet, at Littlecote, casting into a deep swirling pool and hooked a trout which jumped and threw the fly out of its mouth. The fly, which was whitish and called The Irresistible, flew towards us and, Dido snacked at it, thinking, while it dangled there, momentarily, that it was one of the biting flies which had been pestering us. I quickly opened her mouth and was horrified to see about ten inches of the nylon cast round her teeth and the hook, apparently, stuck in the back of her tongue. She tried to spit out the offensive object, snatching at grass and swallowing it, presumably in an attempt to make herself sick.

I decided that it was a veterinary emergency which would need a general anaesthetic, and took her smartly to the car but by the time we got there Dido had ceased to shake her head and splutter. I looked down her mouth but could see nothing. Having decided that there was no longer any point in taking her to the vet at that stage we returned to the river where, as everyone agreed, she seemed to be absolutely normal.

It was the general view, including the river-keeper's, that Dido must have spat the fly out but I remained greatly worried that the sharp barbed hook might be sticking somewhere in her throat or gut and could cause an abcess, apart from the danger of entanglement posed by the nylon. So during that night both I and my wife visited her to ensure that all was well, as it was on the following morning. Nevertheless, for my peace of mind I decided that I should carry out what is known in hospitals as a stool examination. As is Dido's wont, she had been out early on the lawn and had deposited the necessary specimens, which I dissected with short, sharp sticks, fortunately out of sight of the neighbours.

The investigation proved negative and looked like being the same on the following morning until I reached the last specimen. Within it I discovered a neat, folded packet of half-chewed grass, smaller than a postage stamp, and inside that could be seen a coil of nylon thread. A wash with a watering-can revealed the fly with its hook safely covered by the grass and as sharp and uncorroded as a new fly bought in a shop.

With almost a whoop of delight I carried my prize upstairs to show my wife who was still reading the morning papers in bed. Dangling the fly in front of her nose, triumphantly, I declared, 'Furthermore, to celebrate, I'm going to catch a fish with it!' The feathers composing the fly were a little bedraggled but they could be fluffed up again. So, that evening Dido and I went down to the river. A few fish were rising and within minutes, in the pool where the dangerous incident had occurred, I had a three-pound trout on the fly which had caused it. I greatly doubt that any other angler in history has caught a fish on a fly which has passed through a dog.

With Dido being so magical that anything seemed possible, I thought that, between us, we might gradually collect enough interesting anecdotes to make a children's book called *The Adventures of a Chocolate Dog*. Instead the idea occurred to us that she should write a more serious book, without delay, about the canine predicament as experienced through the eyes, nose and brain of a dog. There had been lots of books about the man/dog relationship and the time had come for a serious book about 'dog's best friend' and how he should be treated to get the best out of the dog/man relationship. Only a dog could produce it. Dedicated to the Greater Glory of Dog, it would be called *One Dog and Her Man*.

Over several months, Dido and I closeted ourselves in my study or conferred on our walks or on the river. It was a pleasure for me to take a breather from the world of spies in the less treacherous world of dogs where there are no 'dirty tricks' and no disinformation. The book duly appeared in June 1991, as written by Dido, with my assistance. It was serialized over three days by the *Daily Mail* with colour photographs showing Dido and me at the word processor. My nadir occurred when it was seriously suggested that in the accompanying TV commercial I should be pictured on all fours with a copy of the newspaper in my mouth. It was the only personal sacrifice for Dido which I have had the courage to decline.

Dido was in demand to take part in television shows, when Gloria Hunniford rated her as 'very professional'. Coast to Coast television sent a team to Hungerford to cover the occasion when she became the first dog to open an account at Lloyds Bank. The local paper printed a picture of the event under the heading 'Barking all the way to the bank'. When her photograph appeared alongside mine in the *Sunday Telegraph* I called upstairs to my wife that we were both pictured there. When she came down to look she was not best pleased that I had meant Dido.

The book quickly reached Number 11 on the *Sunday Times* list of bestsellers and the paperback rights were sold to Bantam Books, which she much preferred to Corgi Books, since one of that breed bit the Queen!

Any doubts about Dido's authorship can be dispelled by looking up her name in the author's catalogue at the London Library for there she is along with Charles Dickens, Daniel Defoe, and Conan Doyle. Further, the copy of her book on the shelves there has a London Library bookplate stating 'Presented by Chapman Pincher and Dido'. When my wife and I were invited to the party to celebrate the reopening of Hatchards, the prestigious bookshop, in Piccadilly, copies of Dido's book were on display — not among the Pets or Animals section but in Biography, surely the essence of one-updogship.

Answering her substantial fan mail, with requests for autographed photographs, has continued to occupy much of my time. I rush downstairs when the postman knocks to find that the package is some kind of edible treat addressed to the senior author. She has opened fêtes and bazaars and been the subject of lectures. I never imagined that I would be trapped into becoming a permanent dogsbody, which my dictionary defines as a drudge.

We had already received a letter of thanks from President George and Barbara Bush in response to a copy of the book sent to Dido's White House counterpart, Millie, a Springer spaniel. So, as the Queen is a lover of Labradors, we felt that Her Majesty might also like to read our book but understood that it was just not permissible to send one to her directly. However, one never knows when opportunity is going to offer and that is just what happened during a visit we paid to Sandringham to watch a gun-dog trial run by the *Shooting Times,* a magazine for which I write. The Queen's head-keeper there, a Scot called Bill Meldrum, is also a famous Labrador trainer and handler and, though Dido did not compete, he took a fancy to her, patting her head when she made friends with Topper, a black Labrador belonging to the Queen, which he was demonstrating. Naturally, I mentioned Dido's book to Mr Meldrum and then sent him a copy signed by us both to a rather impressive address — The Queen's Kennels, Sandringham. He liked it so much that he thought the Queen might too. So, through his good offices a copy was eventually put into her hand. We had signed it 'With loyal respects from Chapman Pincher and loyal love from Dido' and sealed it with Dido's pawprint. In due course we received a letter from Buckingham Palace which read:

> The Queen has now received a copy of *One Dog and Her Man* which you and Dido kindly sent her, and which she looks forward to enjoying. Her Majesty well remembers meeting you, though she cannot recall having made Dido's acquaintance. She sends her warm thanks to you both for your kind thought and for inscribing the book to her.

I then explained to the Palace how, on the one occasion when Dido might have been presented, when we had all been invited to a big field trial in Windsor Great Park attended by the Queen, she had to be left in the car because she had come into season at the wrong moment. As it was warm, all the windows and the sunshine roof of the car, parked close by, had to be left half open and the wind was blowing through in the direction of the ground where dogs were supposed to be concentrating on finding dummy 'birds'. It may have been coincidence but some of the top dogs put up mediocre retrieving performances, beyond the understanding of their owners, perhaps because their minds were elsewhere.

Dido had been able to sign Her Majesty's book, and many others, thanks to the expertise of a Newbury dentist who made a cast of Dido's right paw in dental plastic which was then mounted in the form of a stamp.

Fame touched Dido again in January 1991 when she appeared, by invitation from the Kennel Club, in the Parade of Dog Personalities at Cruft's and was interviewed by Angela Rippon but I knew she was really famous when a letter addressed to Dido, Kintbury, Berks reached her with no delay. (Dido may be a silly-sounding name but, like mine, which is even dafter, people do remember it.)

I always said that she would knock me off the front page and when the paperback of *One Dog and Her Man* came out she had knocked me off the front cover! Instead of the photograph of the two of us which had graced the front cover of the hardback edition, there was only Dido sitting on one of her favourite chairs.

People stop us on our walks, often because they recognize Dido and wish to be introduced, but usually because they have never seen a chocolate Labrador before. Happily the colour is gaining popularity and in 1991 we all took part in a Chocolate Field Day held at Greatworth Manor, near Banbury, the delightful home of Mrs Susan Towers-Clark, who has bred chocolate Labradors for more than forty years. There were fifty-one chocolates and, among them, was Mrs Tower-Clark's chocolate stud dog, Downfarm Bugler. As we all believe that Dido's genes are so special, a marriage was arranged and consummated. Nine weeks later, to the day and spot on for the promotion of the paperback version of her book, she produced seven chocolate pups. They were so winsome that Press photographers competed to take the first pictures of Dido in the wooden container where she suckled her young, the title of her next book writing itself in the process — *A Box of Chocolates*.

While our joint literary activities are fun — Dido's aspirations now include journalism and book-reviewing — her major role, like that of my previous dogs, will always be as a key member of the multi-specied orchestra which composes and plays my endless pastoral symphony.

CHAPTER 12

THE JOY OF BIRDS

Though I was trained primarily as a botanist, birds give as much joy as flowers, because, however familiar they may be, there is always something new to learn about them. I was sure, for example, that robins were everyone's friends but, on visiting a local trout farm, I found that there they are rated as damaging predators. The fertilized trout eggs, laid out on shallow trays in running water inside a building, are regularly pillaged by robins, which also eat the helpless alevins — the newly-hatched trout. Wagtails also take their share, and being riverside birds, may also do so in the wild, but the worst of these egg predators are blackbirds. To scare them, the trout farm owner had set up a stuffed owl!

When a song-bird's nest is pillaged in my garden I automatically blame cats, magpies or jackdaws but, while fishing the Dee at Banchory, I saw evidence of a culprit which I would never have suspected. A wooden tit-box by the ghillie's cottage at Little Blackhall had been broken into by a greater spotted woodpecker which had killed the young and, presumably, eaten them because the box was far too small for its use. When I consulted the *Handbook of British Birds* I found previous records of the woodpecker as having taken young from the nests of tits, house-martins and sparrows.

While enjoying the last evening of the 1991 trout season on the Kennet, I was watching a large skein of Canada geese, more than a hundred, flying in arrow formation a couple of hundred feet up on their way eastwards, probably to the Thames estuary for the night. A smaller group of about twenty came on about six hundred yards behind them, much lower, having got up not far away, but heading in the same direction and honking loudly. To my surprise, the first skein all banked to the left and returned, losing height as they did so. I thought they might be going to land but what they did, and seemingly with great deliberation having come full circle, was to fly eastwards again, gathering up the smaller skein and incorporating it perfectly into the arrow. This impressive example of social behaviour may be common but I had never seen it. Though farmers take a different view, huge flocks of Canada geese, one of the world's largest flying birds, are a glorious recent addition to the southern country scene. To experience the sight and sound of wild geese I previously had to go to Scotland. Now they fly over my house.

To see the collared dove, which deeply puzzled me when I first heard it making its mournful wail in the streets of Montrose more than thirty years ago, I would have needed to travel to Europe. Now it is so common that a pair nests in my garden every year. The Australian black swans which nest on our stretch of the Kennet save me an even longer journey. Sadly, they rarely bring up their cygnets, as the spring is usually too cold for them, though they have been known to succeed. Though smaller and much less weighty than the mute swans, they dominate them.

Spotting an unusual bird is so exciting that with some people it becomes a driving obsession. My most spectacular sighting of recent times was a bittern on the canal at Kintbury, no doubt a bird of passage, though they were resident in the area in living memory. It remains a thrill to me to see a bird I do not know and to deduce its identity, as I did with a pair of snipe-like birds, with slaty-black body and wings and brilliant white rump and tail which I put up on a bank of the Kennet. Though there was nothing green about them I guessed that they were green sandpipers, as the reliable *Handbook* eventually confirmed. Even the little water-rail which survives in a tiny enclosed area of stream within a hundred yards of my house gives me pleasure every time I see it. So do the buzzards which sometimes soar majestically over the village and remind me of an occasion when my interest in such raptors was not well received.

My previous wife and I were motoring on Devon moorland when my daughter then, perhaps, two years old, staged a display of what is rightly termed projectile sickness and which is quite frightening when first observed. Her stomach contents were suddenly deposited with incredible force on the windscreen and dashboard. As I drew into the side and alighted to clean things up my attention was riveted on a pair of buzzards. I reached in for my binoculars and as I stood there gazing at the mewing birds my wife's patience fractured and my explanation that they would quickly be out of sight received poor response.

Birds of prey have always held excitement for me and, while this is understandable with the sight of a golden eagle, a stooping peregrine, an osprey quartering the Tay or a hen harrier in pursuit of Speyside partridges, I remain enraptured by a kestrel hovering by a motorway.

Rarities are, understandably, rare, so it is the birds which are still common that provide most pleasure. I never cease to marvel at the fact that an adult robin, that miraculous package of pertness, smartness and song, weighs little more than half an ounce. Even the dowdy house-sparrow, which I may curse when it picks out the mortar from my old brick house, offers a mind-boggling surprise — a heartbeat of 800 times a minute.

The way that a bird inherits the considerable technology to build a nest through its genes has always seemed incredible and finding nests remains a special pleasure. Other boys used to say that I could smell nests but the truth was that I tried to think like a bird and looked where I would build if I were one. I also learned, early in life, that the way to see nests in bushes is to have the sun in front and to get down and peer upwards. For finding the nests of skylarks, meadow-pipits and other nesters on open ground a friend and I would drag a long rope between us and watch for the sitting birds to flush. The most remarkable nest I have ever seen was a tom-tit's built in a large gramophone horn dumped, mouth-down, in a wood. The busy bird had completely filled the enclosed ground area with moss.

While most people with a garden enjoy watching visitors to bird-tables I wonder how many put out nesting materials? All the fur I brush off Dido goes into the garden as do the cuttings from my hair when my wife trims it. We have fun finding these offerings again in the nests of robins, chaffinches and hedge-sparrows when we remove them at the end of the nesting season, burning them to destroy any parasites. Sometimes they contain peculiar items, one of them tragic. While I take great care not to leave any strands of nylon fishing line on a river bank, cutting any cast-off pieces into harmless fragments, I must have dropped a foot-long piece in the garden. A blackbird incorporated it into her nest, forming a loop in which she eventually strangled herself.

Though the river and the canal at Kintbury are bonuses, with bird-table visits from reed buntings and wagtails, I miss the small lake at my old home which had shovellers and other tame ducks and attracted wild ones. There is something special about lying in bed and hearing the splash-down of wild mallard. The herons were not so welcome not because they ate fish, which I could spare, but because I discovered that they are deadly killers of ducklings. The disappearance of my duck broods at the rate of one every day puzzled me until I lay in wait and watched a heron pouch one.

Perhaps, in retrospect, my concern for my baby ducks was excessive. I once caught my wife's favourite ridgeback killing a tame duck which was sitting on eggs. As this was the fourth offence and I had been waiting to catch her red-toothed, I belaboured her with the dead duck so much that my wife was in tears. But it did not stop the ridgeback from doing it again. Nor were marital relations improved when I asked my wife if she would like the duck to make pâté! As for the herons, watching them teaching their young to fish made up for their depredations and there is much to learn about them. During one hot summer the fish all died for lack of oxygen and after the pond filled up again no herons ever came. Can they, I wonder, detect when water is devoid of fish? They never seem to waste their time.

Among the stone monuments I built at Lowerhouse Farm was an aviary (since alas demolished) so that my wife could breed various cage-birds. They included a particularly beautiful, near-purple budgerigar which she occasionally allowed to fly in the large sitting room. I had warned her, repeatedly, that somebody, one day, would open a window or door and the precious bird would fly out of our lives. So I was not too surprised on going out in the morning, rather late and somewhat irritable, to see it hovering over my car. I put out a finger in the wild hope that it might settle on it and when it did I made a grab and caught it. I marched into the house fuming. 'There you are! I told you this would happen. Think yourself damned lucky . . .'

I stopped in mid-sentence because I saw our purple budgerigar safely inside its cage. The bird I had caught was an escapee and just happened to be almost identical. I have rarely seen my wife so triumphant. The new arrival did not stay long. It was a born escaper and somehow regained its freedom in a couple of days.

Another feathered inmate was Charlie, a talking minah bird which must have previously belonged to a railwayman because it was forever announcing 'I'll go and drive the train now!' He perpetrated his greatest coup at a moment when Lord Forte called in for tea. Superbly on cue, the bird croaked 'Hello Charlie!'

For some reason, that minah bird hated me, making threatening motions and noises whenever I went near his cage but his animosity was nothing compared with that of a large white cockerel, which had the run of the orchard during the day. My feathered enemy had the biggest spurs I have ever seen — at least half an inch in diameter at the base — and a brain that was not to be despised because he invariably figured out some means of attacking me, creeping up behind with great skill then jumping up to bring both legs down with power. If I saw him I would fend off the attack with my wellington boot but, eventually, he got me on the shin with such force that I was seen limping down Fleet Street — my ludicrous explanation for my infirmity being that I had been kicked by a bird. Now, with only a canary for tame bird comfort, I am safe.

While fishing offers wonderful opportunity for bird-watching so does game-shooting, visits to grouse moors, in particular, usually producing sight of some rarity such as a merlin, raven, peregrine falcon or ring ouzel. Buzzards and other raptors are common now that gamekeepers take a more enlightened view of them, though some still shoot anything which threatens their stock, as repeated court cases show.

The oddest birds I ever saw on a pheasant shoot materialized from a wood on Lord Forte's estate near Guildford. As they flew high towards the guns I realized that they had long tails and were unlike anything I had seen at a shoot before. I urged everyone not to fire but the chap they passed over was deaf and fast on the trigger. He fired at one of them and it ended in the wood behind cackling loudly and, hopefully, was not hit as it was not picked up. The birds were macaws ˙ which had escaped from an aviary.

The bird one is normally enjoined to avoid shooting is the occasional white pheasant, for the demise of which there is usually a fine. At one shoot, though, run by Jim Joel near St Albans, there were so many albinos — about ten per cent of the total — that they were treated as normal quarry. Sir Joseph Nickerson had the occasional white partridge on his shoot at Rothwell but the most spectacular all-white British bird I have ever seen was a thrush, though this was not wild but caged in a show.

Understandably, the birds I have spent most time watching have been pheasants, partridges, ducks and grouse, mainly while they have been in flight. Many people think that the grouse and the partridge fly faster than the pheasant but that is an illusion. As with ships, the bigger the faster their potential speed, though much depends on whether or not they have the wind behind them which, on a well-run shoot, should usually be the case to increase the degree of difficulty. With a strong wind behind them, grouse, partridges and pheasants can often exceed 60 m.p.h. In still air the pheasant averages about 40 m.p.h. in established flight. The grouse comes next and then the red-legged partridge followed by the grey partridge. The illusion of the grey partridge's speed is due to its small size and the erratic nature of its flight, coveys appearing to explode at a bewildering rate when they see the guns, the red leg's flight being more direct. The flight of big birds is even more deceptive in the other direction; geese and swans, for example, being much faster than they seem. Even the heron, which seems to fly so leisurely with a wing beat of only two per second, compared with a duck's nine, has been clocked doing 30 m.p.h. in still air.

Aerodynamically, a bird's speed is a matter of weight rather than size for the heavier it is, the faster it must fly to remain airborne. Further, the smaller the wing is in relation to total body-weight the faster it must beat. Being essentially ground-loving birds, even for nesting, and reluctant to fly unless forced to do so, game-birds have relatively short, broad, stubby wings so their wing-beats have to be so fast that they are quickly exhausted, being unable to repeat the performance without a substantial rest. This is particularly noticeable with the red-leg partridge which was called the Frenchman during the Napoleonic Wars because of its propensity to run from the guns rather than fly. In France, apparently, it is called the Englishman for the same reason.

A mile is a long flight for a pheasant and is also about the usual limit for a partridge or grouse. While grouse will move long distances in search of food they usually accomplish this in short bursts. These limitations make biological sense because, being residents, game birds do not have to undertake long flying migrations to breed or to find food in winter. All they need is to be able to fly far enough to escape a predator, usually when alarmed while squatting in undergrowth, and they are well equipped for a quick upward spring and rapid acceleration.

For all birds, there is a speed — about 12 m.p.h. — below which flight is impossible, so being able to accelerate rapidly to reach it is essential to survival. This costs so much energy that even a long-distance flyer like a pigeon becomes exhausted if forced to make more than five take-offs from the ground in quick succession.

There is no virtue for our main game-birds in flying higher or further than they have to, which is why they fly, obligingly, within shot-gun range. It is, perhaps, as well for average shots, as most of us are, that the pheasant, partridge and grouse are all relatively poor flyers. Flying at modest speeds, fairly low and for only short distances, they can usually be driven over guns yet are likely to remain within the boundaries of an estate. This is not to say that they are easy to hit. The flight muscles have to be so big to secure the quick take-off that they account for about half the body weight so the wings can flap only in short bursts. They are then forced to depend on gliding, while the muscles recover, and a gliding bird is a notoriously difficult target because it is also falling, which is by no means always obvious. Even the grouse has to alternate its rapid wing beats with long glides which is when it presents its most difficult challenge as it slips over the contours, swerving and tilting from side to side. What a splendid bird it is and so peculiarly British that if the nation decided to have a bird as its insignia, as the Americans have the bald eagle, it should, surely, be the red grouse!

At the same time it is one game-bird about which sportsmen need have no qualms on the grounds of cruelty because the fate in store for most grouse in a good breeding season is slow starvation, largely because of the innate cruelty of the bird itself. The strongest grouse, which tend to be the older, drive the young birds off their heathered territory to places where there may be little or no food so they are allowed neither to feed nor breed.

Considering the extent to which the grouse is associated with the 'upper class' it is ironic that research should have revealed the existence of a rigid class system among grouse themselves. The upper class grouse, which are the most aggressive, lead a lush life on the richest and most sheltered feeding grounds, the most ruthless having the largest territories and, sometimes, two wives. The middle-class grouse on the outskirts try to fight their way into the upper class and sometimes succeed. Those of no fixed abode hover permanently at starvation level. It is the cocks, those arrogant-looking birds inclined to stand on a rock and cry *Go-bak, go-bak, go-bak* as trespassers approach, which decide which females are to be allowed to marry into the upper class. It is their progeny which decide whether each Twelvth of August will be glorious or not.

While the heather-eating grouse cannot be coddled by artificial feeding, as pheasants are, I have heard of one creature comfort allegedly enjoyed by the birds on a famous North Yorkshire moor. The late Earl of Swinton, who was a distinguished politician, set up a college for enthusiastic Conservatives of both sexes on his estate, near Masham, and took some delight in ribbing the man in charge of it, whom he called the 'Headmaster'! One summer's day, while talking, casually, to a group of local people, including the 'Headmaster', about the prospects for the coming grouse season he remarked that, because of the Tory College, his grouse had a great advantage as they did not catch colds. Asked to explain, Swinton said that owing to the extramural activities of the Tory students there were so many condoms on his moor that the grouse could use them as wellington boots.

For a reason which defies scientific explanation ducks need no such protection — they can stand on ice for days on end without getting frost-bite. It has been seriously suggested that the blood circulating in their legs and webs contains some antifreeze constituent. The flight of ducks is also different from that of most game-birds because, being swimmers, they are poor walkers and runners and, being migratory, their muscles and breathing system are built for sustained wing-flapping. A full-grown mallard which, at two and a half pounds is light for its size, can sustain a speed of 65 m.p.h. for long periods compared with a homing pigeon's 50.

Another aspect of bird behaviour to which I have paid much attention while standing in the shooting line is their reliance on exceptional powers of vision. Most birds depend on their eyes to see their enemies and their food and, because they fly so rapidly, need quick focusing capability. This is especially true of predatory birds, like hawks and falcons, which depend on extremely accurate judgement of distance as they stoop or swoop on their prey. It is the movement of its prey which first attracts the flying predator's attention. The consequence is that, compared with the size of the head, a bird's eyeballs have to be very large, extending so far inwards that there is little room left for the brain. This has limited the development of intelligence since the degree of complexity of the brain is largely dependent on its size.

The prime requirement for game-birds, which are always on the look-out for predators, is all round-vision, which is achieved by having the eyes on the side of the head. As the eyes take up so much room in the skull, there is no room for eye-muscles, so few birds can move their eyes, gulls being exceptions in this respect. Instead, they rotate their necks. This twisting constricts the carotid arteries which supply the brain with blood but it is nicely overcome in birds with longish necks by a little safety bypass, which links the carotids so that if one of them is restricted the other is always open.

Experiments have established that birds have well-developed colour vision without which the bright colours of the cock pheasant, which are plainly for sexual recognition, would have no meaning. So the usual custom of wearing clothes which blend with the country background would seem to make good sense. (The red hats favoured by American game-shooters are to help them to avoid shooting each other.) I have often wondered whether a white or light coloured dog sitting at a peg puts pheasants off. Looking back, there seems to have been an excessive number of occasions when pheasants divided in front of me when I had a very white Springer. My current chocolate Labrador is probably the ideal colour in the absence of any dark green variety.

The lesson in all this for the shooting man is that game-birds' one-eyed, all-round vision is excellent for the detection of movement but, being only moderate judgers of distance, they may well assume that any faraway movement is close and take evading action. A high duck or a pigeon, for instance, will jink at the first flicker or movement of a gun. So, when birds are being driven, the guns will be wise to avoid movement of any kind. The old cock grouse which stands on a rock, having safely brought his covey to rest well in front of the butts, is looking for signs of danger and any bobbing up and down is likely to send the whole lot away. Indeed, the principle of the scarecrow would suggest that even standing still on the skyline is probably a mistake because birds can recognize something that has not been there in the past.

Ducks and geese excepted, most game-birds are active in the daytime and sleep in the dark. They do not see well in dim light, when colours begin to fade, probably seeing more poorly then than we do, so that darkness falls earlier for them. This would explain their reluctance to fly when the last drive of the day has been left too late and suggests that shooting should finish earlier so that the survivors have time enough to feed before going to roost. Partridges certainly see poorly in dim light, as I witnessed some years ago when birds were being captured for experimental purposes by the Game Conservancy at Fordingbridge. Once a covey was detected in the starlight, a lamp could be shone on them and the birds would stay still long enough for a triangular net, carried like a banner, to be laid over them. The backs of the birds were to be fitted with highly coloured plastic strips to enable them to be recognized in flight and the headline on my newspaper account, contributed by the features editor in my absence, reduced my popularity at Fordingbridge — 'Ever seen a partridge in a football jersey?'

While game-birds have no outer ears, their widespread use of alarm calls is proof of the extent to which they make use of hearing to protect themselves against predators and in the defence of their territories. All noisy creatures have acute hearing and game-shots would be wise to take note of it. Talking, laughing or the banging of car doors can ruin a drive, especially as the season advances, because though they may be only bird-brained, pheasants and partridges soon learn to associate noise with danger.

The remarkable capability of pheasants to hear distant sounds such as thunder, blasting or heavy gunfire is well known to country people and when the woods resound, repeatedly, to the cries of scores of cock pheasants I know that a thunderstorm is probably on the way. When salmon fishing with a long carbon fibre rod I have sometimes taken sufficient note of such alarm calls to stop fishing because of the lightning danger.

Many people, particularly town-dwellers, find it hard to understand how someone who loves the countryside and its fauna and flora as I do can derive pleasure out of shooting which, involves killing. The answer, as I shall explain more fully later, is that, like farmers, game-shooters admire and coddle the game-birds which we rear and release but there comes a time when they must pay for their keep and be harvested. It should follow that the true bird lover will stay his gun when anything truly wild appears in range and many do so. Like most shooting men, I took pleasure in bagging a woodcock because it was such a difficult, jinking target, with the much lauded right and left at a pair always being a possibility. For many years now, however, I have declined to shoot them because they are truly wild and are such delightful birds, with the exciting noise they make when flying over a wood in summer and their habit of carrying their young in flight, tucked between their legs. While I did not regard striking the woodcock off my quarry list as a personal sacrifice, the last one I shot will always remain firmly in my mind for a reason which did not emerge until long afterwards.

While shooting at Baynards Park with Alan Bristow one of the guests was the late Reginald Bosanquet, the controversial TV personality who enjoyed putting his gun up but did not do a lot of shooting. I was drawn next to him when a woodcock flew towards us both. I was quicker than he was and downed it in front, to general acclamation from all except Reggie, who said nothing. Several years later I was waiting in the ante-room of Independent Television News in London, chatting to Lord Chalfont about a programme in which we were about to appear, when Reggie strolled in. Pointing his finger at me and with no amusement whatever in his voice, he pronounced, loudly, 'There's the bugger who shot my woodcock!' He had never encountered one since and the event had rankled in his mind. I wonder how often such trivial happenings in the shooting field, or for that matter, elsewhere, which the perpetrator quickly forgets, are the cause of lasting resentment.

CHAPTER 13

MUSIC'S BLISS

The songs of birds formed my introduction to the appreciation of music, which my dictionary defines as 'any pleasant combination of sounds or the art of combining sounds in a rhythmic form for the expression of emotion'. The sounds of ascending skylarks, cock blackbirds and thrushes proclaiming their territorial rights, and even the cock robin's modest but distinctive effort, were sources of conscious delight from my childhood and the emotion was in me, as it still remains, such sounds being potent stimuli for memories.

My parents were musical to some extent, my father having been a flautist while in the Army and, on rare occasions, accompanied my mother, who sang well enough, in powerful soprano, to earn money on local concert platforms. It was music which had led to their union, when as a young miner's daughter in the old town of Pontefract, she had been first entranced by the tall Drum-Major of the Northumberland Fusiliers as he led his band, staff in hand, through the main street on the way to church. Most of the time, though, he was not encouraging and when, in later years, she was in full practice flight he would remark to me 'I think your mother's got her head fast'.

Neither of them did anything positive to stimulate my interest in music and, apart from the birdsong, the only music I tended to hear was the Catholic Mass. Catholic music remains deeply evocative of my upbringing, recalling that specific smell of incense, candles, flowers and swabbed flagstones. 'Kyrie eleison, Christe eleison' I chanted for years with no idea what it meant. Later when I was able to listen to High Mass in places like St Mark's in Venice and St Peter's in Rome I appreciated its grandeur along with the rest of the fabulous theatricality, not a trick being missed. Like pictorial art, music owes a colossal debt to religion and the reverse is also true.

Peculiarly for a boy, I always disliked popular music and jazz, which I continued to find so offensive that my children were denied the opportunity to listen to it when I was in the house. When watching television now I never cease to bless the unknown benefactor who invented the blab-off.

The first experience which led me to appreciate great music occurred while I was paying a Saturday night visit to a cinema in Darlington, when I was about sixteen, and heard a trailer of a rather bad film starring Beniamino Gigli. He was singing *Celeste Aida* and he caused me to feel that strange surge of tightness in the top of the chest — since called the Tingle Factor — occasioned by great music and particularly by lyrical tenors. I saved up and bought the record, the start of a rather substantial collection. In a surge of enthusiasm I later tried to learn the violin and persisted for about a year but it was too late. Instead, I devoted what time I could to listening and soon came to agree, wholeheartedly, with the philosopher Nietzche, that 'without music, life would be a mistake'.

I am in debt to music not just for its pleasure but for helping me to endure the pressures of working long hours, often against the clock. When at home, in the country, I trained myself to write while listening to music and a fair slice of my life has been enhanced by orchestral, chamber and solo instrumental delights played either on the gramophone or radio. For this purpose, the music must not be too intrusive into concentration, which excludes vocal music and any piece which is not already familiar. Conversely, the work should not intrude into the music, as the clatter of the typewriter inevitably did, and, these days, the word processor is much quieter. Fortunately, great music is unique in that it stands re-playing so often without becoming boring, as the regular re-reading of a book would.

Having listened to so many thousands of hours of music — I estimate 20,000 hours just since I retired — taste becomes rather wide and preferences develop for pieces rather than composers. Such wide experience also enables the listener to recognize most front-rank composers from only a few bars of their music, even if it has not been heard before, a private guessing game which gives me great satisfaction when I am right. Indeed, such distinctiveness is a sign of originality and style and I recall discussing this with the delightful, though second-rank, composer, Sir Arthur Bliss. His selection as the most easily recognizable composers was Brahms and Elgar. They are easy but many others, like Berlioz, Liszt, Schubert, Tchaikovsky and Prokofiev are unmistakable.

It is the solo piano works of Liszt which create, most strongly for me, the illusory atmosphere of inspiration when I am writing, more than any other composer, though, no doubt what I select to play varies, subconsciously, with mood. Modern composers, whom I have been trying to like for forty years, never feature because, while an innovator like Mozart or Beethoven gives the impression that he wrote to rid his mind of some insistent melody that was burning into it, most modern composers seem to be fiddling to find a tune and never succeed. When an announcer on Radio 3 or elsewhere needs to make a long explanation of a piece of music, invariably modern, cacophony always ensues.

When working at home I have always liked to alternate a spell of writing with some outdoor manual activity — building stone walls, carpentry or gardening. So it has been fortuitious that my optimum period of concentration at the writing machine has coincided with two sides of a long-playing record.

I have discussed the therapeutic effects of music on the brain with several neurologists and it seems possible that there is some connection with the rhythm of satisfying music and the pattern of the electric discharges on the brain surface — the so called brain waves. Possibly, there is a difference in such patterns between those who like jiving around to heavy beat music and those, like me, who hate it.

A few years ago the BBC paid me the compliment of asking me to appear on a radio programme, called 'Man of Action', in which I had almost two hours to talk about and play some of my favourite music. As I was encouraged to write the script as biography it enabled me to pay tribute to some old friends. I do not think that Sir Thomas Sopwith was musical in any way but, in remembering the hours we had spent together on the Test, he appreciated my dedication of Schubert's *Trout Quintet* to him.

It used to be true that most people living in the country tended to be divorced from live musical performances unless they made the effort to travel to a big city. Today there are high-class musical festivals within reach of all and we are particularly fortunate in being close to the Newbury Spring Festival which features some of the nation's finest orchestras and virtuosi, both native and foreign. The Festival spills over into the village churches, including our own at Kintbury, and the great houses, which are the venues for the chamber orchestras and soloists.

Musicians of the highest calibre can be heard in the long gallery at Englefield House, at Highclere Castle, and other stately homes. The interest in music of estate owners who so often are country sports enthusiasts, gives a further lie to the urban, 'chinless Charlie', bonehead image of such people. Not only do many of them lend their homes for musical events, but some sponsor the performers financially and give them hospitality. One of them, Brigadier Tim Landon of Faccombe Manor, sponsors the excellent Burlington Trio and their performances in the spacious hall of his fine house recall the tradition

121

set by his wife's forebears, the Esterhazys, who were patrons to Haydn. Those who decry 'Bloodsports' as degenerate should know that on the Esterhazy estate it was customary for people to describe a brilliant performer in the field by the comparison 'As good a shot and fisherman as Haydn'.

Admittedly, there are occasions when the highly personal nature of musical enjoyment displays itself in an offbeat country manner. At a recent concert in Newbury's St Nicholas Church I sat near a local sporting squire during a performance of Mozart's *Sinfonia Concertante*, which featured delightful counterplay between the violin, played by Norbert Brainin, and the viola played by Peter Schidlov, with the two performers standing close together, fiddling furiously away. At the end, the old gentleman applauded loudly and observed to me, 'I thought it sounded and looked like a couple of cock pheasants having a go at each other'. To some, musical appreciation is a more cerebral process than to others but he had clearly enjoyed it.

My own musical peculiarity is my inordinate love of bagpipes which many people cannot stand. The skirl of the pipes and sway of the kilt cause such an upsurge of pleasure in my breast that I suspect I must have some Scottish genes, which is not improbable as my father's forebears lived not far from the border and some raiding, hairy-kneed Scot may have 'had his way'. The full dress uniform of some of the Scottish regiments could look ludicrous, with every peacock device pressed into service, but they get away with it, probably because of their reputation as fighters. In that connection, a musical friend of mine, Bill Harries, who sponsored a famous Welsh male-voice choir, was anxious to find a suitably impressive uniform in which to dress the singers. He looked everywhere for inspiration but gave up because, as he put it, 'The Scots have collared the lot!'

Poor Bill! Having made a fortune in business and bought a country estate, he was longing for a knighthood for his services to Welsh music but his chance was remote until, suddenly, it became a certainty when the Government was looking for Welshmen to honour to mark the investiture of the Prince of Wales. Sure enough, the letter from Downing Street arrived but Bill died suddenly before the honour could be accepted. I can think of nobody who would have loved it more.

Inspired by the success of the provincial and country music festivals, a few enthusiasts have extended the principle by offering great music in country hotels. A courageous pioneer in that direction has been our friend and former neighbour, Connie Ward, who initiated the highly successful concerts at Cliveden, the former country estate of the Astors, and at Kinnaird, her Perthshire home, now a hotel. While staying at Kinnaird for salmon fishing recently, we were superbly entertained by the entrancing talent of Ofra Harnoy, the beautiful, young Israeli cellist who had been flown in by Mrs Ward with the distinguished pianist, Michael Dussek.

Similar successful initiative has been shown by Ann Hutley who has mounted a series of public musical entertainments at Wintershall, her Surrey home. The timbered hall, which must have echoed to the sound of itinerant minstrels and mummers centuries ago, is now, regularly, the setting for piano music by artistes of international repute and many of us who thought we knew something about music have learned a great deal more there from the instructive commentaries and performances of people like John Lill.

Beaverbrook's musical interests were limited to hymns, which he liked to sing, and to what he called 'jingles'. He had a choice of 'jingles' on old gramophone records and one of them figured in a hilarious episode when the Beaver wished to express his deep suspicion of some new American enterprise being favoured by Anthony Eden, then Prime Minister, whom he disliked. He telephoned the Editor from Cherkley to say, 'Call me back in ten minutes and I'll give you the title of the leader for tomorrow's paper'. The Editor did so but all he could hear was His Lordship urging on the butler to wind up the ancient machine. Eventually he heard the reedy strains of *Working for the Yankee Dollar* and the phone went dead.

Beaverbrook's limited interest restricted my musical endeavour as a journalist to one occasion — the opening of London's Festival Hall, which had a scientific twist because of the daring acoustical construction of the building. My report dwelt on the way that sound engineers had tuned up the hall with screwdrivers. Nevertheless, the Beaver had a major influence on my musical education. The numerous foreign trips I made at the expense of his newspaper enabled me to experience performances in many of the great opera houses and concert-halls of the world — from *Aida* in the ruins of the Baths of Caracalla, in Rome, to Mozart in Salzburg; from the sailor-suited Vienna Boys' Choir to Donizetti in the elegant Fenice Theatre in Venice; from Granados in Madrid to Chopin in Warsaw; from Jussi Bjoerling in Stockholm to Lauritz Melchior at the 'Met' in New York.

Lord Sieff provided my wife and me with a very special musical memory on our honeymoon trip with him to Israel. One of the celebrations in his honour was a concert by David Oistrach, who was visiting Tel Aviv. His beautiful rendering of the Beethoven *Romance No 2 in F* was dedicated to Lord Sieff and, as his guests from England, we were included. But a much more intimate honour was to be made, later, by a string virtuoso of comparable stature, the late Paul Tortellier.

As my wife was deeply involved in the Newbury Festival, we were privileged to give a night's accommodation to Tortellier, whom I had long admired and whose performances figured in my record collection. Over breakfast, next morning, he began to question me about the 'Peace' women at nearby Greenham Common with whom he expressed considerable sympathy, even suggesting that he might like to go and play for them. He then announced that he had composed both the words and music of a Hymn to Peace and insisted on performing it, possibly in the hope of changing my pro-nuclear views. In the confines of our modest hall a cello was produced and tuned. Then, to his own accompaniment, he sang to an audience of two — my wife and me — until the arrival of the daily help who was startled to see a tall, lean stranger with hair like an aurora borealis fiddling away and stridently singing under the grandfather clock. Sensing another convert, the maestro insisted that she delay her chores and listen as he re-started the Hymn. He played more tunefully than he sang but, in his inimitably pleasant and very French way, he got his message across in several forceful verses.

The Queen occasionally graces the Newbury Festival but the most charming story about her musical associations, retailed to me in the shooting field by a witness, concerns a performance of *La Cenorentola* at Covent Garden by the opera company of La Scala, Milan. When the leading singers were presented, a large, over-enthusiastic baritone commented, profusely and with many gestures, on Her Majesty's beauty and especially on her smile. To save her embarrassment, someone took her arm to lead her away but she broke free and returned to the Italian with, 'You were saying — about my smile.' Sadly, as her ladies-in-waiting confirm, few people, dare to take the liberty of paying her the compliments which are music to any woman's ear.

A clue to Princess Margaret's musical taste came my way when I drove her from a yacht in Cowes to lunch with Sir Max Aitken. I had the radio quietly tuned to a Mozart piano concerto and she, imperiously, switched it off. Her nephew, Prince Charles, who learned the cello, might have left it on, as might his predecessor, the Duke of Windsor, who played the bagpipes. My association with the Duke was limited to a brief encounter at the end of a garden party at the British Embassy in Paris, when his grey topper had been mislaid in the vestiaire. 'I would hate to lose it because it is a memento of happier days', he explained, smilingly but wistfully, I thought.

Few non-musicians can have spent more time listening to great music than I have. As a further joy, when I am fishing, walking or even standing in the shooting line, melodious movements intrude themselves and I can usually run through them, almost in their entirety. Then, there are special days, even in winter, when the whole landscape resonates in harmony of its own accord and the reason for so many 'pastoral' masterpieces by great composers who loved the countryside becomes self-evident.

CHAPTER 14

TRAVELLER'S JOY

I am indebted to Sir Thomas Sopwith for much wise advice and on the subject of foreign travel he urged me to do as much as possible while I remained young. So many people plan to travel in their retirement and then find that they have lost the desire to go or cannot afford it, he explained. I entirely agree and would add that, as far as possible, travelling should be done, in line of duty, at the expense of some large organization for then one can go in style and stay in comfort beyond one's private means. In my case, it offered another means for staying out of the office and of reducing the load of commuting to and from London.

The lot of the roving foreign correspondent sent on assignments by the foreign editor is not enviable, in my opinion, as it is the enemy of home life. There were times when international conferences on science, medicine or defence required my attendance but, much more often, I was able to choose where to go after finding a story which would be exclusive and would eliminate the deadline stress because there would be no competition. Such a trip, which I recall with special pleasure, was a journey to the village of Brunnwinkl, on Lake Wolfgang, near Salzburg, in Austria, to meet Professor Karl von Frisch who had discovered how bees communicate. His wooden chalet, decorated with stag-horns was like a set for a Franz Lehar operetta and the white-haired professor himself looked the part in Tyrolean deerskin breeches and grey-edged green jacket. His story seemed incredible — that a foraging bee which has discovered a good source of nectar can tell its hive-mates exactly where it is by dancing in a particular way. There was no doubt, however, that, by meticulous experiment, some of which he repeated for me, he had proved all his extraordinary claims, including the fact that from a quick glance at any patch of blue sky a bee can tell the exact position of the sun and so get its bearings even on a cloudy day. The word 'beeline', implying the shortest route between two points, predates von Frisch's discoveries, so people in the past seem to have realized that bees could be sufficiently well informed about a honey source to fly directly to it, though they did not know how.

Having spent enough time in Salzburg, I seized the chance to pick up some personal war reparations by fishing in the private trout lake belonging to Krupp, the German armaments magnate. He had made the angler's paradise, called the Hubertesee, by damming a stream where it runs through a gorge in Alpine foothills and stocking it with thousands of rainbow trout. His keeper did not like it but shrugged, helplessly, when I said that I was an English officer without declaring that I had left the Army. Everywhere I looked over the steep banking I could see fat trout basking in the sun. My borrowed Austrian spinning lure, a beautifully machined mother-of-pearl and gilt affair, looked more like something to hang from a watch-chain than a bait but it was clear from the first cast that the fish were fascinated by it. At every throw, dark shapes, looking more like Herr Krupp's torpedoes than fish, followed it to within rod reach, only to turn away at the last moment.

The trout teased me that way all morning until I came to the one place on the lake where, because of the shadow of pine trees, the fish were no longer visible. At the first cast there I hooked a trout which went off like a rocket and danced itself to exhaustion by skittering along the surface on its tail. During the next ten minutes I hooked a fish every time I threw the bait. Then I lost one and though I continued to fish there for half an hour I did not get another pull. As soon as I moved to a sunlit spot the trout renewed their game of baiting me. After a break for lunch I moved back to the shaded area and, again, the first cast produced a trout. The fun lasted until I lost another fish when earnest interest in my spinner dramatically ceased. The practical lessons seemed to be — if you can see the fish the odds are that they can see you: if you lose a well-hooked fish move away and come back later.

As I had a plane to catch that night I had no time to eat any of the nine fat trout that I kept. A pity! I can think of nothing that would have tasted sweeter than trout poached from Herr Krupp's strictly private pond. But I kept the extraordinary spinner which was to work wonders for me on another river in not too dissimilar circumstances.

For most journalists foreign travel means moving to foreign towns but in my field the venues, as with Brunnwinkl, were often deep in the foreign countryside, so deep on occasion, that few of the native inhabitants had been there. Such a venue was Emu Field, the area of desert in South Australia, formed of red clay, not sand, which had been chosen for the test-explosion of the first British atomic bomb in 1953. It gave me my first opportunity to see the huge wedge-tailed eagle, swarms of parrots and many other birds which had only been names to me. It also gave me the first experience of an Australian breakfast which I had no desire to repeat — curry and whisky at 5 a.m. after an all-night flight.

The hospitality arrangements were rather better three years later at Maralinga, the permanent nuclear testing ground in South Australia, which has since been the focus of so much bitter argument concerning the alleged effects of radioactive fall-out on those taking part. The fireball caused by a bomb located on top of a steel tower, was more impressive but, oddly, more memorable for me has been the image of clouds of pinkish parrots flying round the tower and perching on it. Known as galahs, which, because they are allegedly stupid, is also Australian slang for idiots, they seemed likely to earn their name as the countdown to detonation proceeded towards zero on two mornings, before sudden changes in the weather aborted the tests. On the third day, when the bomb was exploded, there was not a galah in sight. Maybe they are not so stupid.

Maralinga taught me that there are professional drawbacks to being abroad and I enunciated Pincher's Law — when out of touch, the amount that a journalist gets into his newspaper is inversely proportional to his distance from the office. As the RAF director of the operation, the late Air Vice-Marshal 'Ginger' Weir, was a friend I was given information and facilities denied to my rivals. These included a flight over the bomb crater a few minutes after the blast to see the effects on various test structures which had been erected. I filed an exclusive account of this experience but to little avail. While I was in the air Ginger told the other correspondents that he was calling the explosion, which had been timed for 5 p.m., 'The Five-o-Clock Rock', an allusion to rock and roll which was then all the rage. The night editor in London was so taken by this utterance, which I had not heard but which headed the story sent over by the Reuter man, that my copy was relegated to the bottom of his report.

He would not have demoted the copy I could have sent him had I not been sworn to secrecy. Before the test I had spent some time in Sydney with a man called Joe Fallon whose original ancestor there had been an Irish political convict. Joe, who was so proud of him that he had his handcuffs on show in a glass case, had befriended the lonely, young Prince Philip when he had been a junior naval officer on a destroyer visiting Australian ports, long before he had met the future British Queen. They had remained in touch over many years and there was a steel filing cabinet full of letters which had passed between them. I had heard about this cache, which Joe would never let anybody examine, and for some reason that day, when I mentioned it, he suggested that I might look at it while he was having a nap, provided I never printed anything about it. I spent an enthralling couple of hours reading racy material which, at that time, would have made international headlines. Joe could have made a fortune out of the collection but, presumably, destroyed it before his death.

Whenever the Royal couple, or Prince Philip alone, visited Sydney they never failed to contact Joe and he was in embarassing public difficulty, as a result, the next time I visited him. The weather had been unbearably hot and, as the Queen wished to swim in privacy, Joe was asked, by an aide, to lend the pool at his large house in Vaucluse, a snooty area of the city. As Joe was unwell he had not bothered to clean out the pool so, explaining the situation, he asked the fire brigade to do so. Newspapers, who happened to dislike him, printed the fact that his pool had been cleaned at public expense and hounded him for an explanation which, loyally, he never gave.

Years later, when I was able to mention my friendship with Joe to Prince Philip, he spoke of him with great affection.

My welcome at Christmas Island, in the Pacific, to watch the colossal fire-ball created by Britain's first H-bomb was warm because of my service in helping to prevent the threatened Japanese interference. I enjoyed myself in Honolulu before and after the explosion but what I remember most clearly is a remark by a senior scientist when I gasped at the enormity of the explosion — 'Compared with the energy in just one tropical storm it is like a fart in the night.' Though I suppose it proves nothing, I have witnessed four atomic explosions, flying low over one of them shortly after the blast, without discernible ill effect.

Though I was never to see an H-bomb dropped in anger I did witness the excitement of a nuclear scramble as fully-loaded bombers took to the air in a mock retaliatory attack on Russia. So, I can reveal, did the Queen who normally remained as aloof as possible from weapons of mass destruction because of their political sensitivity. In total secrecy, during a visit to the USA in the 1980s, the Queen's plane put down for fuel at the Strategic Air Command HQ at Omaha. By previous arrangement, she then witnessed the scramble and even spoke, by telephone, to the SAC Commander who was airborne in the control plane. Had this become public at the time, the media would have had a field day with guaranteed political repercussions from Moscow. The event which, I believe, has not been made public before, was a further example of the secrecy which governments can maintain if they wish. I learned about it through my practice of asking any retired defence officials I meet if they can recall any highly newsworthy event which the media missed completely. It came from a retired US Air Force general whom I met in Florida while visiting an alligator sanctuary!

Such officials relish such coups against the media as much as journalists enjoy penetrating their security, and they have often responded with some item which would certainly have made my day. One such was the furore in Whitehall when the Navy feared that a small vessel, called *Throsk*, carrying nuclear warheads had been hijacked by the IRA. The nuclear weapons pioneer, Sir William Cook, a wartime friend and Berkshire neighbour, could not restrain his mirth as he told me about it in answer to my routine question.

While any association between rocket missiles and fossilized Venice would seem unlikely, it took me there for a delightful week to cover an international space-research conference, staying with my wife in one of the splendid hotels on the Grand Canal. When I awakened on the first morning my arms were covered with insect bites. I blamed mosquitoes from the canal and made sure that all windows were shut on the following night. Next morning the bites were even more numerous so I flung off the sheet and, sure enough, found an obnoxious bug bloated with my blood. I put it into an envelope and went down to see the manager with whom I had already made friends. He was appalled when he saw my arms and ordered the housekeeper to close and fumigate our modest room after transferring our luggage to what looked like the Papal Suite. After the bug had been examined at Venice University the manager insisted that I must have picked it up at Torcello, the nearby island, which we had visited to see the magnificent mosaics in the Catherdral there, but my bites were too numerous to have been inflicted by one specimen. Anyway, when the bill eventually came there was no charge for my wife's stay and other welcome reductions. Should one carry one's own bug?

While sightseeing in a foreign country can be rewarding in itself, such visits are enormously enhanced if one has the luck to be accompanied by a person of outstanding influence in the area. I have mentioned how I met the first Lord Sieff, of Marks and Spencer fame, at his pheasant shoot the day after I had married my present wife. He asked her why we were not on honeymoon and got the reply that, as I was not one to miss a big pheasant day, that ritual was being delayed. Next day, he announced that, for a wedding present, he was sending us to Israel, where he and his family had done so much. Furthermore, he would be coming with us as there were to be festivities to celebrate his peerage. It meant being abroad for nearly three weeks but my editor agreed that the chance of meeting the Israeli leaders in such circumstances was not to be missed.

We spent time in Jerusalem, Tel Aviv and on kibbutzim but the rest was devoted to exploring the country with guides, particularly archaeological sites like Jericho and Meggido, which had just been names to us. While roaming the ruins of Ashkelon I learned that the Crusaders had so enjoyed the local breed of onions that they took some to Britain, where the name Ashkelon became corrupted to escallion. So, for the first time, I realized why in the north, when I was a boy, spring onions were known as scallions.

More majestic than the pyramids of Egypt, in location, concept and power to evoke the distant past, is the mesa of Masada where Israeli soldiers take the oath to defend their country. Instead of being the tomb of one tyrant VIP it is a memorial to common people who preferred death to slavery. For it was on this flat crag, which drops on its eastward side 1300 feet into the Dead Sea that, in AD 73, the last of the Jews holding out against the might of Rome staged a heroic if forlorn act of defiance. At the same time it was the scene of a brilliant siege operation by the Tenth Roman Legion. To stand on the summit and see the Roman camps and siege-works below, with even the shacks of the camp followers still discernible, was to witness history as it happened nearly 2000 years ago. Only the shouts and the blood seemed to be missing.

Flavius Silva, the Roman Governor, who was also a determined general, decided to reduce the fortress. With a force of 15,000, including Jewish slaves, he built a wall round the base of the entire rock to prevent the zealots escaping. Then he threw up a ramp of stones and earth 600 feet long reaching to the summit. With a battering ram on top of the ramp he breached the walls. Rather than be captured, the defenders killed their wives and children then drew lots to decide who should kill the men and then commit suicide. When the Romans entered Masada it was a burning ruin and more than 950 people lay dead there. Among the debris archaeologists found marked pottery fragments which could only be the fatal lots.

I had not thought of Israel as a centre for watching wildlife but it stands on the main migratory route of many birds, like the black stork, and hundreds of herons and other fish-eating birds congregate on the carp-farms. By the roadsides flocks of goldfinches dart in and out of the orange plantations. Hoopoes are common and even in the back-gardens of Tel Aviv there are giant azure kingfishers which hunt lizards. I saw jackals and hyenas but failed to see a leopard, though a few still exist there.

My wife and I thought that such experiences could never be repeated but they were, a few years later, when the late Lord (Victor) Rothschild and his wife, Tess, whom we had met at Lord Sieff's country home, invited us to spend ten days with them in Israel. 'Don't bother to bring any money,' Victor said. 'Everything will be provided.' It certainly was, including a helicopter to take us to the Santa Caterina Monastery, deep in the Sinai desert and at the base of the mountain where Moses is said to have received the commandment tablets and where, ludicrously, one is shown the original bush which burned without being consumed. The sun was so hot that the helicopter could not take off in the late afternoon with the full load it had carried in the morning. So I was left behind for a couple of hours and began to explore the rocky scrub around the monastery until an Israeli major from the small garrison there sent a scout after me, explaining that the Bedouins were in the habit of firing at anyone who might be a Jew.

Through Victor, we met most of the Israeli leaders, who were cock-a-hoop after their stunning victory in the Six Day War. I asked Ezar Weizmann, who had commanded the Air Force, about the danger that Soviet fighter-pilots, then stationed in Egypt, might become involved. Pointing to a Russian monastery, visible on a hill, he said 'If they want to fill the cemetery there that's their privilege'. Later, I learned that three of them had already been shot down over Israeli-held territory and duly reported it.

Taking supper with Teddy Kollek, the perennial mayor of Jerusalem, I noticed one table companion who seemed familiar but was not entirely recognizable. It was David Ben Gurion minus all his prominent hair. He had just cut it off because someone had offended him in the Knesset.

Sadly, apart from Lake Galilee, where we had no tackle, no fishing was available in Israel. Happily, it was readily available shortly afterwards on Lake Naivasha, in Kenya, where we were guests of the late Jack Block and his wife who owned several of the major game parks. The fish were fairly small bass but Jack made their pursuit more exciting by deliberately incensing a huge bull hippopotamus, which had a harem close by. I was not amused by Jack's close passes in the small boat for, had the engine stopped, the hippo could easily have capsized us. More to my taste was the young hippo, called Sally, which lived in the lake by the next bungalow, the home of Alan Root, the wildlife camera-man. Sally regularly came onto the lawn in the evening and her friend there was a tame aardvark called Million, from the old Al Jolson song 'Aardvark a million miles for one of your smiles . . .'

All the lakes in the stupendous Rift Valley offer exciting wildlife, flamingos in particular, but the most thrilling Kenyan lake in my experience was Lake Turkana, formerly called Lake Rudolf, the home of the gigantic Nile perch. My first fish was a tiddler of 50 pounds which did not do much but the second was in the 200-pound class and sadly broke the hawser-like nylon because the boatman had set the reel wrongly. It was the biggest fish I will ever hook.

Easing away my sorrows by sitting in a hot spring outside the hut where we were living, I was joined by Bruce McKenzie, who had flown from Nairobi. He immediately told me, in confidence at that stage, a story which I knew could grab the headlines throughout most of the world. A few days previously, three Palestinian Arabs equipped with Russian anti-aircraft missiles had alighted from a car by the perimeter fence of Nairobi Airport shortly before an El Al jet, with many Jews aboard, was scheduled to land on its way from Johannesburg to Tel Aviv. Mossad, the Israeli intelligence service, had alerted the Kenyan equivalent of the SAS and the terrorists were captured. Their car contained grenades, sub-machine guns and other weapons which had been smuggled in from Uganda.

A couple of days later, two West Germans, a man and a woman, using South American passports had arrived, as Mossad had predicted, to see what had gone wrong. They were arrested and when the woman was examined she was carrying instructions about other airliner targets for the Palestinians written in invisible ink on her abdomen. Bruce explained that while the operation had been a triumph it created severe problems for the Kenyan Government. To try the five terrorists would bring reprisals with which they might not be able to cope and, under Kenyan law they could not be quietly executed. The Mossad man in charge had offered to take them to Israel to stand trial and, as we spoke, they were already there.

It was another case of really hot information coming my way in the countryside — which could hardly have been more open than on the wild shore of Lake Turkana. I was unable to use it for five months but when I did so, in the context of the Entebbe Raid, it had maximum political impact by proving how Uganda, and Idi Amin, in particular, had assisted Palestinian terrorists.

The fluke of finding Bruce in a giving mood, as we relaxed in the hot spring, was the only reason why I had learned that story and it supported my conviction that a great deal goes on in the world which never becomes public and remains secret even from historians.

While Bruce McKenzie's generosity did not bring me a really big Nile perch, it did get me my first 30-pound salmon. Over the forty years that I have fished Scotland's rivers I have never caught a salmon weighing thirty pounds or more. In Norway, where the family of Bruce's wife had a beat on the turbulent River Driva, in the Sundalsfjord, I caught one on my first day there — a fresh-run 31½-

133

pounder. To rebut the charge of trumpet-blowing let me record that on that same day only a mile higher up river somebody caught a 56-pounder, while 64 is the record for the beat I was fishing.

Salmon run big in Norway yet to the eye accustomed to Scotland's salmon they do not look so big. On six occasions on Scottish rivers, I have convinced myself that the fish I had just landed was a thirty-pounder. And on three of these the ghillies, with all their experience, agreed with me. So much so that we celebrated the achievement with the ritual dram of whisky. The fish were long, deep and in fine condition but each time we hung them on the scales-hook back at the fishing hut they were short by one or two pounds. In Norway the reverse occurred, depriving me of much of the thrill of fulfilling the thirty-pound ambition. My fish, a cock in superb condition and so lately out of the sea that it had sea-lice on its shoulders, was long enough but seemed to lack the necessary depth and I judged its weight as no more than twenty-five pounds. Indeed, when my host passed by on the bank and inquired if I had been lucky I replied, 'I've got one that's not a minnow but it's not a whale either.' I was delighted a few hours later when the scale turned at 31 pounds but it was not the same as knowing it the moment it was grassed.

Sadly, because of excessive sea-netting, I missed the best years of the Norwegian salmon fishing but, thanks to Charles Forte, I did experience the best of the fishing in Iceland. For many years he hired a beat on the Haffjardara river on the west coast but, one season, being unable to go for business reasons, he offered it to my wife and me. We have never forgotten a minute of it. Using a concoction of red wool, fur and stiff cockerel 'whiskers', looking like a small shrimp or prawn, I took four salmon out of my first allotted pool and could not get down quickly enough to the next pool, where my wife was fishing, to tell her of my good fortune. She also had four and was playing a fifth, which she lost.

We skirted an unfishable region where the river expands into a shallow lake set between the cones of a dozen miniature extinct volcanoes, some with their tops blown off in prehistoric blasts and with the lava they produced solidified and weathered into grotesque shapes. My wife then waded gently into the Kula pool while I fished the Stone, a much bigger pool which was alive with leaping, rising salmon, some of those below the big boulder that gives the pool its name being monsters well over twenty pounds. The salmon that jumps is rarely a taker but one lying by it quietly sometimes is, so I fished the pool down twice from the right bank without a touch and before wading across to fish the far bank I sat and looked around. It was a botanist's paradise with wild pinks, orchids, bedstraws, woodruffs and several flower species I had never seen before. The boggy sheep land between the lava flows was dotted with the waving white mops of cotton grass. Ringed plovers, dunlin, wagtails and whimbrels were feeding by the water's edge. A couple of incredibly tame ptarmigan surveyed me from a tussock.

As I waded the fast water to reach the other side two Arctic terns dive-bombed me as a warning to keep away from their one chick which had survived the depredations of the black-backed gulls. The wind had freshened and was blowing upstream, as it would for days — difficult for casting and bad for fishing. Iceland would more aptly be named Windland but it blew some good — it grounded the mosquitoes which can make fishing unbearable on a really quiet day.

I decided to try a larger version of the same fly, which we called the Monster. It produced two splendid fish which fought like tigers. A enormous salmon heaved itself out by the side of the boulder and I foolishly wasted half an hour trying to entice it. You can sometimes bully a salmon into taking a fly which you cannot with a trout but this one had the sulks. When the Land-Rover arrived to take me away I found my wife had caught three making seven for the morning while I had six.

The afternoon's fishing in the lower part of the river below the fishing lodge was different again. In the biggest pool, called the Sheep, thought by some to be the best in the world, I hooked five salmon on long lines and lost all but one of them. I ended the day with seven fish while my wife had nine. It was to be our best day out of eight. The wind and weather turned sour and the salmon became dour. On the last day I went 'up the mountain' to fish the mouth of the lake in which the river rises and the five little pools on the way. The experience was exciting and enchanting. Five salmon beached and three hooked and lost.

Our total for the week was ninety-one for which, after the first day, we had to fish hard. The salmon in Iceland can be as irritatingly unobliging as anywhere else. But I have met no finer fighters.

In the following season I tried the Monster on the Tay taking two fish with it when other flies failed and now use it regularly as a fall-back fly. Iceland was the apogee of my salmon fishing, to date, and with the decline of the salmon population there has since been a succession of nadirs but, as the unexpected can still happen, I press on whenever I can. Fortune may smile again, as it did on the afternoon of 4 September 1980 with an unexpected telephone call which, eventually, took me on the longest and most productive country trip of my writing career. Had it come a few minutes later it would have gone unanswered for my wife and I would have gone fishin' and the opportunity, which was to result in an international, political and legal furore, would have disappeared. Fishing has brought me some memorable scoops but it almost deprived me of that one.

The call was from my old friend Victor Rothschild who, cryptically as usual, urged me to get myself to Cambridge right away for a meeting with some mystery man who was staying with him. As the man was due to leave next morning he offered to send a chauffered car for me. I went and the man turned out to be Peter Wright, later to be known as 'Spycatcher', a retired officer of MI5, the secret Security Service, burning with a vindictive desire to reveal the follies and scandalous behaviour of his old colleagues. He was also desperate for money to save an Arab horse stud-farm which he had set up in Tasmania.

That evening I agreed to write a book, based largely on Wright's material, and that, provided I could find a publisher, we would share the royalties with his half being paid directly by the publisher, not by me, through an arrangement to be set up by Lord Rothschild, who was then a banker. Wright declined to give me any substantial information unless I went out to interview him at length in Tasmania which I did, at my own expense. His home proved to be a wooden shack made from two apple-pickers' huts set in a small-holding and I could see how, remote from the exciting life he had led and with an inadequate pension, he had stewed there in the sticks, while sitting on secrets which he knew were saleable. For nine days I listened in wonder and made notes while he poured out MI5's most sacred secrets. Never in the long history of the British secret service had any outsider been so privileged. A few people called on horse business and whenever they were strangers both Wright and I wondered if they might be snoopers for MI5.

On returning to Kintbury I wrote the book rapidly, working in long shifts, and wondering, during my 'thinking' walks with my dogs what MI5 would do if they got wind of it. Unknown to me, they did more than that. They got hold of a copy of the script and, had I known the level at which secret meetings were being held about it in Whitehall, with the Prime Minister, Home Secretary, Cabinet Secretary and the Director General of MI5 in attendance, I would not have slept as soundly as I did. For reasons which were later to seem grossly mistaken, it was decided not to suppress the book and when it appeared in March 1981, under the title *Their Trade is Treachery*, the repercussions dominated the national newspapers for days. The Prime Minister made a statement to Parliament and set in train the first independent inquiry into secret service security for twenty years.

While Wright, who, by agreement, was not named in the book, lay low in his shack, my village was invaded by television, radio crews and reporters. Wright's only intervention, which was not very clever, was in the form of a most urgent cable about his money delivered to me by my wife while I was standing in a field of turnips during a partridge drive. Such are the exigencies of the investigative bumpkin!

Six years later Peter Wright was to re-issue the facts already in *Their Trade is Treachery*, in a book under his own name, entitled *Spycatcher*. It contained little that was new, apart from fictitious allegations about a plot by up to thirty MI5 officers to undermine Harold Wilson and his government. Wright, himself, admitted that the 'plot' story, which boosted publicity and sales, was a monstrous exaggeration, when interrogated about it later on a 'Panorama' programme. Had the goverment ignored the book it might have caused only modest stir. Instead, to ensure that all past, present and future secret service officers could be assured that the British government would never condone the sale of its security and intelligence secrets, it took steps to have *Spycatcher* banned by the Australian courts.

During this long process, which failed ignominiously for the government, my village was once again invaded by the media because Wright's case was based on the argument that as the government had not banned my book it should not ban his. In the result, all arguments fell apart when *Spycatcher* was published in America with such publicity, world-wide, that it made Wright a millionaire, though he preferred just to make additions to his shack, rather than move. Because he had beaten the British 'Establishment' he became something of an Australian folk-hero, visited by fans. My country peace was invaded in a less flattering manner.

To further Wright's case in the Australian court, certain Labour Party politicians in the British Parliament had been induced to call for the prosecution of myself and Lord Rothschild for 'corrupting Wright, with an offer of money to secure highly sensitive secrets', something we had never done. By persistent questioning, the Attorney-General was pressured into agreeing to an investigation and for three weeks, on and off, a pantomime, hatched up in Whitehall by some of the highest in the land, was to be played in Kintbury village, providing me with reminiscences I could never forget.

Lord Rothschild and I were, separately, interrogated for sessions of several hours at a time by a Detective Chief Superintendent of Scotland Yard's Serious Crimes Squad, investigating possible breaches of the Official Secrets Act. The more observant of my village neighbours were not slow to identify as 'coppers' two men in blue raincoats always arriving precisely at 1.30 p.m. I was grilled, sometimes over tea, scones and strawberry jam, on every aspect of Peter Wright's damaging statements in the Australian court but had no problem in rebutting them with documentary evidence and witnesses. As I had predicted to the detectives, the investigation was eventually ended when it could be taken no further without the interrogation of certain individuals, including a former Chief of the Secret Service, which was not permissible, even to the police, because it would have revealed secret machinations inside No.10 Downing Street. To their annoyance, the case against Lord Rothschild and myself collapsed, without so much as a whimper from the Labour MPs who had whipped it up and exploited it. Parliament was told that no evidence requiring the prosecution of either of us had come to light.

As a finale to their interrogations the police had produced a search-warrant and insisted on examining the private files in my study. As they were so voluminous I suggested those that were relevant and included one bearing the name of an official so senior that, when they examined its contents, I knew that the case against Lord Rothschild and me would collapse totally, as it did. I also realized that its examination would be likely to have an important political consequence; involving a departure from high office, which duly occurred. Once again, modest events in a quiet little village had produced an explosive repercussion of national consequence in Whitehall.

The whole affair, which had been intriguing, exciting and not without its humour as well as its danger, had created such widespread interest that I was reminded of my journalistic colleague's comment when I told him that I intended to continue my undercover activities in retirement — 'What, in Kintbury?'

CHAPTER 15

MAGIC MOMENTS

An element of uncertainty is essential in all sports but there is no field sport in which it plays such a dominant role as fishing, where there are so many factors out of the control of the participant. One is the weather but, such are the uncertainties of angling, that even the most unpromising weather could provide a memorable day even, when fishing for grayling or salmon in winter, ice forms in the rod rings. So uncertain was my entry to what was to be the prime sport of my life that I nearly missed the opportunity which might never have recurred.

As with so many things which have meant so much to me, I became a fisherman by accident. I met a boy who was keen on it and, rather reluctantly because there was a competing invitation, I went with him as an observer. The only thing that was hooked that day was me and it was for life. I have often wondered why this happened and can list several important reasons. As an only child, I was essentially a loner and fishing fits a loner's requirements for quiet and solitude. Further, I have never derived much enjoyment or satisfaction from watching anybody else do anything, however brilliantly. I was never taken with competitive sports, possibly because I did not excel at them, and always preferred what is now called 'doing one's own thing' as and when one wishes. I was regularly in trouble at school because I would always rather go fishing than play for the first eleven at cricket, which I did on occasion.

Fishing suited my temperament as it requires total personal involvement all the time, unlike team games where one is intensely involved for only brief periods, when design or chance brings one in contact with the ball. The idea that fishing is 'slow' and requires great patience may be true for an observer but not for the participant who never knows what the next cast may bring. From the moment the fly or bait first touches the water there is always glorious uncertainty that what I call a 'magic moment' may be about to arrive. The joy of all angling, whether for salmon, trout or coarse fish, derives from such magic moments when a fish decides to take a fly or bait. A lifetime's fishing is compounded of tales of the unexpected which are the subject of bantering disbelief in all countries because, in fact, the oddest things do happen on rivers, where one is usually alone.

That all-round country sportsman, Sir Thomas Sopwith, used to express the uncertainties of angling by saying 'With fishing there are no rules'. That has also been my continuing experience since, when quite young, the 'no rules' nature of fishing was demonstrated one summer evening when I was worm-fishing for trout in a clear, shallow stretch of the River Tees, near Croft. Wading in what was a favourite stream, I cast the worm so that the current swished it round the boulders. As I was re-baiting the double hook a horse appeared on the bank ridden by a groom in breeches and rubber boots who dismounted and, to my astonishment, splashed into the water beside me, dragging the horse in after him. Every trout within a hundred yards must have heard the clatter of the horse's hooves as they slithered over the cobbles and I asked him, angrily, what he thought he was doing. 'Hardening the horse's legs,' he replied. 'Cold water is good for a steeple-chaser's legs.'

I was about to curse him when I felt a sharp tug at the line which was dragging in the water about ten yards downstream. I struck instinctively and the liveliest trout I had hooked that season leaped out of the water. After a tussle in which the line became entangled round the horse's legs and the groom got a boot full of water, I netted the trout under the horse's nose. It weighed one pound three ounces, a big trout for that river.

So many strange things happen on a river that my wife has been able to collect and publish a large number of extraordinary but true anecdotes in support of Sir Thomas's assertion. I have witnessed several of them. For example, while I was fishing the Blackhall beat of the Aberdeenshire Dee, as a guest of the late Jock Leslie, his son, then aged about seventeen, hooked a large salmon while spinning in the neck of the Roe Pot pool in fairly high spring water. He was using a golden sprat — then the standard bait — mounted in a transparent plastic device which had a large, stiff loop to which the nylon trace was fastened. After a few seconds the line came back without the bait and the youth was soundly — and rightly — berated by his father for having tied a faulty knot. Having been shown the knotting technique once again, he cast the bait into the same place and hooked a large springer which he played successfully and which, I believe, weighed 22 pounds. The fish was the original one he had hooked and the treble of the second bait had chanced to slide into the loop of the golden sprat protruding from its mouth!

The uncertainties make fishing unique in the number of excuses it offers for failure — the conditions were too bright or too blustery; the water too high, too low or too coloured; the balance between air temperature and water temperature was wrong; there were no flies on the water; everything looked right but the fish were sulking and wouldn't look at anything.

Being non-competitive, fishing turned out to be an excellent sport for a journalist because there is more than enough competition in his working life for him to desire any in his leisure. Izaak Walton, the acknowledged father of angling, called it 'the contemplative man's recreation' and non-fishers seeing anglers watching floats on canal banks and lake-sides might reasonably assume that, indeed, it is a recreation so peaceful, so quiet and so slow that it enables one to contemplate. But I do not believe that is what Izaak meant at all. I think he meant that angling was an ideal recreation for the man who has to contemplate a great deal in his work, for the truth is that angling, of any kind, demands such concentration that it is almost impossible to think about anything else. If the mind begins to wander, the chances of catching freshwater fish are greatly reduced because they are not in the habit of committing suicide by hooking themselves. So, if properly pursued, fishing is an ideal sport for the contemplative man because, while he is doing it, he is able to avoid all contemplation and so recharge his mind. It is partly for this reason, I believe, that fishing is easily the most popular of all outdoor participation sports, being pursued by more than four million people in Britain, quite a lot of them women. Of these, less that a million fish exclusively for trout and salmon, the rest pursuing 'coarse' or sea-fish.

'Gone fishin'!' has long been a reason for getting out of the way in time of trouble because there is nothing like the peace of a river for forgetting problems and restoring sanity. During a major professional crisis in my life — and that of Harold Wilson — which became known as the 'D-Notice Affair', my Editor was astonished to find that I had disappeared on to the South Esk, near Montrose, to fish for salmon. Understandingly, having tracked me down by telephone, he left me there.

There is plenty in fishing to contemplate about when one is not doing it and much of its pleasure derives from reading about it in the abundant literature — rightly listed in libraries under 'Fine Arts' — and in preparing and generally playing about with tackle. I acquired this bug as a boy, devouring every book I could lay hands on and making such tackle as I could not afford. The father of my closest friend then had a sail-making business and we used to raid his store-room for waterproofed materials and thread to make tackle-books to hold hooks, flies and casts, pending the day we could buy proper ones.

Another aspect which has always appealed to me is the fact that while there is always something to learn about fishing, it is not too demanding on skill. A reasonable degree of competence in casting a line and the other mechanics is not difficult to acquire and form, which bedevils so many sports, especially shooting, is never a problem. The other attributes most essential to success, the abilities to concentrate and to observe can be cultivated and, perhaps came naturally to me to some degree.

While casting can be learned from a good teacher in a few sessions, what I call water-craft comes only with long experience and is the main reason why some anglers catch more fish than others. Anyone can see a rise — the circle which a trout makes when taking a natural fly off the surface of the water — but for every fish that betrays its whereabouts in that manner the truly observant angler can spot more which disturb the water in other ways. It may be a small bow-wave, a slight humping of the water or a change in the surface ripple not discernible to the unpractised eye but immediately noticed by the angler with water-craft. It involves learning to think like a fish, on which I spent so much time that my father predicted that I would end up with fins.

While there are no rules there are some generalities. My experience tells me that if fish are rising and refuse a fly after inspecting it, one should present a similar fly of smaller size rather than change to a different pattern. It usually works, with fancy flies or any others. I have also found the reverse to be true on occasion — if a small fly fails to interest a trout a larger pattern may do so. Too many anglers stand too near the water's edge when standing a couple of yards back and fishing a longer line would be more productive. When nymph fishing it usually pays to let the fly come down naturally without moving it, though that does work on some days.

When fish are not rising it does not necessarily mean that they are not hungry. They may still rise to a fly unless they are asleep or torpid, as it seems, they often are, when it is very difficult to interest them in any lure for the simple reason that they are not conscious of its presence. The experience of fish farmers shows that when trout are starved, as may often happen in the wild, their oxygen requirement and general metabolism are markedly reduced. So contrary to the common assumption that food shortage should make them more active so that they can look for food, they may become torpid. After a longish hungry period, trout are prone to remain inactive for quite a while even if there is a sudden supply of food, such as a large hatch of fly. What, then, triggers off such torpid trout to feed? A rise in water temperature can rouse the fish. After a cold April with trout hardly in evidence, a warm May morning can bring the river alive, but there is much more to the mystery of what makes fish take. In the interests of sport it might be better never to resolve it but I will never be able to resist trying.

I was fortunate in realizing, from my earliest expeditions, that fishing takes one to marvellous, hidden places otherwise unlikely ever to be encountered and that nothing tastes better than a hard-boiled egg or a pork pie on a river bank. When I was eleven and, in those days, only just out of short trousers, I wrote to a gentleman called Sir Guy Wrightson who owned a stretch of the River Tees, near Hurworth, requesting a day's fishing. He kindly agreed and, believing that I might meet him, I decided to press my grey flannel trousers, something I had never attempted before. Unfortunately, I pressed them down the seams and then had to press them in the proper way so that they ended up square. I did not meet Sir Guy but did meet his brother, who was most kind and did not comment on the trousers. His reception encouraged me to aim high in the future regarding fishing venues, which I have done ever since.

One thing for all anglers to remember, especially beginners, is that there are almost always more fish in a river, lake or reservoir than one suspects. When I lived at Croft there was a large pool by the road bridge over the Tees which was rarely fished because it looked lifeless. One day during a very hot spell, thousands of quite large fish, mainly chub and dace, rose to the surface there in need of oxygen. Locals who had lived there much longer than I had were astonished.

On another occasion when I was living in Farnham, Surrey I went to fish a small, shallow lake, nearby, very early on an August morning because I needed some small roach to use as pike-bait. The surface was shrouded with mist and through it I could see a large number of small black objects moving over the surface which turned out to be the noses of large carp which were sucking in air. I forgot about the pike-baits and set about trying to interest the carp in my worms dangled from a trout fly rod. I caught seventeen of them in about three hours weighing about ten stones, the biggest being a 12-pound mirror carp. The lake was regularly fished but nobody had known that it contained any carp.

This capability of fish to conceal themselves adds still further to the glorious uncertainty of angling for while a stretch of water may look dead it may be alive with fish and one never knows what the next cast will bring — maybe the fish of a lifetime. So, one must always keep pegging away for nobody catches fish idling on the bank.

Like many others, I began as a bait fisherman, trotting maggots and worms down fast streams on the Tees and Swale. To this day the smell of maggots in sawdust, which the fishermen on the Kennet-Avon canal near my home sometimes permit me to indulge, is wonderfully nostalgic, scent memories being strong with me. There was something magical in watching the float as it bobbed down the stream taking the bait in search of trout, grayling or dace, or, on occasion, as it lay in a deep backwater which was the haunt of chub. I became reasonably proficient but, as in all walks of life, there were a few outstanding local exponents of the fine art who, almost invariably, could catch more fish than anyone else on the same water. What gave them this edge could not be discerned by watching them and, inevitably, they attracted rumours that they had some secret concoction with which they anointed their baits. One suggested that it was a secretion from a heron's legs, which, allegedly, attracted fish, a possibility which has probably never been tested. Another nostrum, vouchsafed to me by an old man who had written it on the back of a Woodbine cigarette packet, was oil of rhodium, which could be bought from the chemists but, as I discovered, did not work. I suspect that these experts were just that little bit better at every aspect of the game — casting, controlling the float, seeing movements of it which others might miss, striking at the right moment and minimizing disturbance to the water.

I did discover one killer bait which may be generally unknown. I had been ferreting on the river-bank and it was the practice to gut the rabbits before taking them home. We threw the entrails into the water to get rid of them and it was soon aboil with huge chub tearing at the unexpected offering and, no doubt attracted from their lairs by the smell of it. I could not wait to try rabbit gut as a bait in a chub hole, dropping in the main part of the gut attached to a stone to attract the fish and putting a couple of inches of small intestine on a large hook. I was quickly into a chub of four pounds, quite large for that river, and caught several more but the process was too smelly for regular use.

The fly-fishers on those streams were highly critical of the use of ground-bait by maggot fishers but, in those days, there would be literally millions of flies floating down the river providing the fly-men with free groundbait while maggots cost money.

Transferring to fly-fishing was not difficult for me because one could do both on the northern rivers. It was only when I moved south that a choice had to be made and even then I managed to keep my bait fishing going as well by joining a club near Farnham, in Surrey which had trout water and lakes stocked with what are given the unfortunate name of coarse fish because most of them are poor eating. I never ceased to smile when opening letters from the club secretary

At home at Lowerhouse Farm, Christmas 1973, with four close friends.

Entering the 'Flying Car' with inventor Bob Fulton – before the near-fatal crash.

With Sir Thomas and Lady Sopwith at Compton, their country home – 1978.

The reluctant teacher far left back row – i/c cricket at the Liverpool Institute.

The author's mother outside his beloved Comet Hotel.

The author aged three – in winter garb.

The author aged ten outside the
family sweetshop in Darlington.
Boots were standard then.

beginning 'Dear Coarse Member . . .'. It was only when prime stretches of southern chalk streams became available to me that I opted entirely in favour of the fly which has never failed to give me pleasure.

Like so many ancient arts, which become something of a religion, fly-fishing is encrusted with fallacies and prejudices. One of the latter is the rule, common on many waters, that it is permissible to cast a fly only at a rising fish or at one which can be clearly seen and appears to be awaiting flies. This means that a person who travels from a long distance and finds the river dead cannot legitimately wet his line. It is a rule often honoured in the breach and rightly so. If one knows that a position, say under a tree on the opposite bank, regularly harbours a good trout, what is the point in straining to 'observe' it, which is often impossible, and may reveal your presence? Casting a fly to places which knowledge or river-craft tells you are likely to hold trout is called 'fishing the water' and is volubly condemned by purists, though I have seen some of them doing it when believing they were unobserved.

Puncturing established fallacies by experiment can be a joy in itself and prime among these is the concept that the only proper way to catch a trout on a fly is to offer an exact imitation, in thread, fur and feather, of the floating aquatic insects on which the fish happens to be feeding. In my experience this is a myth which has benefited tackle shops more than fishermen. There are almost 1000 accepted patterns of trout flies in Britain and Ireland alone, yet I and many other anglers, who originally felt that we needed to carry a supply of many of them, have reduced our favourite dry flies over the years until we are down to two or three, which catch all the trout we can reasonably expect in almost all circumstances. The same is true of nymphs, the sub-surface insects of which there is now a great profusion of artificial copies, many of them intended for still waters and some likely to catch more fishermen than fish.

Whatever the trout are really taking, with the exception of the miniscule insects called 'smut', a few favourite patterns in which we have confidence, properly fished, will catch enough of them. These favourites vary from angler to angler and good bags are regularly caught on quite different flies on the same water on the same day.

Another absurd spin-off of exact imitation is the requirement of special materials, often difficult to obtain, for tying the near-perfect copies. When I was fishing in North Yorkshire, there was a man called George Kirkup who could catch more trout on fly than anyone else. One of his favourite flies was the dotterel and yellow made from feathers taken from the dotterel, a kind of plover, which, even then, was a rare visitor to Britain. It was common talk that Kirkup caught his fish because he had a supply of dotterel feathers, which he had, but his secret lay in his skill. Presented by him, his dotterel and yellows would have been just as effective if tied with a near substitute.

The argument that the fly must closely imitate a specific insect is torpedoed by the fact so many trout can be taken by 'fancy' flies — tyings which are not intended to represent any living insect. The most widely-used of these, today, are the patterns invented by the American angler, Lee Wulff, who simply thought that trout might appreciate a meatier morsel than the usual, thinly-dressed offerings. The variations of his fuzzy patterns — the Grey Wulff, Red Wulff and Royal Wulff — probably account for more trout on English chalk streams than any other though they were developed for American waters. Other killing American patterns are the Irresistibles, which are among my few favourites because their fat, deer-hair bodies make them float all day and they simulate sedge flies.

What the inventors of fancy flies realized, as most of us do who have watched trout feeding in shallow water, was that they are opportunistic feeders, taking anything they fancy, so all that a fly needs to do is to create an impression of a takeable shape and size when seen through the surface film. If it looks like an insect and the fish is intent on feeding it will rise to inspect it and if it approves of what it sees it will suck it in. This, of course, is why a crudely tied or battered old fly often does better than a pristine fly on which the tier has spent such effort. It happens to create an impression more interesting to the fish. A nymph fished below the surface offers closer inspection by trout yet they take some extraordinary objects, as they will with wet flies.

The exact imitation fad requires the angler to be something of an entomologist. Many purists carry a long, narrow spoon devised for extracting the marrow from bones and, therefore, convenient for inserting into the stomach of a captured fish to withdraw the contents which, hopefully, will reveal what fly the trout has been feeding on. On the odd occasions when I have tried or witnessed this endeavour it has revealed a mass of insects and snails culled from the river bottom, which supplies most of the diet of any trout. On the rare occasions when the stomach contains only one type of insect it is because nothing else was available.

The exact imitation theory is further undermined by the behaviour of trout during a hatch of mayfly. Very often they will ignore the real article and take an artificial imitation. Indeed a sizeable Grey Wulff will often do the trick and it is not really like a mayfly.

146

I can see the added attraction of catching a fish on a fly one has tied oneself, and better still invented, as I have done myself with a nymph. But, while the extremists are entitled to do what they wish, they are zealots who carry their beliefs too far and should not try to foist them on others. After all, the purpose of fly fishing is simply to fool a trout into rising to an artificial fly believing that it is some kind of natural food. On most waters this is difficult enough without penalizing oneself with ritual fads, especially these days when big hatches of natural fly are so rare.

Another myth which experience explodes is the assurance given to the young by so many oldsters that if the dry fly drags against the current, as it comes downstream, it will look so unnatural that any trout will be scared by it. I believed it and recovered my fly the moment that the wind or current made it drag until I first went to fish the Compton beat of the Test owned by Sir Thomas Sopwith. When fish which were clearly interested in a fly refused to take it, the old river-keeper there advised, 'Make 'un draag a little.' I did so and immediately the trick worked. What it does is to give the fly some appearance of life or a trout may take it believing it is about to fly off. The heaviest drag of all is applied to a fly when the line is being wound in yet it often proves attractive to fish which have ignored it until that moment. The reel seems to impart an action which cannot be simulated by pulling in the line. Sometimes trout, especially rainbows, will take if the fly makes a small splash as it hits the water though not if the line does. It attracts the fish to inspect the cause of the splash and maybe gulp it in. The 'dry' fly that hits the water with a splash may be almost half-sunk, a condition which often induces a fish to take when a fly cocked upon the surface film is refused.

The reluctance of many trout to take a fly can often be traced these days to the fact that they are regularly fed on food-pellets, not only during the winter but in the early spring when they might lose condition if cold weather reduces the food supply and fish stocks are high. As a result many people have tried to tie a fly which simulates a pellet and, with Sir Thomas Sopwith's approval, and under the eye of his keeper, several of us who fished his stretch of the Test made various experiments. The late Lord Portal of Hungerford, who headed the RAF during the war so successfully, even made one out of a section of a Rawlplug but nothing ever rose to it. I tried an actual pellet in some thin plastic tubing with a hook super-glued on to it and that was totally ignored. It has been suggested that some of the American flies with fat, brown deer-hair bodies are mistaken for pellets but I have proved that is not the case. A handful of floating pellets thrown into a pool would bring up trout, ravenous for them, but a fly cast among them was never taken. Maybe scent is involved because a bare pellet simply attached to a hook would be swiftly taken and I know of one early morning poacher, on another river, who was caught in the act after I had reported catching two trout which had vomited pellets when these were not being fed to the fish.

Another fallacy, peculiar to southern rivers, is the belief that fly-fishing is impossible when the water weed is being cut because it has become too thick and extensive, as it may do several times in a hot summer. Great rafts of tangled greenery floating down to the hatches, where it is raked off onto the bank or diverted into a gully, make casting difficult but can provide one of the most exciting times to fish. On one very bright morning I had a guest to fish on the Kennet and little was happening until down came the rafts, because some extra cutting had unexpectedly been required. Soon, big trout began to move below the rafts and on the edges, feeding on the shrimps and larvae which were quitting the cut weed. We had several of them in short order using a nymph, though it is possible to take trout on a floating fly on such conditions by placing it between the rafts when the fish are moving. That way I caught my biggest brown trout to date, one of six pounds nine ounces which was a record for the beat until my wife committed the offence of catching one of eight and a half pounds.

Once the fish is hooked, the problem is how to play and land it without being caught in the floating rafts which will surely break the cast. That is easily resolved — by thrusting the tip of the rod under the water and playing the fish down there. One needs to be agile but it makes for additional excitement — and satisfaction when victory ensues. I always pray that the odd slivers of weed which wrap round the cast will not slide down to the fish because, once a trout is blindfolded by weed it gives up, whatever its size.

Floating weed, of which there is always some on a chalk stream, tends to get caught up on the piles of bridges. Where I fish on the River Kennet there used to be a wooden pony bridge which sustained one of the most productive pools for large brown and rainbow trout which fed off the weed and liked the protection. It was pulled down and the pool lost both its charm and its fish population. The wooden piles of small river bridges also harbour aquatic insects and crustaceans and are hatching places for the larvae of flies, making them a good feeding ground and, therefore, good taking places for trout. Big fish also like the shade and the sense of protection which bridges provide. Fish lying under a bridge are often inaccessible to the angler or, at least, are difficult to reach and they appear to know it. If hooked, they stand an excellent chance of escape by using the bridge

piles or arches to break the cast. This, of course, increases the angler's·
challenge and I have had memorable tussles with hooked fish which
have gone downstream while the bridge has made it impossible to
follow them. I have hooked both trout and salmon that have moved
upstream through one arch and then downstream through another,
taxing ingenuity and river-craft to prevent the almost inevitable
breakage.

While anglers also find bridges handy for crossing rivers, active
railway bridges should never be used for that purpose, as I discovered
in my youth when I decided to cross the river Tees by a bridge on the
London-Edinburgh main line. Until I was more than half-way across I
did not realize how small the clearance is between a train and the
bridge parapet and had to make a run for it in waders as an express
thundered towards me. I do not think that I would have made it with a
modern high speed train. It was, I suppose, a bridge too near or at least
too handy.

A bonus joy of angling is the wildlife which, because of the quiet of
the sport, one witnesses, usually at unexpected moments. While coarse
fishing I have had a kingfisher use my rod as a diving platform. I have
seen an otter surface within a yard of me while wading. I have seen a
bat fall in the water and flop its way safely to the bank. When I was
fishing the River Tees, while it was slightly flooded, a rabbit hopped
across a sandbank towards the water's edge within five yards of me,
sat for a few moments and then very deliberately entered the water,
swam out into the stream, paddled about there for a while and then
swam back again. It rested on the sandback, shook off its excess
water, as a dog would, and then hopped back into a wood. I have
watched a large trout play for twenty minutes with a big, dead
grayling as a dog would with a bone.

Such joys are intensified if they are shared with a wife who also
fishes, as mine are. A certain Earl of Warwick neglected his wife to
the ruination of his marriage in order to go fishing but that is no longer
necessary, even when salmon fishing, for now there are rods so light
and reels so free-running that the wispiest girl can cast as far as a man.
Not only is it more agreeable for both of us to be on the river together
but I no longer fear a 'rocket' for fishing almost until dark.

Like so many women who take up angling my wife is lucky and
became hooked when she caught a 13-pounder on her first day.
Shortly afterwards, I returned from a day's trout-fishing with Sir
Thomas Sopwith on the Test, where the keeper for many years had
been an elderly man called Ted Hill. I said to my wife, 'You will be
sorry to hear that Ted Hill dropped dead the other day, while he was
playing a salmon, lower down the Test, at Nursling.' Her response was

immediate and telling. 'Did they get the fish?' I knew then that she had been hooked for life. With further experience she quickly became a potamophile, to coin a needed term for those of us who are besotted by rivers.

CHAPTER 16

THE MYSTERIOUS SALMON

In my varied experience, the take of a salmon is the single most exciting moment life has to offer — bar none. One is rarely aware of the size of the freshly-hooked fish until the battle has been on some time. With all forms of fishing hope springs eternal but on a salmon river one never knows what a deep, dark pool may be holding or even a shallow swirl, for it is extraordinary how a quite enormous fish can hide itself. In Scotland, where I have caught most of my salmon, the backdrop of heather-covered hills, the resinous scent of the bankside pines and the piping of oyster-catchers as they sit on granite boulders surrounded by frothing water complete the formula for felicity.

As well as being the most exciting game fish encountered in fresh water, the salmon is also the most mysterious. Once in the river from the sea it does not feed before it spawns, living off its accumulated body fat and other reserves, with its stomach always being empty and eventually degenerating to a thead. So nobody really knows why it ever strikes at a fly or a bait. Imagine a salmon entering a river like the Tay from the sea. From the moment it passes through the estuary, if it escapes any river nets, there are so many anglers, after the season opens in January, that there is hardly a moment of the day when some fly or bait is not passing its nose. Though it is wide awake while making its way upstream it may refuse them all. Then, say at Dunkeld, many miles upriver after rejecting literally thousands of opportunities, it grabs my fly. Why? Nobody really knows. The sight of a fish-like object flashing by may stir some recent memory of gluttonous meals in the sea and trigger off an instinctive grab. This may well explain why prawns and shrimps, recently encountered in the sea, can be so deadly to the fresh-run fish that they are barred on many waters. Presumably salmon feed until the last moment in salt water, including the estuary. With worms the take must be more deliberate since a salmon will mouth one for a long time before swallowing it. Sometimes salmon cannot resist mouthing a worm, a maggot or even a cigarette-end passing over them, though the morsel is usually quickly rejected.

I suspect that what happens is that hunger and the requirement to feed may exert themselves in certain circumstances but the swallowing reflex has been almost entirely suppressed. Additionally, the aggressive instinct against anything invading a salmon's immediate living space triggers off the snap, though this would not explain why salmon will sometimes rise to a dry fly on the surface and can be caught in that manner. Nor does it explain why a salmon will often move from quite a distance from its station to take a fly or bait, as when a flashing spoon-bait cast far upstream and spun down much faster than the current sometimes proves irresistible, with a fish pursuing it and taking it, most excitingly, when it is barely a rod's length from the angler.

Frequently, there can be hundreds of salmon lying in a river pool yet they not only all refuse to take a lure but totally ignore it. Standing on a private metal bridge over the South Esk near Montrose in the days — not all that long ago — when the salmon were stacked like sardines, I have watched them sway gently in the current to avoid a passing lure but otherwise behave as though they did not see it. The fact that their tails and fins were moving at a rate which kept them stationary in the current was no more a sign of wakefulness than the fact that our chests move up and down when we are asleep.

The salmon-fishing innovator, Richard Waddington, believes that in many instances, most or all of the salmon in a pool are fast asleep and he may well be right. Fish certainly do sleep, as aquarium-keepers and fish-farmers can testify. Their fins move automatically just enough to keep them stationary in the current, but oblivious to their surroundings, though any commotion soon arouses them. I have often seen trout which were clearly asleep. After all, what do dogs — and many humans — do when they are bored? Salmon must be bored stiff waiting, sometimes for weeks, for a flood to urge them upstream to their spawning grounds. Being unable to digest anything they have no interest in, food and their metabolism — and therefore their activity — may be progressively reduced to conserve energy supplies. Salmon fishers soon learn what a waste of time it is to cast for the salmon which has become 'potted' — the fish which has been lying in the same place for weeks and occasionally flops out in some reflex way. The fresh fish, not yet being in that condition, is a much more likely taker but it too, must soon behave in a way which conserves the accumulated fat reserves that will eventually be needed for spawning.

Having come so far, a salmon has every reason to sleep long hours to recharge its muscles from its reserves for the continuing struggle upstream, especially as it has no interest in sex until it reaches a spawning bed, high up the main river or in its tributaries. I have always suspected that the occasional salmon which fails to fight but comes in 'like a log' has muscles which are still tired out, not having had the opportunity of sufficient rest.

We know that one thing which stirs the salmon into action is a rise in the river level. Somehow, the fresh water triggers off the urge to swim upstream and the release of energy is quite spectacular, considering the rate at which they travel against strong water. It is also common knowledge that salmon take best when the water is falling again. Perhaps, while resting immediately after an exhausting surge upstream, they are still awake enough to see a lure but, shortly afterwards, will go torpid again until the next flood. While they are alert, the take of one salmon may trigger off another in the same spot which might help to explain why more than one salmon may be taken from the same lie.

The unpredictable way in which salmon, and other fish, will suddenly come 'on the take' and then go off — has puzzled anglers for centuries and science has offered no answer to date. In the first Icelandic salmon pool I tackled the first cast of the fly, standing well back on the dry pebbles and made more to judge the distance than in earnest, produced a lively ten-pounder. The second cast produced another, so did the third and the fourth, a fifteen-pounder. It seemed that there could be no end to it but there were no more takers though I fished the little pool down again and could see fish flashing their silver-green sides. I fished that pool on five further days and never raised a salmon, though they were there all right.

It is a further mystery why salmon are more likely to take a fly or bait in some pools while others which look equally promising and hold as many fish are notoriously 'stiff', as the ghillies say. Maybe 'stiff' pools, are just good dormitories!

With certainty, one can only say that for any salmon there is a magic moment when, after refusing literally thousands of lures which may have sped past its nose, it will suddenly elect to take yours with the pluck at the line which is without comparison for excitement, though, of course, many, perhaps most, manage to reach the spawning grounds without being tempted. Whatever the trigger mechanism, nobody can predict when the moment may occur. Having travelled thousands of miles from its feeding rounds, surviving numerous predators at all stages of its life and evading the nets of man it makes that pointless strike which is likely to be fatal.

I hope that this mystery of the magic moment never will be solved for it is the ever-present possibility that the next cast may produce it that gives salmon fishing its enduring charm and explains why salmon-anglers are prepared to pay inflated prices to fish what are now near-empty rivers.

The life history of the salmon remains surrounded by many other mysteries in spite of all the research on it. One of them is the reason for its habit of rising or showing, which is a better word. Salmon frequently break the surface of the water, like porpoises, as they 'run' upstream, sometimes hurling themselves out in the process. When they are resting briefly in a pool they sometimes surge up from the bottom in what is called a head-and-tail rise and may do so repeatedly. When they have been confined by low water to a pool for weeks they repreatedly flop about, sometimes hurling themselves clear of the water for no reason anyone has yet deduced. They are not trying to rid themselves of skin parasites, as is commonly believed, for they do not have any. It may be no more than *joie de vivre*, an expression of fulfilment that they are on the way to the culminating event in their lives, but I suspect that it is what is known in other animal species as displacement behaviour — irrational activity, like the dog chasing its tail, which is an expression of frustration.

Research may produce a surprising explanation which nobody has thought about, just as it recently showed that the salmon's upstream run is not as direct as generally believed. Fitting salmon with radio transmitters and tracking them has proved that they sometimes travel back downstream for many miles before turning to run upstream again.

Solving any of these mysteries may not be without its danger. In 1949 I wrote in the *Daily Express*, 'A project to discover the swimming routes taken by salmon in the North Sea has been permanently shelved by the Scottish fishing authorities. They fear that if these became known the sou'westered men who fish for a living would find it too easy to trawl up homing salmon long before they got within line-reach of the sporting angler.' It seemed a sensible precaution but, sadly, one that was soon to be negated in the most dramatic way. The American atomic-powered submarine, *Nautilus*, was carrying out trials near Greenland in anticipation of the day when submarines carrying intercontinental missiles might be able to hide under the ice then break through it to fire them. The crew noticed thousands of fish standing on their tails feeding on plankton adhering to the underside of the ice. They were salmon and news of the discovery of their main Atlantic feeding ground was published with the inevitable result — the Greenlanders began to fish for them with nylon nets, catching them in such numbers that the inroads soon began to show in a massive reduction in the numbers of salmon returning to British, Irish, Canadian and European rivers.

A salmon mystery which has engaged attention recently is the explanation of why women catch so many of the really big ones. The British record rod-caught salmon, weighing 64 pounds, was caught by a woman, a ghillie's daughter, called Georgina Ballantine in 1922, and a number of other very large fish have fallen to women. This has led to the suggestion that female sexual scents, known as pheromones, are wafted into the water and somehow stimulate the fish to take. How this happens with a lady in chest-waders and with other heavy clothing is not explained. Miss Ballantine was not wearing waders. She was sitting in a boat and it was her rod, one of two protruding from the stern as her father rowed gently against the current to let the lures down slowly over the lie, which was the one partonized by the salmon. She was probably not even holding the rod and any pheromones would have affected her father's lure as well as her own.

Nor, as the theory is also supposed to apply to trout fishing — my wife currently holds beat records on the Kennet with an 8½-pound brown on dry fly and a 10½-pound rainbow on a nymph — can anyone explain how such scents are carried upstream to penetrate the water in sufficient quantity? Still, it has been responsible for some good ribald laughs. Recently when a group of us were fishing the Tay and my wife hooked a salmon almost immediately there were anguished downstream cries of 'Waft some down here!'

The likeliest explanation is that women, being more patient, fish a pool more slowly and there is little doubt that a persistent angler can increase the likelihood of a magic moment by presenting the bait or fly *slowly* in front of a salmon as it moves down and across each stream and eddy.

River-craft accumulated over the years, plus the ghillie's advice, will tell an angler where salmon are likely to be lying for there is no purpose in fishing empty water. On every stretch there are long-established 'lies' where the depth, nature of the bottom and the current encourage salmon to rest, the place where Miss Ballantine's monster was hooked being one of them. They are usually associated with large boulders, with their tops showing or, if totally submerged, revealing their presence by a ripple on the surface. Bridges tend to be much beloved by salmon, their metal or stone supports creating eddies in which tired fish like to lie, being able to hold their station there without much effort. For some reason they tend to be good taking places if the fly or lure can be placed there. Many beats have a Bridge Pool and it tends to be productive, being a good holding pool for fish waiting for the next flood to urge them upstream.

Time of day can also be important; the gloaming, that extended twilight peculiar to the north, frequently yielding a fish which has eluded capture all day. Shortly before the darkening, on a summer's evening especially, I have seen pools suddenly become alive with activity lasting about twenty minutes. A fly let down into the commotion rarely fails to produce a take from a salmon or sea-trout. Why it occurs nobody knows for it happens only spasmodically, some darkenings passing without a sign of life.

Another mystery which nobody has been able to explain satisfactorily is the salmon's ability to be highly active and put up a strong fight in very cold water. It is a general rule of the animal kingdom that body chemistry is slowed down by low temperatures and quickened by higher ones, yet I have hooked lively salmon in river water so cold that ice formed in the rings of the rod and even under the water. Indeed, until twenty years ago, the cream of salmon fishing in Scotland was for the spring fish, starting in February, and necessitated wading up to the armpits in near-freezing water for up to eight hours a day in gale-driven sleet, with floating ice slabs threatening to knock the angler off balance. How I loved it!

While the axiom that there are no rules applies to salmon fishing more than to any other form of angling, there are a few generalities worth observing and one of them is the fact that in cold water salmon tend to lie deep down and must be sought out by a deeply sunk lure. For this reason it has been the general custom to fish in the colder months with a fairly heavy spinning bait, the fly being reserved for late spring, summer and autumn. Now, with the availability of fast-sinking lines, springers can also be caught on a deep-sunk fly.

Salmon almost certainly have some degree of colour vision but the multitude of different coloured baits and flies which are on sale is unnecessary. In my experience a golden or yellow bait is best for coloured water with brown or back being more successful when the water is clear. With salmon flies, the colour concept has been used to ludicrous excess for more than a century, with every kind of tropical feather being pressed into service. The salmon fly is a misnomer since it does not represent any kind of insect but, if it represents anything, it is a small fish. The only exception I know are flies tied to look like prawns or shrimps like the black-eyed prawn fly, or 'Monster', which my wife and I used in Iceland with such success, but it still caught salmon when its eyes and tail had disappeared and it was no more than a blob of wool with a hook in it.

To illustrate how haphazard the colour fetish can be, a friend of mine invented a fly, which he called Old Charlie after the former owner of a beat on the Oykel river, who liked his liquor. The body is made of floss silk the colour of old port; the wing of deer-hair reminiscent of Grand Marnier; the head of sealing wax, the colour of sloe gin; the hackle coloured like apricot brandy; the golden pheasant tail resembles Château Yquem dessert wine; the gold ribbing recalls champagne; the jungle cock sides represent Black and White whisky. It now catches fish on many rivers in northern Scotland mainly, I suspect, because anglers there persevere with it.

One of the best salmon fishers I ever met, the late Ken Robinson, who ran the Inchmarlo beat on the Dee, used to say that he didn't mind what colour his salmon fly was so long as it was black. Richard Waddington recommended bright yellow, but only because it enabled him to see the lure in the water.

With both baits and flies size is more important than colour and if sport is slow it usually pays to go smaller. However, there are occasions when a bigger lure does the trick, as I discovered when I fished the Grimersta, a fishery consisting of a short, small river and a chain of lochs on the Island of Lewis. The regular fishers there and the ghillies were convinced that it was essential to fish with very small flies, less than half an inch long. I did not have any and, as nobody offered me one, I fished with the summer flies I would have used on the Dee. I caught ten salmon. Nobody else caught more than three and some had only one. As I left some of them were begging larger flies. The records of the Grimersta fishery showed that, in its great days, many of the fish had been caught on huge flies tied on single hooks three inches in length or more. Surely in eighty years, which is but a moment in evolutionary terms, the salmon has not changed its taking habits. It is only man's fads which have changed.

When Sir Thomas Sopwith died he left me his salmon fly-book containing flies which are all large, some of them enormous. I have been tempted to try them but their eyes are made of gut which is now likely to be weak and they are too precious to risk.

Although the 'fly' is a misnomer for a lure, fly-fishing for salmon has assumed a snob value, as it has with trout. There are many who decry those who spin, even in heavy water. I used to watch one of them 'fly-fishing' the little South Esk in March with three big tube flies fitted together to make a truly enormous lure. On the Spey I have been provided with long 'flies' with lead wire inserted in them. Such flies are really poor spinners and the only point in using them is to enable the angler to fish shallow water it might be impracticable to spin and to provide the indisputably extra pleasure of playing fish on a fly rod. I have to admit, however, that one does feel superior if one can say that a salmon was caught on a fly.

In that connection it is instructive to know that the Queen Mother, a devoted salmon angler, was adept at catching them on a worm, which requires considerable skill. I hooked my first salmon, on the Welsh

Dee, while fishing for trout with a worm. I did not manage to land it because the very fine cast became overladen with weed and broke but that is not why I don't like worm fishing for salmon now. For reasons unknown, the salmon takes the worm into its throat and that is the time to strike, meaning that the fish is deliberately played with the hook in its gullet, which is not appealing.

While worms are barred on many waters, prawns and shrimps are allowed and are now responsible for the capture of an increasing proportion of rod-caught salmon. Some anglers are even permitted to use floats when shrimp fishing, the requirement of some owners being to encourage almost any method that will increase the catch at a time of salmon scarcity.

However caught, every salmon leaves the angler with a satisfying memory, strongly associated with some pool or stream, usually with a name reaching back into the centuries. In Scotland they are marvellous, evocative names like Kelpie, the Laird's Cast, the Roe Pot, Two Stones, Grey Mare, the Otter, names as famous among anglers as Tattenham Corner or Beecher's Brook are in the racing world. Some fishermen have become so attached to certain pools that they have left instructions in their wills for their ashes to be scattered on them. Sir Denis Mountain, owner of the superb Delfur beat of the Spey, recounted to my wife and me how this last request of a former tenant ended in hilarious disaster. His favourite ghillie had agreed to scatter the ashes into the Otter pool, assisted by a clergyman and several other locals suitably attired in dark suits and ancient bowler hats. As the ghillie moved down the steep bank he slipped into the river, crying as he surfaced, 'Oh, my God, mercy aye! The urn and ma hat's awa!'

A quirky request? Perhaps, but understandable to any salmon fisher and almost conventional compared with the last wish of an inveterate shooting man. His ashes were loaded into a number of twelve-bore cartridges which were then fired by a group of his special friends at his favourite pheasant stand!

I have enjoyed salmon fishing in England and Wales but there was a special magic attached to the Scottish rivers like the Spey, the Aberdeenshire Dee, the Tay and the South Esk, where many of the happiest and most exciting hours of my life have been spent up to my waist in running water. In a narrow, weedy river like the Test, once a salmon is hooked it has nowhere to go and is soon out on the bank. The Wye is large but its long stretches of clay-bank are more reminiscent of a canal. On a Scottish river, which is usually fast, wide and boulder-strewn, the fish take off into the strong water and the battle is long with many a rod-bending run and often a leap as they make cunning use of the current and every available obstacle. So, to me, one day on a Scottish river is worth a week on any other in Britain.

Though Miss Ballantine's 64-pound Tay salmon may go unchallenged for another seventy years I have a less exacting ambition within the bounds of fulfilment, as I so nearly proved. In the billiard room of the Kinnaird Hotel there are seven salmon in glass cases all weighing over forty pounds and one of fifty. There is just enough space on the walls for one more and I would dearly love to fill it. Fishing with a heavy, flashing metal bait called a Toby on the Kinnaird beat I hooked a salmon which came into the side and showed itself in the deep water. 'It could be forty', was all I said and the ghillie, Bob Grant, did not disagree.

After a long, tough fight Bob managed to gaff it because the bank was too steep for it to be beached. My hopes remained high as it was slung onto the grass but were quickly dashed by Bob's cry, 'Oh hell, it's a razor-back!' What he meant was that the fish, which had certainly weighed forty pounds when it had come in from the sea, had been so long in the river that it had lived on its muscles as well as its fat and lost so much weight from its back that it scaled only twenty-eight pounds.

Still, to date, that space in the billiard room remains challengingly vacant.

CHAPTER 17

SALUTE TO SHOOTING

For those who begin to shoot when young there is a major difference between the country boy and the town boy. To the country boy, as, happily, I was, interest in shooting can come naturally, almost mindlessly, arising out of being taken ferreting, beating or mooching round with a farmer's son equipped with a family gun, perhaps with the offer of an occasional shot. There used to be plenty to shoot when rabbits, hares, pigeons and partridges were common on arable land and wild duck shooting was easy to come by before so much marshland was drained.

A town boy's interest is more likely to arise through a father who happens to be keen. Today's town boy has one advantage in that he can easily start with clay pigeon shooting, either because his father takes him there or he joins a club. This means that he gets shooting lessons, while the country boy is more likely to 'pick it up', as I did and, therefore starts with a lot of basic faults, which are not easy to eradicate when serious shooting becomes available.

I and many like me, were never even taught the basic rules of safety and I sometimes shudder at the risks we took crawling through hedges or negotiating fences with a loaded gun. Until I learned better, much later in life, I believed that the safety-catch was sufficient protection when, in fact, with the catch on 'Safe' the gun is still cocked, the firing pins being held back only by slivers of steel which can become worn. It astounds me, in retrospect, that my father, who had been a professional soldier and expert rifle shot, did not appear to worry when I went out on my own, in my teens, with a shotgun. A more sensible attitude was that adopted by the father of my neighbour, Richard Astor, who recalled, 'When I was ten, my father sent me over a fence twenty times, watching me unload, pocket the cartridges and handle the empty gun.'

The desire to own a gun can, I suggest, be described as 'natural' for any male because some degree of the hunting instinct remains in most of us. The fact that it was the males of a tribe who did the hunting — agriculture was probably invented by women — surely explains why so few females shoot game. While many country girls have hunted the fox for generations, few have stood in the shooting line, though more are doing so in this allegedly enlightened age, perhaps making the transition through their growing interest in clay shooting. I had one friend whose greatest joy on a shooting day was to 'get away from the women', particularly his own wife, but on many major shoots wives are more than welcome, if only to liven up the lunch and brighten up the field with their trendy shooting togs, which some wear even if they turn up solely for the food and drink and then depart. I have no doubt that having a vivacious and convivial wife has helped me with repeat invitations. It is, however, advantageous to have a wife who does not shoot because it is difficult for anyone to offer two invitations to the same family on the same day and, to save the embarrassment of not being able to ask the wife, the man, too, may be excluded.

Being conservers by nature, many women, perhaps most, dislike killing birds but killing is not the main motivation for most shooting men, any more than it is for farmers who rear beef cattle. I have encountered a few 'killers' who derived pleasure out of shooting anything but for the great majority the satisfaction arises out of the challenge posed by difficult targets, which cannot be fully simulated by any artificial means, and the pleasure of meeting it by the steady improvement of skill. Clay pigeon shooting can be helpful in providing practice in gun-mounting and timing, but the trajectories of clays, which are always decelerating, are predictable, while every bird is different in that respect and is usually accelerating.

The true satisfaction of a day's shooting resides in the few memorable birds when one was able to rise to a particularly difficult challenge, rather than in the total. This was brought home to me many years ago on an outside day at Highclere, when scrubby downland was being beaten to put a few spectacularly high pheasants over the guns, ranged wide apart, far below. The highest bird of the day was clearly going to pass over me and from such a distance that I had all the time in the world to miss it. Further, it was the only bird in the air and even the beaters had stopped to see what would happen to it. As I was appearing to take no action there were cries drawing my attention to the bird, which seemed to be getting smaller by the second, but I had steeled myself to put the gun up at the last moment, push it through and fire. I don't think anyone expected me to hit it but down it came, whirling like a sycamore seed, to cheers all round, especially from my host, the late Lord 'Porchey' Carnarvon, who loudly predicted, 'You will remember that bird all your life.' He was right.

When the weather and conditions are right, the birds are flying well and one is feeling good and on reasonable form there is very little in the world that is more rewarding. And, if at the end of the drive, all the shot pheasants could resurrect and walk into the wood the guns would be delighted.

Shooting also provides 'relaxation', meaning, essentially, a complete change from the usual daily round. Two of the major objectives of game-shooting are to get away from stress in any form and away from crowds. It is an ideal sport for those, like me, who are unable to relax by doing nothing. One definition of relaxation is 'becoming less tense' and it is fortunate that a relaxed attitude of mind is conducive to good marksmanship. There can, however, be negative effects for those who get into a stew when they are shooting badly, frustration producing the reverse mental effects to relaxation.

Those who work in towns derive the additional advantage of a change of scene. Shooting takes its devotees to marvellous places, many of them secret valleys, woods and dells hidden from the public gaze. Usually the drives, which, like salmon pools, have memorable names, have been laid out long ago on rising ground for challenging presentation and have a special beauty. As often as not, there is a big house and one of the great privileges is to lunch there and see it as it is lived in and, on occasion, to stay there. The ardent shot is privileged to spend much of his time literally out of the ordinary world, especially when he is on a grouse moor, and much of the sport's charm resides in that.

For most of us the main health benefit of a day's shooting is, unquestionably, mental. Some shooting men, who may feel a little guilty about how much they spend on their increasingly expensive sport, excuse it — to themselves and to their wives — by regarding it as a sound investment in their health, as it gives them exercise and gets them into the fresh air. The rough-shooter, walking ploughed fields and miles of hedges, and the wild-fowler, slopping and sliding about in shoreline mud, obtain a significant degree of exercise and that is also true of those who shoot grouse over dogs but with regular participants at driven pheasant and partridge shoots the situation is very different. The four-wheel-drive vehicle has reduced the amount of walking so much that my calculations on several driven shoots averaged out at no more than a quarter of a mile from vehicle to shooting peg. This means that the total distance walked in a six-drive pheasant or partridge day averages about three miles — little more than most men would walk getting to and from the office and moving about inside it. Those who have loaders do not even carry their guns and cartridge bags.

Four-wheel-drive vehicles, which can usually get within a few hundred yards of any line of butts have deprived even the driven grouse shoot of most of its scope for exercise. It is still usual to climb to the top butts — halting for breath on the way while pretending to admire the view — but many shoots have caterpillar tractors to transport guests there and I have even seen a helicopter pressed into that service. (Oddly, it did not disturb the grouse, which ignored it.) Even young grouse shooters wonder how their predecessors managed to cope with a trek of several miles to the moor followed by long walks, over rough terrain, from drive to drive.

Mounting and swinging a 6-pound gun in a heavy pheasant drive can involve more than a 1000-foot-pounds of work in the day, providing substantial exercise to the arms, shoulder muscles and a lot more of the body. When the recently deceased Jim Joel, more widely-known for his racing interests, ran his so-called 'drawing-room' shoot, on the edge of St Albans, the final drive offered so many pheasants that some of his guests, who all had loaders, were forced to rest during it through sheer arm fatigue. It was quite a sight to see avid shots, like the late Lord Dilhorne, allowing bouquets of birds to stream over him while immobilized on his shooting-stick. Happily, such occasions are rare and likely to become rarer with the growing objection to large bags.

Any day's shooting is more beneficial to the body than hugging the fire but the main health advantages are surely psychological. Relief from the working environment with a break from stress and competition is better than a floppy rest and no sport excels shooting for providing it.

Some urbanites may also benefit from breathing less polluted air for a day, but, in my opinion, the advantages of country air are largely illusory. In a small country, like ours, the wind quickly spreads industrial pollution, as witness the descent of power-station sulphuric acid as acid rain in the remotest places. The common belief that it is the change to 'fresh air' which makes a visitor feel pleasantly tired is fallacious. Those of us who live in the country breathe fresh air all the time and feel just as fatigued. And why should breathing cleaner air make anyone feel tired, when the reverse should be true?

The fact that the health benefits of shooting are considered at all is essentially the result of fairly recent media publicity together with medical advice from our GPs. In my youth all the jogging one sees in both town and country would have raised derision, even cat-calls, as would exercise centres and fat farms. Being rotund and rosy were regarded as signs of robust health. However, there can be no doubt that regular and demanding exercise is highly beneficial but, to be effective, it needs to be more exacting than most shooting provides.

Indeed, there may be negative health aspects to a driven day's shooting if the benefits of the modest exercise are more than neutralized by the intake of food and drink. Limited though it might be, the exercise increases appetite and, together with the ambience of good fellowship round the table, most people are inclined to eat and drink more than is good for them. Most of us, at some time, have been members of shoots where a sandwich lunch in a barn or under the greenwood tree was thoroughly acceptable but the warm environment of a house or shooting lodge is very welcome to most guns, especially in bad weather, and makes for pleasurable relaxation and good fellowship. However, coupled with the 'elevenses' which many shoots serve, the extra intake of calories may more than replace the ounces of excess weight burned off by the activity. At Broadlands I experienced the ultimate in 'elevenses' when, after the first stand, one of the guests sent his driver-butler round with vintage champagne and a tray bearing hard-boiled eggs cut in half and a large tin of the best caviare!

Most shoot hosts and hostesses pride themselves on the quality of the lunch, making it one of the highlights of the day. Particular care is taken in grand houses on commercially let days to encourage the guns to return in future seasons. The farmhouse lunch can be even more excessive for it is no coincidence that so many farmers figure among the fat of the land. (One of my jokes at such lunches, when the table groans with food and drink, is that one of the good things about shooting is the way it makes one rough it.)

For foreign visitors, in particular, the lunch in the dining-room of a stately home, with the owners present, can be a major attraction. However, most people attend a shoot primarily to let their guns off and lunch, however excellent or entertaining, should not be so protracted that it interferes with the afternoon drives. An excessively long lunch usually means that the last drive starts too late for the birds to fly well or has to be cancelled. Pheasants, partridges and grouse must be given reasonable time for an evening feed before they settle for the night and it is most unsporting when guns with full stomachs force them to sleep with empty crops.

One should make some effort at interesting conversation at lunch for there is no better place for initiating and cementing friendships. Taciturn guests, who are not uncommon, will not escape notice. It pays to have conjured up an interesting topic with an amusing new story which can be woven in, but as a rule, these should not be *risqué* if there are women present. Some men have the panache to carry these off without offence but I have found it wiser to avoid acquiring a reputation as a fount of smut. While dining with Sir Max Aitken at Cowes, after a shoot, I was foolish enough to follow up one or two stories told by Uffa Fox, the yacht designer, who was notorious for his lack of concern for female sensitivity. I was feeling in a good mood because Max had just invited me to join the *Express* main board but, after that dinner I heard no more about the directorship.

While the sensible shot will ration himself regarding alcohol I have seen many others take the view that, having paid for it, they might as well have it. A non-drinker, as I have been for many years now, is often surprised at the number of times that glasses are refilled as the port and sloe gin go round and round. I do not know of any scientific investigations into a possible link between drink and shooting accidents but it would be surprising if there was none, because alcohol affects both co-ordination between hand and eye and the general judgement of vital factors like distance. With the hostile attitude of some police forces towards shooting, guns would be prudent to curb their intake considering that many of them get straight into their vehicles after lunch to go to the next drive, which is often along a public road. While the Sopwiths offered only cider at the lunch table, they served a pre-lunch rum cocktail of such strength that, in my drinking days, I always avoided it when shooting. I sometimes sampled it when fishing with them and then staggered into the neck of my pool on the Spey or South Esk, which was perhaps more foolhardly than going to a grouse butt.

Unlike fishing, which is essentially a lonely sport, most forms of shooting are social and much of the pleasure in it derives from the other people involved. Most experienced shots agree that the people one meets in the shooting field are every bit as important as the quality of the quarry and on occasions when I have seriously thought of giving up shooting the realization of how many friends I would be unlikely to encounter again quickly changed my mind. As all who have belonged to a syndicate know, the compatability of a group of people destined to meet for eight or nine full days together in all kinds of weather is crucial and difficult to achieve. A difficult member, usually one who is always finding fault, can seriously detract from the pleasure of the rest. The shooting know-all who cannot resist telling the keeper, or the field master, how he should have done this or that drive can be a menace. An angry keeper, and the beaters who tend to be his friends, are unlikely to give of their best if their efforts are derided.

Over the years I have known a number of shoot-owners who took pains to ensure that their guests on any particular day would be compatible. They all had some friends who were 'difficult' with each other and, so, would not be invited on the same day. This could hark back to some unfortunate incident in the past — in the shooting field

165

or in their private lives — which made two guns like two bits of sandpaper rubbing together. I was often surprised to learn how trivial the fall-out had sometimes been, but hosts were not prepared to take any chance of spoiling the atmosphere of geniality which gives shooting its particular joy. Sometimes it was the accompanying wives who posed the problem or even dogs which had taken a dislike to each other on a previous occasion.

Temperament is, surely, the root factor conditioning compatibility. Shooting must be fun and anyone who cannot take its ups and downs without being miserable and even-tempered is unlikely to make a good field companion. A common cause of gloom is a succession of poor pegs when the rest are getting their share of the birds and maybe more. On many shoots where numbers are drawn there is one which puts its unfortunate possessor into 'Siberia' for most of the day. It is often said that the luck of the draw evens out over the season but that has not been my experience. I drew the dreaded number so many times that I left one syndicate. Conversely, there are some people who, almost invariably, draw good numbers while a few seem to attract birds wherever they are. 'I could put Major X in the middle of a ploughed field and the pheasants would still stream over him', was how one Hampshire keeper expressed this enviable propensity to me. If consistently 'out of it' one should grin and not fume but, as a fairly regular recipient of such bad luck, I confess to the difficulty of keeping a smiling face and not giving tongue. The attitude of my friend, Alan Milton, is more constructive — with not much to shoot at he looks around, counts his blessings and tells himself how fortunate he is to be present.

Much of the pleasure of a shooting day derives out of good-natured badinage and anyone lacking a sense of humour or a capacity for being ribbed without taking offence is rarely welcome for long. One can be keen without being too serious. Nobody I have ever met devoted more painstaking attention to his shooting days than Joe Nickerson yet the atmosphere was always light-hearted. On one occasion, for instance, Joe had fitted out his Filipino servant, Eusebio, with a large flag to serve as a flanker on a partridge drive with the instruction to wave it whenever he saw any birds coming. Having withdrawn his services for one particularly productive drive, Joe was puzzled when no partridges flew towards him while patronizing everyone else. Turning round, he spotted Eusebio standing behind him waving his flag. Nobody laughed louder than Joe.

While an amiable eccentric can be a fount of laughter — I stood next to one man whose loader carried a soda siphon to squirt at his dog if it whined — the shooting field is no place for practical jokes.

Any habit which carries the smallest degree of danger cancels out all the good qualities an individual may possess. Firing at low birds is the commonest crime and some people seem incapable of resisting the temptation, especially if they have had nothing to shoot at for a while.

Firing at other people's birds, which is usually an expression of greed, must be the commonest cause of friction in a line of guns. Most of us have erred in that respect but the character who makes a habit of it can ruin the day. While 'wiping the eye' of a neighbour may be satisfying, the highly competitive individual is generally unwelcome. There are some who think that competing for a bird enhances the fun but for those who are embroiled in competition in their work, any more in the shooting field is the last thing they need. A really compatible group will shoot as a team.

Regarding another aspect of competition it is a grave error for the average shot to be annoyed with himself because he is unable to compete in performance with what are, virtually, professionals shooting four days a week or more. The best one can do is to admire their virtuosity and learn what one can from them, revelling, perhaps, in the privilege of being included in the line with such greats. To become known as a good and stylish shot, if one can, is a positive social accomplishment and generates admiration, in spite of the vocal antipathy of some people to the sport, these days. The fact that King George V was widely regarded as one of the best game-shots of his time redounded greatly to his credit with ordinary people, though, these days, Prince Charles comes under criticism, mainly from the ignorant.

The size of a shooting team has great impact on compatibility. Eight or nine is usual, because the individual price of a gun in a syndicate would be too high if there were less, but this can be too many if they have to be packed into a small area. Also, too many guns in a line can be unfair to the birds.

Crowding can be overcome by double banking, with say five guns in front and three behind. Some of those in front take pride in ensuring that nothing shall pass. When a friend saw me taking a stand for a heavy drive behind the late Keith Showering, of Babycham fame, who was a nailing shot, he suggested that what I needed was a good book! He was right. On the other hand, when I joined a new syndicate and was back gun at the bottom of a steep hill, an elderly farmer at the peg in front of me insisted that I change places, saying 'You'll have more fun where I am.' I suspected that he wanted the better quality birds behind but I had utterly misjudged him. As I was to discover, his kindness was a byword.

167

Joe Nickerson reckoned that seven was the maximum number of guns anywhere and, in his later years, he was almost always down to five or less on his pheasant shoot at Rothwell, only the most productive pegs being filled. The joy of being 'in the thick of it' at every stand, as I was so often, is unforgettable and with fewer people in the field one became acquainted with them more deeply. Even on his wild partridge shoot in Spain he would defy convention there and have five guns, or sometimes only three, compared with the common number of ten to fourteen. Only on one occasion — and for an off-beat reason — have I wished there had been more guns in the line. Shooting with Joe and four others at Nombela, his Spanish shoot, near Toledo, the long drive was interrupted by some problem which we could not understand but which suddenly became evident. There was a tremendous pounding of hooves and we were confronted by a group of wild bulls racing towards us. While the English stared, their Spanish loaders disappeared up cork trees. To have seen fourteen of them hanging from boughs, complete with cartridge bags, would have been even more memorable than seeing five.

Many shots have found the social side of shooting to be profitable to their business lives, as I have, providing professional contacts they would never otherwise have met. When I have been in syndicates I have been able to invite others, senior civil servants and Staff Chiefs being loath to pass up a day's shooting while, perhaps, not being prepared to join me more publicly for lunch in London. Additionally, shooting generates an ambience of good fellowship more conducive to the loosening of tongues than the most fully licensed meal. The many thousands of cartridges I have expended have been an excellent investment in many ways.

Governments are not averse to using shoots for diplomatic purposes and General de Gaulle utilized the famous Rambouillet pheasant shoot that way. I once heard Harold Macmillan describe his experience there, when Prime Minister. De Gaulle stood behind his chief guest and murmured 'Missed again!' every time he did so.

One diplomatically inspired day is imprinted so indelibly in my mind that, after twenty years, I can recall every extraordinary detail. The events began on a morning early in September 1972 with a telephone call to me from Julian Amery, then Minister of State in the Foreign Office. He told me that a very important Arab, who was visiting Britain, had asked to be provided with some duck shooting near London. The only person whom I thought could supply it was my neighbour, Alan Bristow, who was then running the helicopter company which he had founded and still bears his name. I knew that he had not put out his reared ducks, as they were not ready, but I thought there might be some evening flighting of wild mallard, teal and Canada geese from the large lake on his Baynard's Park estate, near Cranleigh in Surrey. I explained to Alan that Julian would not have contacted me had the requirement not been important and he responded with enthusiasm when told the visitor's name. He was Sheikh Zaid, ruler of oil-rich Abu Dhabi and the elected spokesman for other Emirates on the Persian Gulf. In more recent times he has become more widely-known as the main shareholder in the BCCI bank which crashed in 1990.

A few days later the Sheikh, with a substantial retinue, appeared at Baynard's Park for an evening flight, which turned out to be disastrous because no ducks or geese appeared in quantity before darkness fell. Alan Bristow was deeply embarrassed but so well-mannered was the Sheikh that he personally telephoned his thanks on the following morning and asked to be invited to shoot again. This time Alan decided to take no chances with the wildfowl and organized a partridge shoot, having put down a substantial stock of red legs which were not due to be driven for a further three weeks. Four Arabs were to shoot in the line and I was invited, along with the late Freddy Burden, the Tory MP, who was eventually knighted for back-bench services.

When the Arabs arrived I was surprised to see them in their robes, the only concession to the field being green wellies. The bearded Sheikh Zaid was particularly impressive in his grey-brown robe and large, matching turban, while the others wore the more usual white robes and head-dress. The odd man out, sartorially and tempermentally, was an Italian in an electric-blue suit who was the Sheikh's official photographer.

Realizing that his foreign guests had probably never encountered driven partridges, Alan had erected large hides made of straw bales on each of the drives and built so that the occupants could not swing their guns, dangerously, through the line. Having spent time among Arab tribesmen, I was not surprised when these safety measures were swept aside, for there is nothing that the desert Arab enjoys more than letting his gun off. The Arabs' reaction as each partridge flew towards them was equally predictable. Every one of them fired at the bird, irrespective of its distance, and it succumbed in a cloud of feathers. This treatment was also meted out to any young pheasants which flew over and Alan's repeated cries of 'Partridges only! Partridges only!' was misinterpreted as congratulations egging them on to further carnage.

As each bird rose the beaters wisely made themselves as flat on the ground as possible. Then, the most adventurous would raise his head to ensure that the barrage had halted and the hesitant march forward was resumed. A further safety problem was created by one of the Arabs who was accompanied by his young son. Every time he shot a bird the boy ran from the hide to retrieve it, with other guns still firing, until warned by Alan to desist. We awarded the accolade for courage, however, to the Italian photographer who crouched or lay on his back in front of the Sheikh's hide, taking action shots whenever a bird approached.

Freddy and I repeatedly found ourselves next to the Arabs while Alan, who did the placing, was as remote as possible on the end of the line. Whether by accident or cunning design, it was Freddy and I who occasionally had to take evasive action as low coveys breached the line and guns were swung through at them. Admittedly, Alan was less expendable and, perhaps, he was just being sacrificially hospitable.

The break for lunch, staged in the middle of a farmyard, was almost certainly unique in the annals of British shooting. Intent on making his guests feel at home, Alan had put up a large tent with imitation palm fronds sprouting from the poles. There were colourful scatter cushions on the floor while, outside, a sheep was being roasted on a spit.

My wife, who had joined us for lunch, was seated next to Sheikh Zaid and, though they could understand little of each other's speech, she established friendly rapport by feeding grapes to him. After the roast lamb he insisted on providing Arabian-style coffee offered in little cups. Having savoured this beverage in palaces in the Yemen and Dubai, I had already been able to advise her as to the protocol — accept a second cup or the host will be offended but decline a third or he will think you greedy. The coffee seemed to have some special potency, because, after we had banned the ladies from the field on safety grounds, they spent the afternoon falling about in giggles on the cushions.

The shooting continued as before to the delight of the foreign guests as covey after covey of partridges and the occasional young pheasant came forward. By the end of the day three beaters and a keeper had been slightly peppered but when lavish compensations were eventually handed out it was those who were unscathed who felt aggrieved.

Clearly, the experience had done such wonders for foreign relations that Freddy Burden wrote a poem suggesting that he and I had earned the OBE. It had also been a significant day for Alan Bristow's business relations. He was already deeply involved in providing helicopters to service the oil industry and it was no surprise to me when he was soon in business in Abu Dhabi with the ruler, who was being referred to, affectionately as 'Sheiky-baby'. The Sheikh had been well pleased and the Foreign Office was delighted as diplomatic relations had been cemented and commercial relations forged.

Though I am heavily in debt to people who have invited me to shoot over the years I was able to repay Joe Nickerson to an extent which surprised both of us. While shooting several days a week, Joe had managed to build up a highly profitable seed-breeding business, producing new strains of wheats, barleys and other crops which were heavily in demand both in Britain and abroad. At that time my friend, Victor Rothschild, was the Chief Scientist for the whole of Shell's operations and had told me that the company was feeling guilty about taking oil out of the ground in places like the Middle East and putting nothing back in. He said that thought was being given to supporting the breeding of crops specially suited to places like Iran and Victor had already discussed the principle with the Shah, who was a personal friend and had responded keenly. I mentioned this to Joe, while shooting with him, and he asked me to arrange a meeting with Rothschild, which I did, bringing them together over dinner. Not long afterwards, Shell bought a considerable stake in Joe's seed-breeding business, providing him with his first major capital for use in other ventures, and eventually bought him out completely when he wanted to sell.

One problem with shooting is that it can become compulsive sometimes, perhaps to the point of fanaticism. It was not unusual for Joe Nickerson to shoot grouse for three days at Wemmergill, to be motored back to Rothwell in Lincolnshire, to rise early next morning to shoot wildfowl, attend to business in the afternoon, shoot duck in the evening and then be motored back to prepare for more grouse shooting the following day. Repeatedly he assured his friends that he was still as excited on entering a grouse butt or reaching a pheasant stand as he ever had been. He was so devoted to shooting that he felt deprived on a day without any. Sometimes when he woke upon a non-shooting day which had been set aside for rest he would feel an urgent need to have a few shots and would make sudden arrangements for two or three drives of pheasants or grouse with him, his wife or son or just himself in the line, if a 'line' of one is possible. He did the same with duck flighting on an island in the Humber estuary which he owned, though one-man shooting is common enough with wildfowlers.

Soon after his seventieth birthday I was grouse shooting with him at Wemmergill and, between drives, he said to me 'I intend to do another five years and go on even longer if I can. You see, with me, shooting is a religion'. It certainly dominated his life as it did with other famous shots before him. Best known of these was the Edwardian, Lord

171

Walsingham, who ruined himself and his family financially through shooting and providing it for others. A former Earl of Leicester never went to the outside lavatory near one of his big drives without a loaded gun because he had once been there unarmed when a woodcock had flown over him. The mind of an acquaintance of mine was so steeped in shooting that if he went to the loo without success he would say that he had a blank drive.

The Edwardian shot whom Joe, secretly, tried to emulate was the second Marquess of Ripon who is rated as probably the greatest bird-marksman of all time. Immediately before dropping dead on his grouse moor in 1923, Ripon, formerly known as Lord de Grey, shot fifty-one grouse and a snipe in the last drive. In his life-time he accounted for 550,000 head of game. Nickerson shot about half that number but when all the factors are taken into account there was little to choose between this matched pair. They were both exceptionally fast and accurate and their enthusiasm remained unimpaired by advancing years.

When past seventy, Joe Nickerson had a pulley with ropes inserted in the ceiling above his desk so that, while working there, he could keep his arm muscles in trim. While still shooting six and sometimes seven days a week — he could shoot wildfowl on Sunday — he did not neglect his several businesses, arranging matters so that he remained in control, even before the days of the car telephone. It is quite astonishing how many businessmen shoot three days or more each week from 12 August to 1 February. I have never had that opportunity and would not have wanted it. Two days a week for me have always been ample.

Enthusiasm paid off for Joe in never-ending enjoyment. I know of one extraordinary instance where it paid off in worldly goods, the recipients being a most happy couple who are neighbours of mine in Berkshire. When young, the wife had a bachelor uncle who owned a large estate with a superb seventeenth-century house, with contents to match. He was very keen on shooting and she enjoyed picking up there with her dogs while her young husband, who was an excellent shot, was often invited as a guest. There were nephews, who did not shoot, and other nieces who did not pick up. The keen couple, who never thought they were in line to inherit anything from the uncle, assuming that the nephews would benefit, were suddenly told by him that they would get everything, including the resources to run the estate, which they have done with obvious success. Both assured me, as we sat at a shoot lunch in their magnificent dining-room, with the ancestral portraits looking down, that their stunning good fortune was entirely due to their joint enthusiasm for shooting!

CHAPTER 18

THE ENIGMA OF FORM

There are very few people in any field of sporting endeavour, from village cricket to stately home shooting, whose performance does not suffer from the mysterious factor generally known as 'form'. As television repeatedly exposes, some of the most professional exponents of football, cricket, golf, tennis, snooker and darts can suddenly slip from the heights of stunning performance to the despairing depths and none of them are able to offer any convincing explanation for the fall. All they can say is that they are 'off form' which explains nothing because, in the dictionary sense, form simply implies level of performance. Considering the huge sums invested in competitive spectator sports which are all manifestly affected by the form of the players, it is surprising that no organization seems to have sponsored any serious research into it. The spin-off from any discoveries to shotgun shooting would be very welcome because it is bedevilled by form, as I can testify from frustrating personal experience.

Being in or on form implies a high level, with 'off form' being a blanket expression to cover various degrees of ineptitude. Most serious exponents of any sport usually know exactly what they should be doing, especially if they have had professional tuition. When 'off form' they are simply unable to do what, on other days, comes almost naturally. Such a slump may last for only a short time but can sometimes endure for weeks.

If driven to pick out the one essential element of performance most likely to be responsible for the ups and downs it surely must be timing which, of course, is partricularly crucial in sports involving a moving target. When batsmen are off form it is usually because they are not timing their shots accurately and this is the main problem with shooting men. In cricket or shooting, whether of game or clays, timing is absolutely of the essence, the smallest error being likely to lead to a poor result or total failure.

The bird missed behind might have been hit in the head had the trigger been pulled a fraction of a second earlier. What is it that conditions the sense of timing? Timing is a function of the brain, nerves and muscles. Physiologically, it boils down, basically, to co-ordination between the eyes and the muscles controlling the necessary movements of the limbs, and form varies with the efficiency of that co-ordination. My observations, mainly in the shooting field, would suggest that some people are born with a heightened sense of timing and those less well endowed in that direction are rarely able to reach such a high level of performance however much they practise. I think that most people would assume that this certainly applies to outstanding batsmen. So it is not unreasonable to believe that it also applies to outstanding shots.

There is a close similarity between the arts of batsmanship and shotgun marksmanship. Like well-bowled balls, the birds come at various speeds, heights and angles and, like the elegant cricketer, the elegant shot will have different strokes in his repertoire for dealing with each type of bird to best advantage. I do not happen to know any outstanding cricketers who are great shots but I have stood in the line with a few whose professional reputations depended on the same quickness of reaction and power of concentration. The former racing driver, Jackie Stewart, is such a shot and so was the late Graham Hill. Fighter aces depended on their ability to hit a fast-moving target and some, like Johnnie Johnson, were fine shots.

When expertly accomplished, each stroke of bat or gun is unhurried, graceful and a delight to watch. In both sports there are exponents of varying degrees of excellence, consistency being an essential component. There are also specialists, those who excel at a particular type of ball or bird, and all-rounders who are capable of dealing with any type of challenge. Some shooting specialists maintain their high kills-to-cartridges ratio by selecting the kind of bird at which they happen to excel, sometimes pretending not to see a bird which they think they might miss, while all-round shots take on difficult birds at every range and angle, not being afraid to miss.

While the major co-ordination seems to be between hand and eye, in reality it is between the eyes and the whole muscular system, the position of the legs, the shoulders and the. general balance being of comparable importance. The correct nervous signals have to be sent from eyes to brain and from the brain to almost the entire muscular system, which has to be involved for the body to maintain its poise and balance. Part of the process is conscious — the ability to judge the target's distance, speed and precise position in space, whether it be a ball or a bird, and the timing of the intended contact, though, with long practise it becomes almost a series of reflex actions.

Even the greatest exponents have to practise to maintain the accuracy of their timing, which can quickly degenerate. It is no coincidence that the best shots shoot several days a week. Nevertheless it is an oddity of form that one can leave something like shooting for months and then perform brilliantly on the opening day — perhaps better than at any time later in the season!

Accuracy in sports depending on moving targets involves split-second judgement and decision so that all the physical actions occur at the right moment. It involves conscious judgement and decision-making, which both devolve on the brain and nervous network so that the signals coming in from the eyes are correctly interpreted and the right messages are sent to the muscles.

Another component of performance is the so-called kinaesthetic sense — the awareness of changes in the position of various parts of the body which enables the shot to watch the bird without having to check the position of his arms and legs and to gauge his movements without looking away. Like vision and hearing, this sense may be better developed in some individuals than in others.

Cricket and snooker commentators are apt to remark, 'A momentary lapse of concentration!' when someone makes a bad stroke or fails at an easy pot, but what does that really mean? Concentration implies bringing all the required factors — the senses, brain and muscles — to a common focus. Yet when a player fails he may be trying as hard as ever. Indeed, as all shooters in particular know, trying too hard can be counter-productive and on off-form days conscious concentration does not necessarily put it right. In other words, poor form may be due to an excess of concentration. This also shows up in another country pursuit — pub darts. As a one-time player myself, long before it became an international sport, I know how counter-productive trying too hard can be. I invariably put up my best performance when taking virtually no aim. However, while one can try too hard, being half-hearted is even more devastating. In shooting, one really needs to want to succeed every time the trigger is pressed which, I suppose, is a definition of keenness or enthusiasm. The pheasant that looks easy is often missed because of failure to summon up sufficient enthusiasm for the shot.

Paradoxically, relaxation, which would seem to be the opposite of concentration, is regarded by most shooting instructors and manuals as a necessity for consistent performance. Being tensed up, either mentally or physically can ruin performance. This is very noticeable with batsmen during their early minutes at the crease when they tend to be tensed up and awkward. I suspect, however, that relaxation refers mainly to attitude of the mind rather than to muscles, which should, obviously, be under some degree of tension to respond with speed and accuracy.

There would seem to be a link between relaxation and temperament which is an aspect of personality. Some shots, who tend to be above average, seem immune to loss of temper which is fatal to accuracy. If they chance to have a bad spell they do not go to pieces as others do and quickly recover their composure and their form. One would expect the phlegmatic to be less affected than the excitable. Yet many unabashed extroverts consistently shoot very well. The phlegmatic shot probably gets over a bout of form more quickly, however, because he is less likely to lose heart which, as I know only too well, can be catastrophic.

There are a very few shots who seem to be hardly affected by form at all. They may miss a few birds on the trot but never have a whole day in the wilderness of despair. Perhaps they are natural shots, meaning that they were born with neuro-muscular equipment which is relatively unaffected by any circumstances. Or, having had the advantage of expert tuition from childhood and unlimited practise since, the whole process has become so ingrained that it hardly ever goes wrong.

The way that form can fluctuate even on the same day — from stand-to-stand on pheasant shoots for instance — may well be connected with mood, to which most mortals are subject, some more than others. (The differences in form between drives may, on occasion, also be due to the fact that the birds are flying differently, though they appear to be more or less the same. Sometimes it is the birds which are on form!)

Mood may be an effect of the hormone system, the group of glands, such as the adrenals and thyroid which, by the rapid production of powerful chemicals, can crucially affect the entire metabolism. These days, the phrase 'getting the adrenalin flowing' is common parlance and some sportsmen can be seen 'hyping' themselves into an aggressive mood by deliberately stimulating the flow. Feelings like apprehension, anxiety, excitement and irritability, which can all affect performance, are due to the impact of hormones, the system being so complex and so changeable that it is never exactly the same.

I have always blamed the rapid changeability of mood for the odd fact that there have been a few individuals in whose presence I always shot rather badly. The first syndicate I ever joined was run by a peppery, one-eyed retired colonel who spent most of his time walking with the beaters, but whenever I was in his view I was bound to miss even the easiest bird. Maybe I was trying too hard to impress him but it is possible that some people exert a dampening effect, making others feel apprehensive.

The other factor widely used as an excuse for continuing low performance is loss of confidence. Again, commentators are apt to say when a player is off form for a long time, 'He has lost his confidence' and this is sometimes admitted by the players themselves. But again, what does it really mean? Confidence is the feeling of certainty that when the stroke is made or the trigger pulled the target will be struck correctly or, in other words, it is being sure about the timing. In shooting it is also about having faith in the first aim, which is usually the best aim.

A feeling of confidence is said to heighten muscle tension and mental alertness, resulting in quicker reactions. It should also reduce hesitation, which can be fatal to timing, but it has to be more than just a state of mind. I have often set off for a day's shooting full of confidence and strode out to my peg feeling sure that I could down anything that came — usually as a result of having shot well on the previous occasion — and have then put up a most disappointing performance. I have also done the reverse, travelling to a big shoot full of foreboding and then shot well. In fact, in my experience, the challenge of being exposed to the big occasion can enhance performance though, sadly, it has also done the reverse for me.

Dealing with the first few birds effectively can make a tremendous difference to the whole day, as can missing them. As with a batsman whose first two boundaries are achieved with sweet strokes, one's confidence soars through the knowledge that one's timing is right. However, most shooters will agree that one can become too relaxed and over-confident, missing the easy bird, as the batsman gets himself out with a lazy stroke.

Nobody has been able to explain why confidence should vary so much from day to day. The ups and downs of fitness may be partly responsible. One would imagine that being off-colour would undermine confidence and superficially it does. Yet I have gone shooting feeling tired or full of a cold, and fearing that it must affect my performance, but have then shot well. My suggested explanation of this is that when the body is incubating an infection the body temperature is raised slightly and, until the germs get their grip, this stimulates the body chemistry which governs hand and eye performance.

Another factor which would be expected to affect co-ordination is sleep. It would be reasonable to expect that one would shoot better, for example, when refreshed after a sound sleep than when still tired after a bad night. In one of the few experiments carried out on clay shooters, scientists found that the quality of sleep had little observable effect. In fact, those who had been deliberately allowed little sleep did rather better.

The ageing process is another factor which affects most skills. It is obvious why the performance of those engaged in sports involving sustained physical effort and rapid reaction time should deteriorate with advancing age. Presumably it progressively erodes the neuro-muscular co-ordination but one might expect experience to offset any decline in that direction, at least for quite a while. Ageing certainly reduces the speed with which one can react to a pheasant suddenly appearing over a narrow woodland ride or to a grouse at a butt, though this can be offset to some extent by using lighter guns of lesser bore. Joe Nickerson foresaw this, moving to 20-bores in his late fifties, then to 28-bores and to watch him engage down-wind grouse or exceptionally high pheasants and partridges with these 'pea-shooters' was to witness near perfection. Lord Forte, using 20-bore shotguns, is undoubtedly shooting much better at eighty-four than he would have been able to do with 12-bores.

Why ageing should impinge so quickly on performance in unhurried games like snooker is difficult to understand. The competitive spirit — the urge to succeed — is an important component of performance in such a professional sport and this usually decreases with age though whether that is due to declining inability to compete or to boredom with having to go on doing so is another question.

Drugs are another factor which has generated much recent publicity, especially in the world of athletics. Alcohol is the most widespread and the large body of experimental research into its effects on hand-and-eye skills prove it to be generally deleterious, especially concerning the all important matter of judgement. This, of course, is the scientific basis for the police activity against drinking drivers. Nevertheless, many shots are convinced that they shoot better after a couple of drinks. A few go out in the morning badly hung over from the night before and perform brilliantly. Alcohol is not a stimulant as commonly believed, but a depressant of the nervous system, making it more sluggish, and there may be something in the belief that anything which relaxes the body and mind is good for form. Perhaps, until there is experimental evidence, a wise rule might be to have the odd drink if you are shooting badly but not if you are shooting well. My old friend, Julian Amery, claims that if he has not been shooting too well before lunch, a drink usually puts him right for the afternoon and that he always tends to shoot better after a licensed lunch. Perhaps it is a matter of relaxation. Abstaining from alcohol completely, as I have for ten years now, has not materially improved my performance.

Experimental physiologists and psychologists have unravelled most of the mysteries of fatigue, especially in connection with repetitive tasks encountered in industry and the armed forces, and have compiled a list of dos and don'ts which have proved of great benefit. So 'form', which must also have a physiological and psychological basis, should yield to the same processes of investigation. Yet, having scoured the literature of behavioural psychology I have found only a couple of papers on the subject of form, though, once its causes were understood, solutions should be much easier to devise. It might even be possible to produce a formula for form which would enable sporting men and women to check their circumstances and, hopefully, pinpoint their deficiences.

Clay-shooting would seem to be the easiest available and cheapest medium for experiments in which circumstances could be controlled and varied. Its exponents confirm that it is a sport definitely affected by form and those few experiments on the subject — carried out by the Medical Research Council — made use of it. The mental and emotional state of volunteer subjects could be varied at will by the administration of drugs.

Some of the initial physiological work might be undertaken with animals, such as working dogs or racing greyhounds. Though horses would be expensive experimental subjects, the results of the research would be of profound interest to trainers and punters for no creature, save, possibly, man, is more affected by form. Indeed the 'form book' is required loo reading for serious students including, I am informed, HM The Queen.

No doubt, there are some who would prefer to allow form to remain a mystery because it contributes so much to the 'glorious uncertainty' of a game and if every player was always on form games might become tediously repetitive. That might be true but I, for one, could do without the problem when it lets me down in the shooting field, as it has so often. One of the reasons I like fishing so much is that, except for Spey casting, form hardly ever comes into it.

CHAPTER 19

GOOD FORM

O scar Wilde, who was a competent shot before other interests took up all his time, once said of a social acquaintance, 'He has dined everywhere — once!' So it is not difficult to imagine what he might have said about the type of guest prone to gaffes in the shooting field — 'He has shot everywhere — once!' The perfect shooting companion probably does not exist but we all need to strive towards that description and, having made most of the possible mistakes in a long shooting life, I feel well qualified to write about them.

The first essential is to appreciate that any invitation to shoot is a great privilege, especially these days when costs are so high. As shooting is essentially about fun and good fellowship it is invidious to introduce any financial considerations but one cannot fail to be aware of the huge costs of providing a day's sport to a team of guns which are an unspoken expression of a host's generosity. While excessive gratitude can become embarrassing, there are ways of showing it and being punctilious in answering invitations early and being determined to fulfil them once they have been accepted are two of them. Most of us have committed the unpardonable sin of withdrawing from an accepted invitation because a better one has become available, but a host who suspects what has really occurred or happens to learn the truth is unlikely to repeat his offer.

Only really dangerous fog or deep snow provides a legitimate excuse for failing to appear on the grounds of weather. The elderly gun may wish to cancel on awakening to hear a dreadful forecast but nevertheless should go. A last-minute cancellation usually creates an irritating nuisance for the owner, with frantic telephoning to find a replacement because, if there is a gap in the line, pheasants have a habit of streaming through it. One of the virtues of shooting as a form of physical recreation is that it forces its adherents out into the open air. They have to get up and go unless genuine illness or some domestic crisis makes it truly unwise or impossible. I have experienced some of my best days when the weather looked so appalling that I was tempted to cancel. Once, I had to be rescued by snow plough on the way but the birds flew magnificently.

The person who is invariably late is only too common in the shooting world and is a nuisance to everyone if the beaters are already out preparing the first drive. I admire the host who starts on time, penalizing the late-comers by depriving them of the first drive, whatever their status. I recall one day when the tardy guest was the then young Prince Charles and the pheasants were literally heaving in the fir plantation into which the beaters had driven them. The keeper warned his employer that he could not hold them there and, with royal protocol rightly set aside, the drive was started. As I had been placed next to the missing Prince I was asked to shoot at his peg until he arrived. It was the best and I enjoyed myself, more than usually, until, late in the drive, His rather breathless Royal Highness appeared and I ceded the position, gracefully, I hope.

A sensible insurance against being late for an unfamiliar shoot is to find out exactly how to get there and how long it will take, allowing extra time for the traffic on weekdays. It is surprising how often a map provided by the owner is inadequate, especially as regards the actual entry to the shoot and the precise meeting place. All too often I have found myself calling at cottages — usually empty — to ask the way. It is hateful to arrive at a shoot to find that the numbers have already been drawn so, usually, I am too early, when I always pull up out of sight until a few minutes before the stipulated time of arrival. That allows time for a dog to avoid the embarrassment of depositing an early morning offering on the host's lawn. When I had the pleasure of shooting at Ramsbury Manor, in Wiltshire, someone's dog — once mine, in spite of my precautions — almost invariably sullied the magnificent frontage, requiring the eagle-eyed host to send for his servant and a shovel. Hosts have a habit of appearing just before the offence can be removed and an admission of responsiblity makes a bad start to the day. Even if the shoot meets in a field or farmyard or on a moor it still pays to take precaution. At one of my first meetings with the formidable Lady Sopwith, when I was most anxious not to offend, my Springer had laid an enormous offering just where her driver chose to pull up her Range Rover. It seemed that she must step in it but, loving her own dogs to the extent that they both slept on her bed, all she said, while dodging it, was 'What a marvellous tuppence!'

My angriest encounter was with two Labradors sent out by a picker-up. They both ran immediately to my peg and urinated on my gun cover. One then returned and did the rest on it.

While a useful and biddable dog can help to secure invitations, a misbehaving dog can do the reverse. The dog most likely to give offence is the one that is never pegged down but always ought to be. While steady for a drive or two, it eventually takes off into a wood, into the kale or into the next parish after a running pheasant or a hare. The hapless owner usually compounds the offence by bawling his head off during a drive when quiet is required. In my sad experience it is generally best to keep silent until the drive is over if the dog is out of sight in the hope that some keeper or beater will catch it. I am fairly sure that a dog, no longer with us, ended my appearances at a Surrey shoot because of complaint from the keeper.

A missing dog can hold everybody up, especially on a grouse moor, and though it may come back with a bird to the delight of the owner, the host is rarely pleased whatever he may, or may not, say. Another common nuisance is the dog that picks up pheasants and then drops them in a wood because other dogs may then decline to touch them and they may be left. The reverse is the bully dog which seizes a bird from another one or forces it to drop it. Submissive dogs are disinclined to argue but the conflict can end in a tug-of-war which is rather appalling when the bird is a runner.

Another threat to field friendship is the dog that squeals or barks at the peg — usually with excitement when the pheasants start to fly — or seems to be rehearsing for the Covent Garden opera. Nothing is more likely to upset neighbouring guns, especially if they happen to be serious about their dogs, for the habit is contagious. Sadly such a dog should be barred from the line, though it is astonishing how some people continue with noisy dogs.

Nobody should arrive at a shoot with a bitch that is on heat or near it but, before I knew better, I took mine, which was almost finished, having garnished her heavily with Anti-mate. My host greeted me with 'Dear God, is that smell you or your dog?' I deserved it. There are, of course, some dogs that are so randy that they will mount almost anything and can be a great nuisance.

Two dogs which hate each other, especially bitches, will never get on. If they both inadvertently turn up at the same shoot the two owners should toss up for which is left in the car at alternate drives. Nobody has the perfect dog, which is too much to expect, but we all tend to be somewhat blind, and deaf, to our own dog's faults. So, if one finds oneself dropped from a list for no obvious reason, perhaps one should ask, 'Was the fault mine or my best friend's?' Though my dogs have served me well and lovingly, they have made most of the possible mistakes and have occasionally been the cause of friction.

Few shoots go by without minor irritation from dogs picking up other people's birds for, when a shot has his own dog, he may be more annoyed by having his birds picked up than by having them 'poached' by a greedy gun. There are those who can barely wait to send out their dogs to pick up anything they can find to put at their own pegs or on their butts, though the habit has to be endured with good grace if the offending animal belongs to the owner, who ends up on a big drive with a huge pile of birds. The Spanish scene is notorious for this with the *secretarios*, the hand-pickers, scrabbling for everything, irrespective of ownership, so that some guns can inflate their kills on the score-card. One grandee has been known to carry a gun while picking up and to fire warning shots to scare off any *secretario* with the temerity to threaten his score. The late Archie Coats, the legendary pigeon shot, told me that when he was partridge shooting in Spain a Spaniard who had hit nothing during a drive asked him for seven of his which had fallen near his butt so that he could claim them as his own. Archie obliged him. Lord Lambton's recipe was to throw the handful of birds he had managed to rescue at the chief offender but you need panache, and perhaps even a title, to carry off such a gesture. The safest response for most of us to shooting greed of any kind is to suffer in silence and to appreciate that it is only those of us who are without sin who are qualified to throw the first bird!

While personal turn-out may be no reliable sign of shooting ability, it is a guide to character and the individual who arrives with the last shoot's mud on his footwear, over-trousers, or even on his shooting-stick, does not go unnoticed. Wherever the late Reginald Maulding turned up to shoot, the shoes or boots which he produced from his car bore all the mud from his previous excursions and he made a joke of never cleaning them because it was a waste of time when they would only get muddy again. Though he had one of the finest minds in the Cabinet his laziness was a by-word, and possibly cost him the premiership, as Lord Whitelaw has recorded in his memoirs.

While some hosts make a point of describing the ground rules of the shoot, some omit to do so and any new guest should ascertain, perhaps from the keeper or another guests, what the custom is regarding the shooting of partridges, woodcock, ground game and foxes. For many years I have been unable to shoot a fox, probably because it looks too much like a dog, and, if a host calls for one to be shot, I usually ask my neighbouring guns to oblige, or my loader if I have one. Often I pretend not to have seen 'Charlie' though that excuse soon becomes obvious. Most shoots I attend forbid the shooting of rabbits and hares on safety grounds and, for me now, it is a pleasure to watch the hares approach the line and get safely through it.

When a host has gone to great pains and expense to put birds over his guests he is not likely to be pleased when they sail over and guns are not ready at their stands because they are gossiping. Conversely, he may not warm to the over-keen shot who fires at an early bird while others are still walking to their pegs, on safety grounds alone. It is usually wise to refrain from shooting at pigeons in a drive before the gamebirds begin to show. It probably does no harm but some owners think it does and that is what matters.

It is sensible to assume that, whatever you do, the host will notice it. This will particularly apply to loud talk, laughing at the peg, cursing a dog or slamming car doors.

Greed in the shooting field can take many forms but the errant behaviour which causes commonest offence is firing at a bird, usually a pheasant but often a grouse, which is the prerogative of a neighbouring gun. Few of us are entirely immune to that temptation or of deluding ourselves into believing that we made an honest and forgivable mistake. We are all familiar with, 'Sorry about that but I was already committed when it turned,' and may well have used it ourselves. 'These curling birds are very tricky, aren't they?' is another gambit like, 'I thought you hadn't seen it,' or 'I couldn't see you over that hedge.' In my experience greed, to which too many of us are prone on occasion, is the commonest cause of the loss of invitations. Some guns are such regular offenders that, whenever one turns up at a shoot the rest fervently hope they will not be drawn next to him. Sadly some greedy shots are so thick-skinned that they are immune to criticism or requests. I know one habitual offender who, being deaf, pretends to be even deafer. On being castigated at the end of a drive he puts his hand round the injured party's shoulder and says, 'I'm glad you enjoyed it. So did I'.

Usually, in the interests of the host, it is best to put up with an uncontrollable or deliberate display of greed and hope that he will notice and take some action. Sometimes the host needs to intervene because the greedy gun can be dangerous. Joe Nickerson had a sophisticated way of dealing with the problem when he was a guest. During a drive he would fire two shots in the air at nothing and when asked by the offender why he had done it would reply, 'I just thought I'd let you know that I had a gun.' When he was the host he could be rough with his tongue to the greedy guest and the common consequence was to be dropped for several years or never to be invited again. It is curious, though, that many with well-deserved reputations for being greedy shots continue to be invited. The late Lord Soames, a much-missed friend of mine, revelled in that reputation, never making any excuse or apology, and was consistently asked again because, otherwise, he was such entertaining company.

It is a wise rule never to shoot at birds which a neighbouring gun in the line has allowed to pass because he considered them to be unsportingly low. A certain duke was barred from one fine Wiltshire shoot after he engaged every bird which his host had considered to be too low, killing most of them. The owner was not only sickened by the duke's behaviour but told his friends about it. Prince Charles even disapproved of high birds which he had missed with both barrels being shot behind him by a neighbouring gun and told me so after I had erred in that manner a couple of times, having found the pleasure of wiping the future King's eye irresistible. If I remember rightly, he thought that, having survived two shots, a bird had run its fair gauntlet. The Prince imparted his message with charming diplomacy, which has been the hallmark of such Royals, of several nationalities, whom I have been privileged to meet. On another occasion, while standing next to Prince Charles on a difficult drive, I wounded a high pheasant with my first barrel and did the same with my second. The Prince shot it dead behind me and then walked over to apologize. I was delighted that he had rectified my errors so expeditiously but he was concerned that I might be annoyed because the bird was coming down anyway.

The extent to which some Royals will go to avoid causing offence was never demonstrated with more subtlety than by the last Egyptian monarch, the late King Farouk. According to my diplomatic source, the British Embassy in Cairo had a duck-shoot in the Nile delta to which the ambassador regularly asked the Egyptian ruler. The rather weighty monarch was carried, dry-shod, to his position in a large barrel mounted on stilts in shallow water. When he had been installed, several of his servants waded out bearing wickerwork panniers filled with dead ducks, which had been shot elsewhere. These were scattered around the Royal hide, a procedure which made it inevitable that, however many ducks flew over him, or whatever form he might display, the King would end the shoot with more birds than anybody else.

The purpose of this performance might have been to satisfy the King's vanity but diplomatic enquiries suggested a rather more sophisticated explanation. The King and his entourage were anxious to ensure that his hosts would never be placed in the embarrassing circumstance of having to apologize for giving him an unproductive stand. Nor would His Majesty ever be forced into apologizing for shooting badly. In the countryside, anywhere in the world, things are not always what they seem.

The greedy host, though rare, is an interesting phenomenon but understandable, perhaps, considering the effort and money he puts into the shoot. I have known several with their own special method of ensuring that they will usually be in good positions. The simplest gambit is to issue cards giving each gun his position at each stand. These days it can be claimed that it has been done by computer. One old gentleman of this genre would have no compunction about sending his keeper to inform you that a change had suddenly become necessary for the next drive and you would find that perhaps the one good number on your card was to be enjoyed by mine host while, yet again, you were on the outside. Another host, if out of the action on an exciting drive, would push the whole line down two pegs to bring himself into it, with no feeling of embarrassment whatever. A commoner trick, when the host has drawn a poor number at what he knows will be the best stand, is for him to put in a short extra drive, perhaps a bit of kale that produces only two birds. Because of the convention of moving up two numbers after each drive this brings him that much nearer the desirable peg.

At his own shoot, Broadlands, Lord Mountbatten offered the guns book-matches from a tray with the peg number inside. It was well known that he had the habit of keeping the one with Number 4 on it under his thumb because that got him off to a good start on the first drive. A mutual friend of ours, Dick Wilkins, noticed this — as did the others — for it was a standing joke how the host always drew 4, though he passed it off as just luck. Dick managed to secure eight blank book-matches, marked them all No. 4 and substituted them on the tray. When the first man drew No. 4 Mountbatten gave the game away by insisting 'You can't be Number 4!' knowing that he had No. 4 under his thumb.

Any display of dangerous shooting can cancel out all the good qualities which a game-shot is known to possess, though I have often been astonished by the way certain people known to have developed dangerous habits, perhaps through age, continue to be invited for friendships's sake. While accidents are, happily, uncommon I have witnessed the incredible, more than once. I was in the line at a partridge shoot, in Surrey, when a guest rested the muzzle of his gun on his boot while adjusting his dress. The gun discharged, inflicting such injury that the man fell to the ground. We were a long line of guns enclosing the end of a large field of green stuff and, on seeing what had happened, everyone ran to his aid, save one, and an ambulance was soon arranged. Fortunately the injury was repairable and a slight limp was the only lasting hurt. The interest lies in the identity of the man who did not run. It was Reggie Maudling, who was as kind and as caring as anyone there but indolent.

The most memorable accident I ever witnessed is one which is mentioned in almost every shooting book yet seems so unbelievable that one would think it could never really happen. It was the situation in which a cartridge meant for a 20-bore shot-gun is loaded into a wider-diameter 12-bore gun and is then followed by a 12-bore cartridge so that when the latter is fired, the former explodes inside the barrel and shatters it.

This happened on an occasion when a man, so intelligent that he was a judge, brought his son to a pheasant shoot. He asked his host if it was permissible for his son, who was learning to shoot, to stand with him in the line and take a few easy birds, should any come over his father's position. The judge explained that, as an extra safety measure, he would load his son's gun, which was a 20-bore. When the pheasants were high he would engage them with his own 12-bore.

Half-way through the drive there was an explosion. Both barrels of the judge's gun opened up as though they had been sliced lengthwise and then hammered flat. The rib along the top coiled up like a clock spring and the whole heavy breach snapped off and flew past his son's face, shaving off a tiny piece of skin. Had it hit him it could have taken his head off. Such an accident is usually fatal to the person holding the gun but the judge escaped with the loss of the top joint of his left little finger.

The judge had been waiting with two 20-bore cartridges in his hand to load into the son's gun if a suitable pheasant appeared. At the last moment he had decided to shoot the bird himself and, unwittingly put both cartridges into his own 12-bore gun. As the gun was pointing downwards they both slipped past the breech and lodged in the barrels. Either he did not fire on that occasion or, having pressed the trigger without result, assumed that he must have failed to load the gun at all. A little later he then inserted two 12-bore cartridges and when he eventually fired, all four exploded, shattering the gun.

In the autumn of 1991 a young man, shooting in my area, noticed a peculiar noise when he fired a shot but failed to look down the barrel before loading another cartridge. The previous cartridge, which had been defective, had left a wad in the barrel and when he fired the next one, the rib of the gun stripped itself from the shattered barrel and sliced back into his brain, killing him. If a shot does not sound right the barrel should always be inspected.

The low-flying partridge or grouse is the commonest cause of shooting accidents though I used to attend a famous pheasant shoot where the host, now deceased, would often insist, in a loud voice, 'Shoot 'em all, high or low. I didn't ask you here to let 'em go.' To avoid offence one had to conform, to feign deafness or plead inability to hit low birds, which was usually my excuse. The requirement was similar at a shoot in Hampshire, where the tenants wanted every bird shot, and one was criticized for letting low birds, especially cock pheasants, escape. However, it is always best not to oblige, if only for safety's sake.

Many Europeans shoot at low birds as a matter of custom, seeming to take the view that whatever comes is there to be engaged and to let anything pass makes no sense. This attitude was first brought home to me at close range on a pheasant shoot close to my present home near Hungerford, where one of the regular attenders was the RAF's top wartime fighter pilot, Air Vice-Marshal Johnnie Johnson, who held the record for enemy planes shot down — thirty-eight proven combat victories. His most formidable opponent in air battles over Europe had been Adolf Galland, Hitler's personal Luftwaffe hero, who was credited with many more kills, though many of them had been notched up on the Eastern front, where the opposition had been easier. We were all looking forward to watching General Galland display his marksmanship at pheasants and partridges and to the contest between the two highly decorated former opponents, who had become post-war friends, having established that they had tried to kill each other in at least one 'dog-fight'.

'Dolfo can tap 'em', Johnnie replied when I asked him if the general was a good game shot. It was no exaggeration. After the first drive we could all understand why he had accumulated such a wartime record. Any bird that moved at any altitude or speed was downed, though with due respect to safety, while Johnnie observed the British tradition of letting any easy ones escape.

The usual low bird accident is caused by the gun who fires too close to someone else's butt or swings right through the line and discharges his gun too soon or hits a beater, stop or picker-up. The danger of a ricochet is always there when low-flying birds are engaged close to the line. I am perpetually surprised that there are not more accidental shootings, particularly on grouse moors. I have seen guns, beaters, keepers and pickers-up peppered, with all the ensuing denials about responsibility. Such incidents may be forgiven but they are never forgotten.

The reactions to being involved in a shooting accident are often surprising. I knew a man who shot and killed his father yet remained ardent in the field. Some shots are not deterred even when they are the victims. I know one man who lost an eye shooting and remained as keen and as effective as ever.

The most widely publicized shooting incident in recent years was the occasion when Lord Whitelaw, then Deputy Prime Minister, severely peppered his host, Sir Joseph Nickerson, when shooting grouse. Joe's reaction was exemplary. He would never talk about the incident or have it mentioned in his memoirs and when Whitelaw wanted to give up shooting Joe persuaded him not to. When he was in Darlington Hospital, awaiting the results of X-rays, Joe was told that he might have to undergo surgery because there were pellets in his gut but, while examining the photographs, remarked that he did eat a lot of game. Further photographs showed that the pellets were indeed *en passage*.

On rare occasions it is a bird which inflicts the injury and my nose still bears witness to my being severely struck in the face by a grouse while in a butt on Sir Thomas Sopwith's moor at Arkengarthdale, North Yorkshire. I had shot a fairly high grouse in an approaching covey far out in front of the butt and was concentrating on a second when the dead bird struck me full in the face. It was like being hit by a cricket bat for the vengeful grouse does not fall on its victim but strikes with all its forward momentum and, assisted by the wind, it might, in certain circumstances be lethal. My already outsize nose was broken, my eyes blackened and the bird then struck my loader, with enough force to knock him sideways. Having established that I still had a face left, and stuffing bits of a torn handkerchief up by nostrils to stem the blood loss, I carried on shooting. I bled so severely that when the drive was over, some twenty minutes later — but not before — the guest in the next butt ran over asking 'Are you all right?' When I explained what had happened he exclaimed, 'Thank God! I thought you'd been shot.' The gentleman concerned has always been one to get his priorities right in the shooting field.

While shooting on another Swaledale moor, a couple of years later, my loader, who was new to me, asked me to repeat my name and responded by saying, 'Ah! You must be that feller that was 'it on't nose wi't grouse'. Fame indeed!

Lord Mountbatten received similar cavalier treatment when a friend of mine shot a high pheasant which fell on his Lordship's neck and felled him. Instead of rushing to his aid, the gun responsible remarked to his loader 'That must be a first! Knocking down an Admiral of the Fleet!, and continued to shoot.

A visiting foreign Queen was felled, nastily, by a pheasant on the Sopwith shoot at Compton and next door, at Bossington, where I shot for several seasons, the wife of one friend had to be rushed away with suspected kidney injury after being struck on the back by a falling hen pheasant while she was bending down. Elsewhere, a pheasant, still kicking in its death throes, engaged the trigger of a shotgun and shot the man who had brought it down. Not surprisingly, the newspapers had more sympathy for the bird than for the man, who should never have put down a loaded gun.

Though criminal statistics demonstrate, day after day, the lethality of the shotgun, one still sees examples of cavalier treatment in the shooting field — people jumping onto trailers with loaded guns or even entering vehicles, when the driver is in a hurry, while walking guns are regularly seen stepping over wire or negotiating fences with the gun, perhaps broken, but with cartridges still in the chambers. With guns the most remarkable things can happen. One even hears of a gun going off while the owner was cleaning it!

Next to being dangerous with a gun, the worst social sin is to depart with someone else's, as I once did, with unfortunate effect, at the height of the pheasant season. We had been shooting with single guns and mine and that of another guest had brown canvas covers. They were kindly put in our cars by a servant and, foolishly, neither of us checked them until we reached our homes — mine in Berkshire, the other man's in Norfolk, where he was a member of the Queen's Household at Sandringham. As we were both busy the arrangements for the exchange, in London, were complicated and time-consuming. After that I marked my covers with red ribbon. It is essential for every guest, after thanking the host, hostess and the keeper, to ensure that he has every item of his own equipment. Over-trousers left in someone else's vehicles are the commonest cause of apologetic telephone calls and I have offended that way more than once.

Good form in the house-guest demands even more exacting standards than for the 'day-boy'. It is necessary to find out, in advance, whether dogs are allowed in the house and it is safest to assume that they are not, unless invited to bring them in.

The thoughtful guest will be ready to leave immediately after breakfast on departure day. Hanging about can be a nuisance but there can also be serious snags to an earlier departure. When staying at Sandbeck Park with the Earl of Scarbrough, my wife and I announced, on the last evening, that we would forgo breakfast and leave at 6.30 a.m. Our host insisted that he would come down and see us off but, wishing to avoid disturbing him so early, we crept down with our bags and opened the front door, setting off all the burglar alarms. With customary good humour, Lord Scarbrough appeared in his dressing-gown and predicted that, within five minutes, three police cars would converge on the house from different directions of the parkland. They were dead on time and we could not save face by taking off because we would have been apprehended as suspects.

As with all good things, shooting in the 'Big League' does not last forever and when, after several successive years of enjoyment at a shoot, no invitation comes one wonders why. It is inevitable that ageing guns will be squeezed out by the young, which is how most people get into the charmed circle in the first place. The right attitude is simply to be thankful for the past favours. Indeed, the great mystery to me is always why I was ever asked in the first place.

CHAPTER 20

A BREED APART

Ghillies and keepers form a breed apart which should never be allowed to become extinct, though they will do so if those opposed to country sports achieve their objectives of securing Parliamentary bans on fishing and shooting. Scottish ghillies, on salmon rivers, the type specimens of fishing keepers, are worth their weight in expensive tackle for they know where the takers lie and where the snagging rocks are — 'Bonny Scotland!', as they remark when an angler is stuck on the bottom. They know where it is unsafe to wade and they contribute to those memories which are the lasting values of the sport. They can be memorable themselves, through their dourness or hilarious company on the river banks, in their boats or in their huts. Ghillies are constantly meeting different people under conditions where friendship, or occasionally dislike, develops and so become unusually worldly-wise about human nature. Many qualify as 'characters' who are never forgotten by those whom they serve. Like anglers they come in all shapes and sizes and, now, in all sexes. I have encountered a young lady ghillie on the Wye who had spent the previous night in the local disco but performed most creditably. I have also met a lady gamekeeper who is experienced enough to have published a book about her work.

While being loyal they can be irreverent about their masters. For many years I fished opposite the famous Inchmarlo beat of the Aberdeenshire Dee where the old ghillie, Wilkie, had strong views about the extramural activities of his laird. On one bright March day when the ghillie on my side shouted across the water to ask why the laird and his guests were not fishing, Wilkie's reply rang down the river, 'They're awa' ty Edinburgh on a drinking and whoooring expedition.'

The ghillie on my side of the Dee at that time, Frank Brown, is credited with a famous riposte when an angler, who was fishless for the week, caught a salmon almost with his last cast and remarked, 'That fish has cost me £100' — a large sum in those days. 'A good job, then, that ye did'na get two!' Brown replied, disapproving of such a mercenary approach to the king of sports. It was also Brown, I believe, who remarked, looking upstream towards Balmoral, that the Dee would remain unpolluted 'as long as there's a monarch up the glen'. I was not amused, however, by the riposte of the ghillie on the Welsh Dee after he had gaffed out a large salmon before it had time to realize it was hooked and therefore gave me no sport — 'They catch cold if you leave them in there'.

With others the humour tends to be unconscious but, none the less, hilarious for that. When I had the pleasure of fishing the Wye, at Ross-on-Wye, through the kindness of the late Sir Charles Clore, the ghillie there was aptly named Moody. He would follow me down the pools spinning with great skill and shouting 'Damn!' whenever he hooked a salmon, as though he was embarrased, which he certainly was not.

On Moody's beat there was one pool called the Lavatory because, in previous years, there had been a privy there for the use of anglers. It was my favourite pool with fairly fast water which could be fished from both sides — a rather pleasant change from the other canal-like pools set between steep clay banks. Sensing my boredom after a fruitless morning on the clay banks, Moody shouted in a loud voice across the river to my wife, 'Mr Chapman Pincher looks as though he wants to go to the Lavatory,' a remark which, momentarily, she misintepreted. It was, in fact, easy to slip into the habit because, on a later occasion when my wading staff had slipped down a steep bank into deep water, I explained to Moody that I had lost it in the Lavatory, and wanted him to scrabble about in it to try and find it, which would have sounded very odd to a stranger.

Some ghillies are frankly superstitious, sometimes in quite extraordinary ways. One day, while fishing Red Gorton, a famous beat of the Tay, I took a salmon of about twelve pounds within ten minutes of starting to tow a huge plug bait on a long line behind a motor-boat, the recommended but boring method for the height of water we encountered. The ghillie looked dismal as he boated the fish and commented, 'I dinna like that. We won't get another one. You never do when you get one right awa'. Naturally, I was determined to prove him wrong but, though my wife and I caught kelt after kelt, we never hooked another fresh fish all day.

My favourite ghillie, Bob Grant of the Kinnaird beat of the Tay, expressed the same fear when my wife caught a fish almost immediately. He proved to be right too, though the superstition makes no sense whatever. Incidentally, Bob Grant is possibly unique in that he has a big identical scar across the palm of each hand. Years ago he cut his left hand badly with broken glass and, unfortunately a bit was left in. He went into hospital to have it removed after an X-ray had shown where the bit was and, by a stupid error, they operated on the right hand. When they found their mistake they operated on the left hand so he has surgical scars on both. Sadly it happened before the days when patients sued hospitals for negligence.

My least favourite ghillie operated on a beat of the Aberdeenshire Dee for many years and alienated many of his rods by repeatedly demanding whisky. In fact, his introductory remark to my wife and I when we arrived on the first day of a week's fishing, said without humour, was, 'I hope you have plenty of whusky. Because nae whusky nae fush!' Though we provided him with a bottle, he was soon helping himself to ours, though his behaviour on the day the owner joined us was suddenly very different.

It always pays to offer whisky because some ghillies, while saying nothing, will otherwise avoid putting their charges over the best lies, especially when rowing boats. In my experience they represent a small minority and, these day, many ghillies decline to drink at all on the river-bank.

Occasionally one meets a ghillie who is an outstandingly successful fisherman. There was a Deesider called Willie Stevenson who had a battered spinning rod shaped like a banana but, time after time, he caught fish following me down a pool while using the same bait — usually a sprat. Another Deeside ghillie, the late Ken Robinson, was the most beautiful Spey caster I have seen, though, in reality he was a retired businessman who chose to spend his retirement that way. He had a bottomless fund of wonderful stories told with the skill of a professional comedian, so a day when the salmon were scarce or unobliging was one long laugh.

I have learned a lot from Ken and other ghillies, especially about salmon lies. One thing they do most skilfully is to row the boat in big rivers. It looks so easy but I learned how difficult it is when fishing the Norwegian river Driva, which is much more powerful than it appears. The ghillie advised me not to take the boat out when my wife and I decided to fish after supper but it was too tempting. I was soon out of control in the heavy current and we would have been swept down rapids had I not dropped the oars and grabbed an overhanging willow. Sadly, many river boats have now been motorized.

Ghillies do not like it when their advice is ignored and it usually pays to humour them, for example, by trying the fly of their choice, even if only for a short time. On the other hand, it is very satisfying to prove a ghillie wrong, by catching a salmon where he says it is useless to fish, for instance. I have done this several times in the spring when the ghillie has assured me that it would be a waste of time to fish the white water in the neck of a pool but I always carefully avoided making too much of his confusion because, most times, he would have been right.

When I began to fish for salmon in 1950 it was standard practice on every beat I experienced to gaff the fish — really an appalling thing to do if it can possibly be avoided. Now fish are gently beached or netted and can be returned virtually unharmed to the river if not wanted. In the only Icelandic river I have fished the ghillies got in behind the played-out fish and kicked them out of the water, never losing one in the time I was there.

One should never be overawed by a ghillie even if he has spent most of his life on the beat. The redoubtable Lady Sopwith showed how to deal with the ill-tempered ghillie when first taken up to fish the Delfur beat of the Spey. On entering the boat she asked the old ghillie how far she should cast her spinning bait into the famous Two Stones pool. Not approving of women anglers, especially beginners, he replied, somewhat scathingly, 'As fur as ye can'. With that, she put the bait into a bush on the opposite bank and quietly asked the ghillie to go and retrieve it. From then on they became good friends.

Ghillies can be unforgiving, however, if they feel they have been professionally affronted. Fishing Frank Brown's beat on the Dee as a guest of Joe Little, a rumbustious fish dealer from Aberdeen, I was using one of the first glass-fibre spinning rods, which had been sent to me by the makers for test. When the day was ending and we were all due to pack up to attend a theatre in Aberdeen, I hooked a salmon which behaved as though it was really large. Being determined to get it I played it gently, especially as I had begun to suspect that it was foul-hooked. Brown and Joe encouraged me to give it more stick and, as I did so, the rod, which was solid, not hollow as glass rods are now, snapped at the butt. While I operated the reel on the butt, Brown held the severed rod. In the half-light, Brown stuck the gaff into the salmon and heaved it on the bank, immediately shouting, in horror, 'It's a bloody kelt!' It weighed about fifteen pounds and was hooked in the back. It was an offence to gaff a kelt and several people, including two other ghillies who were unlikely to keep quiet about it, had seen Brown do it. Our relationship was never the same.

While some gamekeepers appear to be taciturn, because they find it pays not to say too much, others have such a mischievous sense of humour that they cannot resist an opportunity to display it. Such a man was Alf Fry, the head keeper to Sir Thomas Sopwith at Compton Manor where, week after week, he 'got his cards' from her Ladyship when anything went wrong. Angus Ogilvy was a frequent guest and, on one occasion when his wife, HRH Princess Alexandra, accompanied him and decided to join the beaters for the joy of the exercise, Alf insisted on paying her a beater's wages at the end of the day. She was quite touched as she pocketed the £3 saying 'All the years I've beaten elsewhere and I've never been paid before!' Sir Thomas was greatly amused but called Fry to the presence with a charge of 'I hear you've been insulting the Royals again.'

Gamekeepers, who get little chance to shoot at driven birds, tend to be caustic about sportsmen who put up a poor performance. After one of them had counted the birds shot and the cartridges expended after one drive he exclaimed 'Fifty-four for two! Sounds more like a cricket score.' Another, who was loading for me at a shoot attended by several admirals, remarked, 'You might as well give them bladders on sticks!' However, I have noticed that they may not perform so well themselves when given the chance. There is one drive called The Plantation at Ramsbury Manor where the pheasants used to pour out so high that most of them outwitted the guns. On one occasion one of the several local keepers who acted as loaders to make some extra cash remarked on the poor bag to the resident keeper. Later that season a day was therefore arranged for these keepers to try their skill. Plenty of cock pheasants flew over them and they succeeded in shooting just one of them.

Keepers can also be scathing about what they consider to be amateurs who are brought in to run shoots. One of them was loading for me at a shoot in Suffolk run by a retired Admiral and after I had remarked on the paucity of pheasants at what had previously been a productive stand he said, 'Well, Sir, would you hire a gamekeeper to fight the battle of Trafalgar?'

As with ghillies, keepers' humour is often unconscious, like the unforgettable remark made loudly to me by one, Cotter, as we walked up a field of green stuff in Anglesey 'Don't shoot that cat, Sir,' quickly followed, in muffled tone, by 'Too near the 'ouse'.

Often, one never knows the hidden reasons behind the behaviour of a keeper which may look odd but happens to be soundly based and I have, occasionally, kicked myself when I have learned the truth. I was once stupid enough to give a sharp rebuke to one of Joe Nickerson's staff on his grouse moor at Reeth, in North Yorkshire. I was in the right-hand end butt and a beat keeper was sitting in the heather with a rolled-up flanking flag doing absolutely nothing as several coveys flew over the empty butts beyond me. At the end of the drive I berated him for failing to flag them towards me and, though he said nothing, I found out later that Joe had ordered him to let them pass because, in a poorish season, he was conserving stock for later shoots.

Though I know it only from a second-hand source, a fox-hunting misunderstanding has remained in my memory ever since I heard it long ago. It concerned a gamekeeper who was driving a Land-Rover on his master's estate, which was being visited by the local foxhounds. One of the mounted hunt officials passed by with a couple of hounds, which had become detached from the pack, and he asked the gamekeeper to put them in the back of his vehicle and hold them until the end of the day, which was drawing to a close. The gamekeeper declined, apologetically. The irate official insisted that he take the hounds under threat of being reported for insolence to his master. Again, the keeper expressed his regrets but refused.

That evening he was not surprised to be called to his master's presence for a dressing down but it never came because he had the perfect explanation. Knowing that the owner liked to produce a fox for the hunt on his land and aware, as was the owner, that most of the foxes had been eliminated in the interests of the pheasants, he had taken the precaution of trapping one and had it in a bag in the back of his vehicle. His intention was to let it go at a suitable spot if the huntsmen failed to find which, in fact, they did not. As he explained to the owner, the rumpus if two hounds had been put in the back with the bag-fox was not hard to imagine.

While gamekeepers are almost constantly in contact with lethal weapons, ghillies have a greater risk of being killed in the course of their duties. All the major Scottish salmon rivers have taken their toll through drownings and, in spite of this, most of the ghillies I continue to meet cannot swim. They are forever crossing most dangerous places in boats, sometimes in heavy water, yet are almost certain to drown should they fall in. Fortunately, some of them are now being required by their employers to wear inflatable safety collars which would keep them afloat.

Most technological advances carry penalities of some kind and one which has inflicted lethal consequences on ghillies is the long salmon fly-rod made of carbon fibre. A young ghillie of my acquaintance, on the Middle Blackhall beat of the Dee, was one of the first to suffer the new hazard. While returning from the river, after trying out the new rod, it touched an overhead electric cable and an 11,000 volts discharge killed him instantly. He was alone and his body was not discovered until after nightfall when the ghillie from the next beat, Ian Anderson, an old journalistic friend of mine, was asked to search the bank. Believing that his young neighbour must have had a heart attack, he eventually picked up the rod and touched the cable, receiving a similar shock which threw him down the road. Though burned, he was saved from death by the rubber boots he was wearing. However tragic for a while, life goes on and, later, Ian received from his granddaughter a T-shirt bearing a clenched fist grasping an electric flash and the words 'Grand-dad — Tested to 11,000 volts!'.

River keepers on trout streams are less likely to be drowned or electrocuted but they are constantly threatened by the horrible affliction called Weil's disease, an infection transmitted in the urine of rats. This used to be limited to underground miners but the modern practice of feeding trout on food pellets has extended it to the river-bank. Rats thrive on the pellets and they quickly find any bin which has not been securely covered by a lid. Several river keepers who have handled contaminated pellets have died as a result and, apart from ensuring that bins are covered, they should always use a scoop when feeding the pellets to the fish. Gamekeepers have also been infected by pheasant pellets and grain in dispensers which have been patronized by rats. One of them, on a shoot within a few miles of my home was desperately ill but happily recovered.

A most serious hazard which now besets gamekeepers and ghillies alike is the risk of being seriously injured by violent poacher gangs armed with silenced .22 rifles or .410 shotguns. The abolition of the death penalty for murder and the general spread in the carrying of weapons by criminals, have been followed by an upsurge in violence from poachers who have been disturbed while about their thieving. Like terrorists, they wear camouflaged suits and balaclavas and resort to intimidation of keepers' families by telephone calls. In the present state of the law, especially in England, they are likely to be given ridiculously light sentences if caught, on the usual plea that, being unemployed, they have been driven to poaching to feed their families. It seems unlikely that magistrates will ever regard deliberate poaching as theft because the image of the old villager taking a salmon or a pheasant for the pot still lingers. Most magistrates are loath to take away a car caught in use by professional poachers though it might be stuffed with pheasants or salmon. Poachers are usually on the dole because their night work augments their income sufficiently and they are able to convince the bench that without a car they cannot look for work. In fact, the car is the poacher's main technological asset, enabling him to reach river beats and coverts, which were inaccessible before and to remove his kills and sell them many miles away. Even when poachers are caught with night vision apparatus, silencers, portable radios and high-tech lamps, the courts are inclined to be lenient because, in purely legal terms, poaching is not theft.

Of course, the murderous poacher is not new. There is a lane-side cross near my home in memory of a policeman shot by poachers more than a hundred years ago. It is not long since the keeper on a famous shoot was cold-bloodedly shot in the face by a poacher who was jailed for three years for the offence. Understandably, the victim did not feel very secure when the villain emerged after only eighteen months but he did not have to worry for long. The poacher was given to sexual experiments, one of which involved putting a rope round his own neck. One of them went wrong and he suffered the ultimate penalty.

The keeper who had been shot could hardly be expected to grieve over the self-inflicted death of his old enemy and ghillies of my acquaintance were equally undistressed when they discovered the body of a notorious salmon poacher drowned in his own net. It was one less to force them to spend their nights on watch. They were astonished, however, when not long afterwards, the dead poacher's son was caught netting salmon.

Ghillies are also plagued by tackle thieves who break into their riverside huts and steal anything to hand. I have myself lost tackle that way on the Wye. The huts are sometimes so easy to break into that I have done it myself when inadvertently locked out on a bitterly cold day with the ghillie far away. On the whole, though, fishing huts have afforded me much comfort and pleasure, some of them being such a pride that they could almost be described as palatial, with armchairs in which one can snooze around the wood stove for a few minutes after lunch. I know one — at Dalguise on the Tay — which boasts a chandelier. Another, at Inchmarlo on the Dee, is a chalet with beds, while the main hut on the Littlecote trout water lies athwart the Kennet, providing a splendid setting for an evening rise supper with views through picture windows, upstream and down.

Shooting lodges tend to be truly palatial; the extraordinary Norwegian chalet built for the Longwood shoot by Ronnie Lyon even having showers for the beaters. The walls of the Lodge at Well Barn are replete with stuffed game-birds while those of Kinveachie on Speyside are decorated with the heads and antlers of bigger game.

Like the bent policeman, the crooked gamekeeper or ghillie holds a position of trust which is easily exploited. Some have been caught selling their own deer or salmon while others have turned blind eyes to poachers for a share of the proceeds. Hard evidence that a keeper or ghillie is behaving dishonestly provides the only sound reason for a guest to pass on criticism to his host and, even then, it is a difficult choice which can have unfortunate consequences. A shooting friend who is also a game-dealer knew that I was friendly with the owner of an estate and telephoned me one November evening with information which worried him. My friend's keeper had offered to sell him 200 live hen pheasants and he felt that the owner ought to be told. I had been shooting there and one big drive had produced only three pheasants, at which the keeper had affected total astonishment, assuring his master that there had been hundreds there when he had fed them on the previous evening. Enquiries showed that the keeper was heavily in debt and had been selling birds all over the county. He was duly sacked but the whole shoot was closed down by the disgusted owner — another one off my list! I lost another, which I had attended for many years, after remarking to a guest, who passed it on, that the keeper, who was brilliant at driving the birds away from the guns, was President of the Pheasant Preservation Society.

It was a regularly employed ghillie who showed me a method of foul-hooking salmon with a fly rod which was unbelievably simple, provided there were a few fish in a pool. He assured me that our host, who was renting the beat and had left early, was aware what he was doing because he needed to catch some fish to help pay the rent when the river was low and the salmon were not taking well. That must have been true because my wife and I who witnessed the process could easily have reported the ghillie to our host and he was not in the least concerned that we might.

Few would ever think of leaving a salmon river without tipping the ghillie but many keepers on trout waters, who may do even more work, consistently miss out. It is for the services which we do not see that ghillies and keepers should be tipped, rather than for what they actually do for us, as so much of their work is done in the closed season. Nevertheless, most anglers and shots base the tip on the day in question, which may be poor because of bad weather. It generally repays to err on the side of generosity, especially when fortunate enough to be asked with only five or six guns instead of the usual eight.

Even when a poor day is obviously the keeper's fault, it is customary to give the usual tip but the occasional gun is made of sterner stuff. When a day at a shoot in Norfolk had been a shambles, Guy Moreton, a brilliant shot for whom only the best was good enough, was quietly asked by the other guns, 'What should the keeper get?' Moreton who was already in his car shouted 'The sack!' and drove away.

CHAPTER 21

ENEMIES OF THE COUNTRYSIDE

The countryside is increasingly beset with serious problems and every one of them derives from a single case — the pressure of excessive human population. The cities and towns are expanding remorselessly, gnawing away at fields and woodland. Distant areas of countryside are suddenly condemned as authorities prescribe the creation of new towns and 'model' villages for 'overspill'. In existing villages expansion is contrived by developers using every kind of inducement, device and dodge to introduce their chainsaws and bulldozers — enemies of the environment worldwide. Never send to know for whom the chainsaw whines; it whines for thee. Enormous areas are progressively covered with motorways, airports, industrial estates and science parks, green fields often being cheaper than the refurbishment of existing sites which become derelict. There is a rapidly-growing concept that the remaining countryside, including its farmland and private estates, is a free leisure park for everyone's enjoyment at will.

The rivers have been monstrously polluted by the products of industry and human bodies and their water is so cavalierly abstracted for commercial and domestic consumption that many of them are being reduced to trickles or cease to run at all. The air is so fouled by chemical by-products from power-stations, factories and vehicles that distant forests are dying from the effects of acid rain. These evils all derive from the fact that there are simply too many people for such a small island. And since it is politically unpopular even to point to the main cause, the only measures that can be taken are temporary stopgaps — piecemeal botching.

So long as the population increases, concrete will continue to obliterate the countryside like a lava flow. The M4 motorway, which connects Berkshire and Wiltshire with London, has its advantages but, when using it, the observant countryman cannot help but deplore the colossal swath of natural beauty which it consumed. The same is true of all the other motorways with their adjacent services, filling-stations, lorry parks, supermarkets and the industry and housing they inevitably attract. Country house hunters are quickly made aware how difficult it has become to find a property free from the irritating hum of traffic on motorways or busy main roads. More and more roads are becoming illuminated at night so that there is no darkness over much of Britain, as satellite pictures demonstrate.

The one benefit of economic recessions is the slowing down of the rape of the countryside. When times are good, developers who, enjoy a degree of personal prosperity which seems excessive to others, are ingenious at contriving methods of circumventing restrictions. Sites are secured for light industry on the grounds that country towns and villages need jobs for the young residents. When the industry is not quickly forthcoming, permission is granted for the same ground to be used for houses, which are eventually occupied by incomers, often urban invaders. Any remnant of a field is seized upon for 'just filling-in'. Too many villages are cursed by incomers who buy large houses with several surrouding acres and then eventually wear down the opposition to the building of houses in the grounds. The perpetrator then escapes from the eyesore he has created, moving on to another village to repeat the destructive process there. Developers now proffer inducements such as a 'free' park or recreation centre if permission is granted to build several hundred houses. They are assisted by former town-dwellers who move to villages and then agitate for the amenities they previously enjoyed — street lighting, pavements going far beyond the village and recreational facilities like bowling alleys. The building of golf courses is a currently successful device. Once built, there is pressure to build a club house, then a hotel and staff houses.

Sadly, the economics of farming are encouraging the loss of agricultural land to such 'amenities'. Modern methods of food production are so efficient that less land is needed and farmers are being bribed to set it aside by attractive payments. Further permanent inroads are inevitable as developers press for set-aside land on farm peripheries to be made available for building.

Additionally, the intensive farming methods which have proved so productive have caused massive damage to the overall environment. Thousands of miles of ancient hedgerows have been uprooted to make way for prairie-style farming with the resulting dreary monoculture destroying the once varied beauty of the countryside and the habitats of much of its wildlife.

Weedkillers and pesticides have done tremendous damage to wildlife. The burning of straw to save money has caused such unnecessary air pollution and unpleasant inconvenience that it has, at last, been prohibited by law. Heather moorland has been covered with alien conifers, often to secure tax benefits. Excessive quantities of fertilizers have so increased the concentration of nitrates in rivers that the plant life they harbour has been adversely affected. For the first few weeks of each season the entire bottom of the river Kennet becomes infested with a brown alga which breaks away and rises in floating lumps resembling sewage. Its cause seems to be in no doubt — the excessive amount of nitrates seeping into the river from fields treated with fertilizers to maximize crops. The quantity of fly life on most rivers has enormously declined, possibly for the same reason. Slurry and silage effluent has repeatedly poisoned long stretches of rivers. So deleterious are the results of intensive agriculture than, for many environmentalists and country dwellers, some farmers should be listed among the enemies of the countryside.

River pollution, of course, is centuries old and the extent to which people watched and did little as their waters were ruined by industrial greed is eloquent testimony of the public apathy about their surroundings. At one time every British river was clean enough to carry its quota of salmon. I am old enough to have witnessed the demise of the River Tees as a salmon river — in the later 1920s. Until then some adult salmon had managed to get through the polluted estuary and I recall seeing scores of dead kelts, which had spawned successfully, and being so excited, on one occasion, that I fixed one to my hook and pushed it into the stream to see what playing a salmon would be like. Then a further increase in the cyanide in the estuary from coke ovens there began to kill all the smolts as they tried to get down to the sea. Looking back, it is extraordinary how industrialists were able to do this deliberately and with no penalty.

River pollution is now totally unnecessary in view of technological advances capable of preventing it. Some rivers like the Thames, the Tyne and the Wear have been so greatly improved that salmon have reappeared in them but in many others the deterioration has continued. In spite of new legislation, industrialists are still able to pollute once lovely streams on the grounds that forcing them to purify their poisonous effluents would make their products uncompetitive and threaten jobs. Yet when forced to take preventive action their sales do not seem to suffer. When factories are prevented from releasing their effluent into rivers they often pay a contractor to take it away and dealing with it becomes his responsibility. Some of it still ends up in rivers, as I learned as far back as fifty years ago when, as part of my army duties, I needed to visit the Royal Ordnance Factory at Bridgend in Wales. There was a small but regular amount of extremely corrosive fluid emerging, at intervals, from a pipe and the authorities put out tenders for a contractor to remove it. The lowest tender was submitted by a local man who set up barrels under a tarpaulin and came regularly with a wheelbarrow to take the full ones away. Eventually, the authorities decided that they should find out what the man was doing with the liquid and, with some reluctance, the contractor explained that he was bottling it and selling it as lavatory cleaner which was in short supply. Though this meant that the effluent was getting into some river through the drains the man kept the contract, perhaps as a reward for ingenuity.

Some of the most environmentally unpleasant effluent today reaches rivers through the domestic drains — the foam created by the massive quantities of detergents used in homes. By chance, I was probably the first to draw wide public attention to this new burden as far back as 1952. Because of my interest in fishing I was telephoned by a river mill-owner who reported that huge masses of froth were floating down the River Arun, in Sussex and blowing on to the fields. A water expert had already dismissed the phenomenon as a climatic effect but, together, we traced the froth upstream to a communal laundry which was using large amounts of detergent. Eventually, as the practice spread, the froth began to appear on more and more rivers but, because no solution has been found, many rivers remain befouled by foam.

Another of my individual efforts to draw attention to pollution was less than sucessful. I had the pleasure of fishing a certain beat on a little Scottish river where, in April, the salmon were stacked in the pools like sardines. There was only one drawback — the sewage effluent from a nearby town flowed into one of the best pools and, especially on a warm day, the stench, as well as the sight, could be unbearable. The laird could have brought pressure to bear on the local authority but felt disinclined to do so because he did not wish to be seen pushing his own interests against those of the councillors, who were saving on the rates by failing to install an effective sewage system. The only answer was to try to bring some pressure to bear on him.

One member of the regular fishing team was the then Lord Chancellor, the late Viscount Dilhorne, and his solemn advice, over brandy and cigars, was that one of us should be photographed fishing the offending pool in a gas-mask and that news of that event should be leaked to the local newspaper. Naturally, it would not be dignified for the Lord Chancellor of England to be photographed in such a circumstance and the others all demurred for different reasons. So the short straw was drawn by me. A wartime gas-mask was produced by our hotelier and I fished away in the pool which received the stinking effluent, and was photographed in colour. The event was duly reported in the local paper, commented upon and seen by the laird. Sadly, he did not turn his attention to the local authority. He turned his rage on the anglers who were sacked from the beat, Lord Chancellor and all. Like the laird, we were not amused.

Even more damaging than pollution is the excessive abstraction of water from rivers and the underground supplies on which they depend. Just as African peoples are outbreeding their food supply, residents in many parts of Britain are outbreeding the supply of water. The Kennet is a fair example of the results. A succession of dry seasons has lowered the level of the water stored in the Wiltshire chalk, which usually keeps the river topped up, but, while this could be shrugged off as a temporary occurrence which the weather should eventually put right, there is a permanent threat in the form of the expanding population in the Swindon area. The quantities of water being abstracted from the Kennet and its catchment zones for domestic and industrial use are so great that it is unlikely that the river can ever return to its former level, however hard it may rain. Many of its tributaries, which formerly harboured water plants and the insects and crustaceans that fed the trout, are now too shallow to do so. Some have dried up completely. The re-opening of the nearby Kennet-Avon canal for longboat traffic has seriously exacerbated the problem. It is joined to the Kennet, which feeds it at various points, and every time a lock is used many thousands more gallons are sent on their way from the river to the sea via the Thames.

Describing a stream, Tennyson wrote — and we all believed him — 'For men may come and men may go, but I go on forever'. It is no longer true.

Forty years ago I was able to draw public attention to a particularly scandalous aspect of air pollution when attending a meeting of the British Association in Liverpool. I reported in the *Daily Express*, then with a daily readership of about 11 million, that sulphur fumes were belching from Britain's chimneys at such a rate that 9 million tons of sulphuric acid were being formed in the air every year. Figures released at the meeting showed that the coal-burning power-stations were the main culprits. Re-reading the article I wrote at the time, and to which the paper gave prominence, it was a spirited plea for action by the power-station authorities or by the Government. Yet no action of consequence was taken, the inevitable argument being that removing the offensive fumes would be too expensive. Further, there was little public comment, though, a short while previously, in December 1952, a London smog which temporarily concentrated the sulphur fumes fourfold, had caused more than 4000 deaths. Five years later, the British Medical Association published the results of an inquiry showing that at least 2000 people were being murdered by slow poison in the polluted air of London every year, the number throughout the country probably being about 10,000. The sooty smoke represented 10 million tons of unburned coal. The Clean Air Act got rid of the smoke but not the sulphuric acid. The term 'acid rain' had not then been invented and it took the best part of thirty years for the inevitable damage to forests and lakes to become apparent. So severe is it in some Scottish lochs that they are being treated with large amounts of lime to neutralize the acid, so that trout and other life can, hopefully, thrive again.

The density of traffic on Britain's roads is now so great the exhaust fumes are a major contributor to air pollution. Of course, it is worst in big cities where, in London for instance, in 1992, many people suffered from asthmatic attacks when a blanket of fog concentrated the traffic pollution. It must still be considerable where motorways run through the country. It had been known for centuries that lead was poisonous yet only recently has action been taken to reduce the amount of it belched into the air by petrol-burning vehicles.

The car has done more to damage country interests than just by pollution. Parked cars are ruining the beauty of village streets while villages with heavy through traffic suffer severely in many ways. When this is relieved by bypasses thousands of further acres of land are consumed. To the countryman, the millions of birds and mammals killed by vehicles is sickening.

My first recollection of this slaughter was in the late 1920s when the first real surge of motor traffic killed thousands of thrushes, blackbirds and less common species on the Great North Road, which was littered with squashed corpses. After a few years the numbers of deaths declined, perhaps because the birds became more traffic-wise but the density now is so great that few birds flying low across a dual or triple carriageway have much chance of survival. Bill Meldrum, the head keeper at Sandringham, believes that more than 1000 game-birds, mainly wild pheasants from the estate, are killed on the local highways each year and, from the end of August onwards, most of us who live near big shoots see the mutilated carcasses of pheasants killed on the roads every day. There is a lull in the road carnage from the end of January, but it begins again in the spring, when some of those which survived the previous season appear again on roads.

My estimate of pheasants killed on the roads each season in the few square miles surrounding my village on the Berkshire/Hampshire/ Wiltshire borders totals several thousands. As the victims tend to be well-grown birds the financial loss, nationally, must be huge, making a significant contribution to the overall costs of running shoots. Much of this waste could be avoided if motorists and lorry drivers took reasonable care. Many do not. Most birds can take avoiding action if they see a vehicle approaching at not more than 35 miles per hour. Unless a driver is prepared to slow down to that speed, at least, a bird has little chance. Some drivers, especially the younger ones, derive amusement from seeing a cloud of feathers and will drive through a whole brood — mother and chicks. My wife and I regularly use a back road on which several pheasants are killed every day and we have never hit one.

In desperation, some landowners put up notices about game-birds on the roads asking motorists to take care. Several which were erected near the town of Hungerford, not long after the human massacre there, were riddled with shotgun pellets by someone, possibly a poacher, wishing to show what he thought about them!

While the reared pheasant may never learn to be traffic conscious the rooks watching by the verges of motorways for invertebrates surfaced by the vibration are amazingly agile, though they occasionally push their luck too far. Magpies, making regular use of the carrion, rarely fall victim, their judgement of an oncoming vehicle's speed being superb. Sadly, hares have no such sense and the appalling impact of traffic on their numbers continues unabated, most of the deaths occurring in darkness. How hedgehogs manage to keep their numbers up is a mystery. A survey in Denmark, which is much smaller than Britain, suggested that between 70,000 and 100,000 hedgehogs are run over each year. The premium for peaceful existence is rising — for the birds and the mammals, including us.

Greed for speed is but one aspect of human cupidity which has hit the countryside. Equally offensive, if not more, is the devastation of the natural stocks of salmon by commercial netting in both the rivers and the seas — leagalized poaching in the angler's view. I have already explained how the atomic-powered submarine, *Nautilus*, inadvertently discovered the main feeding grounds of the Atlantic salmon. When the atomic bomb fell on Hiroshima, Lord Beaverbrook insisted that the headline should be 'The Bomb that Changed the World'. It certainly changed the world of the salmon. In no time, the Greenlanders were taking 2200 tons of salmon in a year, many of them immature fish bred in Britain, Ireland and Canada to which they had previously returned to spawn. The lightweight nylon net permitted them to make such huge catches because miles of it could be operated and, being invisible, the salmon could not evade it. The Greenlanders are now down to below 300 tons, partly because they have murdered the stock but also because of controls forced upon them. Serious inroads are also being made by professional sea fisherman using long-line methods. Motor vessels use nylon lines thousands of yards long carrying hundreds of hooks baited with brislings hanging down into the water from the line, which is held up by cork buoys. It takes about two and a half hours to bait and pay out the line which is left to drift with the current for about six hours.

The North Atlantic Salmon Conservation Organisation has reduced the quota which the Greenlanders may take but not what British netsmen extract. Inevitably when the Greenland bonanza became common knowledge, British trawlermen began to take their share as the fish returned to our eastern shores. In 1963 this was prohibited off Scotland by the Scottish authorities in the interests of their rivers but, incredibly, the English allowed trawling to continue off the coasts of Northumberland and Yorkshire. I have never ceased to be astonished as to why the Scots put up with it, especially as almost all the fish taken off the English coast are returning to Scottish rivers to spawn. Only after almost thirty years, when so much damage has been done, did the Government move, in late 1991, waiting until the situation was almost inoperable before deciding on the surgery. Sea-netting of salmon in the North Sea is to be phased out, but only slowly.

Equally reprehensible, in my opinion, is the way that river netsmen have been allowed to continue their slaughter of the salmon. To combat sea-netting, the Atlantic Salmon Trust was formed in 1969 with the prime intention of ending or at least reducing the damage being inflicted by the Greenland nets, in particular. I was invited to become a Council member to give guidance on Press relations and was most enthusiastic until I realized, after attending several meetings, that some of the most influential Council members were commercially involved in the netting of rivers, like the Tay. It seemed crazy to me that people should be asked to donate money to a Trust to stop salmon being caught in sea-nets when one inevitable result would be that the river-nets would catch many of them instead. I argued that before we could legitimately generate publicity to put international pressure on the Greenlanders we should get our own house in order. I received no support on that score so I quit. I did so quietly at the request of the Director, who was a personal friend, and even allowed my name to continue to appear as a member when I should have ensured that my reason for leaving received the widest publicity.

Since then, netting has been progressively reduced on several important rivers, such as the Aberdeenshire Dee, but in almost every instance the action was not taken until the damage became almost irreversible. The netting interests claimed to have been waiting for scientific 'proof' that river-netting is deleterious to stocks. As happened with the decline of the herring, nothing was done in time because various scientists could not agree on the cause. Yet as far back as the 1920s I can remember large herrings being sold out of open carts in Darlington at two a penny! Thousands of tons which could not be sold, even at that price, were used for fertilizer. By the time the scientists agreed that the herring was being over-fished there was little left to agree about. Surely, it does not need scientific proof for netting to be seen as a wholesale killing process which must affect the spawning stocks. A salmon cannot be killed twice.

The effects of netting have been at their most painfully obvious on the Tay, one of Scotland's most beautiful rivers which, with its tributaries, once comprised the greatest salmon waters in Europe. Today, for most of the year, it is virtually empty. I found out why when, in early August 1991, I drove down to one of the netting stations just below Perth after fishing two famous beats in the Dunkeld area which were so devoid of salmon that their owners were embarrassed even to ask friends to fish them. I watched netsmen sweep completely and continuously across the river from both sides. I had always understood that netting was restricted to three-quarters of the width of the river so that there was always a passage for a few fortunate fish, but the netsmen assured me that there is no law to stop them netting right across. Only two men were needed to work the long, lightweight nylon nets — one to steer the motor-boat the other to walk down the bank holding a rope attached to the other end. When the two eventually met again the net was hauled in by a motor-driven winch. As one net was being wound in from one side of the river the netsmen on the other side laid their net, again right across so that no fish had any chance of escape.

In former days, when the boats had to be rowed and the heavy hempen nets pulled in by hand, a team of netsmen could make about five sweeps in a shift. Now two men can make thirty sweeps and in high water have made as many as forty. From 5 February until 20 August, working in shifts, at all heights of water, day and night, save for sixty hours each weekend, the Tay netting stations have taken about 50,000 salmon and grilse a year plus many sea-trout. A netsman told me that they once killed 236 salmon in one shift. As the catch which I inspected showed, only skinny fish can get through the 2-inch square meshes and fish caught by anglers higher up commonly have net-marks or are without a dorsal fin. It is believed that nets have been taking about 96 per cent of the grilse run.

Some of the netsmen were working on a share-cropping basis, receiving the value of one-third of the catch, so they had every incentive to take the maximum. It was commonly believed that these netsmen were small family groups working for themselves, as they have done down the centuries. On the contrary, they worked for companies with shareholders and most of them spent the rest of the year on the dole.

The Tay nets were required by law to remain inactive for sixty hours at weekends — a recent increase from forty-eight — and that would seem to allow some fish time to pass through, provided the river was high enough for them to do so. However, there have been so many netting stations spread over such a long distance that sixty hours was not long enough for many of the fish to pass them all. The highest nets could still catch them when netting was resumed after the weekend. Further, a netsman told me that salmon which get past the netting area on the incoming tide may fall back into it when the tide ebbs, so many which should have passed through are still there to be netted after the weekend.

The result of all this has been a wipe-out in the upper reaches with salmon angling, which was worth more than £100 million to the Scottish economy, so unproductive that even poachers were finding it not worth the trouble and risk there. The numbers of salmon passing through the fish counters has shown a massive decline and the rod-catch has fallen dramatically year by year in recent times. Those who fish the Tay in the autumn may see fish in the river, especially on the lower beats, because netting ceases by law on 20 August. This autumn run can still be large because it has never been netted in recent years and is further proof of the slaughter which river netting has inflicted on the spring and summer runs. Relatively few of the autumn fish reach the higher stretches because they spawn in the lower parts of the river and its tributaries there. So only anglers on the lower beats tend to benefit to any appreciable extent.

In 1991 all the fishing beats in the Tay system experienced their worst season in living memory. That year I achieved an ambition, nurtured by many anglers, to put both a fly and a bait over the very lie where the immortal Miss Ballantine had caught her record 64-pound salmon nearly seventy years previously. The Bargie Stone, above which she had hooked the fish, was still there but the lie was empty, as was the rest of that once splendid beat.

It was the view of the ghillies to whom I spoke that unless netting was drastically reduced or stopped, the Tay would be finished as a salmon river within two years. There is nothing more devastating for the angler who has arrived on an expensive salmon beat than the ghillie's admission, after the first blank morning, 'They're nay there'. At the end of a blank week one of them remarked to me 'You must look on a visit to Scotland as a holiday and if you manage to catch a fish it's a bonus.' Few fisherman are likely to be so charitable, lovely though Scotland be.

On top of all this there is now a serious threat to the smolts, the young salmon which go down from the rivers to the sea at the age of two years or so to feed there and mature before returning to spawn themselves. They are being deprived of their food in the sea by further obscenities. Millions of tons of the sand-eels, capelin and other small fish on which the smolts and salmon rely are being scooped up by the billion in micromesh nets for conversion to fish-meal and oil, some of which has been used to fuel power-stations! In 1989 and 1990 it seems that so many smolts may have died of starvation that the prospect for returning salmon over the next few years could be disastrous. The Perth netsmen told me that, in the past, they would see long, wide ribbons of smolts moving downstream in the shallow water but they had not done so recently. Again, officials are not prepared to move without the 'scientific' evidence, which usually takes many years to acquire. Meanwhile the continuing damage can be fatal. It would be more sensible to take what would seem to be obvious precautions without delay while the investigations are in progress, whatever their result. Too much money given for active conservation is being handed out to scientists who captivate charitable organizations.

The various commercial interests, which have been quick to latch on to the profitable delays interposed by research projects, blame each other for the salmon crisis but the obvious truth is that they are all responsible to some extent for what has happened. It is of little consequence to the fish, or to the angler upstream, whether it is netted off Greenland or at Perth.

With netting increasingly uncommerical on the Tay, it has been possible for an organization representing the riparian owners and angling interests to buy off nine netting stations, mainly below Perth, which, alone, have been taking an average of 20,000 salmon and grilse a year. At least that number should, in future, be able to forge upstream to spawn many millions of eggs, when rod anglers could expect to hook a few of them. For that rosier prospect, anglers and the Scottish economy are indebted to an astute, determined businessman, Sir Alan Smith, a non-fisherman but Tay-lover who, inspired by his angler son Michael, took the problem by the scruff of its neck and pushed the languishing deal through in a few weeks.

If the reduction in netting substantially improves the rod catch over the next five years, as it should, there will be further action to acquire and remove the rest of the nets from the estuary.

The countryside's enemies which I have mentioned so far operate, mainly, within the law. There are others who operate outside it, some blatantly.

CHAPTER 22

LAWLESSNESS AND DISORDER

While salmon poaching by gangs may now be in decline it will surely regenerate if the King of Fish becomes plentiful again. I have a historic flash photograph of a gang of Welsh miners, each armed with a gaff and the night's haul of twenty salmon, some of them huge, taken some seventy years ago. More recently, a more savage picture was sent to me by the Duke of Fife showing some 1500 salmon and sea-trout killed by poachers who had emptied cyanide into his once magnificent stretch of the South Esk.

These days salmon poachers go to great lengths to avoid capture, which has to be red-handed to secure a conviction. They arm themselves with night-vision devices and portable radios, so that lookouts can warn them of the approach of ghillies or police, and some use very old technology to great effect. Recently on the Wye, ghillies received a tip-off and staked out a pool where early morning visitors could confidently be expected. As was later discovered, the poachers had tied black cotton thread between certain trees and bushes where anyone laying in wait would be bound to break it. On arrival they inspected the threads and avoided going near the river's edge and, when apprehended, claimed that they had come to watch the dawn break. Their hidden nets were not found and they were free to poach another day.

I was present on the Grimersta salmon fishery when the keepers discovered a net in one of the lochs with twenty-three salmon in it. What was extraordinary was that a team of students was paid to camp on the fishery to deter poachers but, somehow, the villains had managed, though they lost that haul. I was not really surprised because poachers were openly netting at the mouth of the river, with the police not doing much about it. The poachers were locals while the anglers were 'foreigners', mostly Sassenachs. While I was staying at a busy Scottish hotel which has public rooms and bedrooms looking across the river, a salmon fisher hooked an obstruction which turned out to be a nylon net. Unbelievably, poachers had set it unobserved and had hoped to collect it and its contents.

Though some of the poaching gangs, especially those from Glasgow, are cowardly criminals who will viciously assault outnumbered ghillies or policemen, the courage of some individual poachers cannot be denied. I was once taken to meet a Scottish poacher as he was such a 'character'. He had only one arm because he had lost the other while throwing a Mill's bomb into a salmon pool. On another occasion he had escaped apprehension by plunging into a swollen river in the dark and, because of his disability, had been assumed drowned. Nevertheless, he admitted to us that he would never be able to resist poaching, though under a court order subjecting him to immediate arrest if seen within a mile of any salmon river.

With such men — I have never heard of a female salmon poacher — the requirement to poach is compulsive and they extract pleasure as well as profit from their illicit enterprise. The same is true of the individual pheasant poacher. The late Lord Marchwood told me of his boyhood travail when accompanying his father, who loved shooting driven pheasants on other people's estates but poaching them even more so. After a day in the field it was the boy's job to look out for any stray pheasant on the way home. He would then be required to make the bird fly over his father who would be stalking with his gun. If the bird went the wrong way he received a torrent of abuse.

I have to confess to a considerable degree of illicit pleasure when I poached the first two salmon I ever caught, though it was by accident rather than design. I have described how I acquired two small Austrian spinning baits for trout, beautifully fashioned of brass and mother-of-pearl, and used them to some effect in Herr Krupp's private lake. I had these in my bag when taken for a day's trout fishing on the Tweed, at Melrose, by a young friend when I was visiting Edinburgh on journalistic business. While I was spinning with them, the ghillie on the beat, who was known to my friend, came up and spoke to us but made no comment. His back was barely turned when I hooked a salmon of nine pounds, which I eventually beached. My friend tailed it up the bank and before I could ask what we should do with it, he hit it on the head and hid it in a gorse bush. I was soon into another of the same size which suffered the same fate. We then decided that it was time to go and the problem of getting the fish away was easily solved because my bag was the large hold-all which formed part of my luggage. He shouldered that and strode off downstream while I walked upstream to the car, fishless, in the direction taken by the ghillie. We met on the road without incident and I have kept that secret for more than forty years, save from one special fishing companion, the prankster, Jimmy James. When I discovered that the Scottish friend had moved south and become a fishing instructor and that Jimmy was

213

going to him to brush up his salmon casting, I could not resist giving him the opportunity to stage a coup by having such rarefied knowledge which he used with subtle effect.

Fortunately, since those days, the saleable value of poached wild salmon has been kept at an artificially low level by the impact of large quantities of cheap farmed salmon on the open market but the thieving of fish by the individual poacher will always be with us, especially in times of high unemployment.

Unemployment is also being blamed for the vandalism now afflicting the countryside but, though mindless damage has always been with us, it has never been so widespread or so savage. When walking through the churchyard next to my house I was appalled to see a boy of about fifteen, in the company of others slightly older, defacing the names on the marble village war memorial. When I pointed out that the men named had given their lives so that we could live in freedom, they were unimpressed. A similar gang of louts ruined an ancient brick bridge over an arm of the Kennet by pushing both walls of it into the river. Sluices on the Kennet have been shut tight to cause damaging floods. Taps on farmers' diesel tanks have been opened with consequent river pollution. A historic wooden replica of a gibbet on the Berkshire-Hampshire border, kept in repair by the owner because of its interest to visitors, has been burned down for the second time.

According to some social workers such wanton and costly vandalism, which has reached epidemic proportions, is the fault of communities which fail to provide recreation centres and other facilities to keep the young occupied. Yet recreation centres are a major target for vandalism.

The truth, I suspect, is that the deliberate act of destroying gives a sense of achievement to boneheads who have no hope of creating anything useful and their number has been greatly increased by lack of parental control and falling educational standards. Louts feel secure from parental disapproval if they are caught and magistrates tend to regard their behaviour as 'part of growing up'. Though vandalism costs the nation enormous sums, politicians do not see enough votes in the problem.

There is also a thoroughly evil element in vandalism, as demonstrated by youths who, laboriously, place concrete slabs on railway lines with the obvious intention of derailing trains and string wires across lanes to maim motor-cyclists. Recently, from my bedroom window, I watched two young men upend a heavy drain cover in the dark in such a way that some person, likely to be old, would trip over it, possibly — perhaps hopefully — breaking a leg.

A genre of country-livers, most of whom rank as vandals, are the so-called 'travelling people' — gangs of hippies who do not travel far enough for my taste. With their assumed right to park their ancient vehicles wherever they wish to stay as long as they like and to be immune to laws, both national and local, they are persistent wreckers of the countryside wherever they go. They subsist on their right to draw social security without ever seeking work and to pay no taxes of any kind. Their vehicles are, for the most part, unlicensed and unroadworthy. When finally forced to depart they leave environmental damage and filth which has to be paid for by the law-abiding local people.

In May, more than 1000 of them, with their dogs, have encamped on the centre of Hungerford Common which, contrary to popular belief, is private land belonging to Hungerford Town. Under by-laws agreed to by the Commoners, anyone else is liable to prosecution for parking more than fifteen yards from the roadway. They are permitted to drive unlicensed vehicles which would never pass an MOT test. Until recently, the police made no effective effort to control them and gave the impression that they were afraid of them. In advance of 1 May 1992, when the hippies threatened a repeat performance to celebrate the pagan feast of Beltane, whatever that might be, the police thwarted them but only by sealing off all the roads around the Common to the considerable inconvenience of local residents and decent visitors. The cost of the operation, involving police reinforcements from other areas and a helicopter, must have been enormous. Meanwhile, these hippies continue to parasitize the system and their social security money is often delivered to them.

The police have also been negative about 'acid house' parties when hundreds of rock and drug addicts have invaded country estates and taken over barns for their unwelcome activities, often doing criminal damage to property in the process. Police called to two such occasions on land belonging to a friend of mine advised him to put up with the inconvenience, the damage and the mess and, above all, not to provoke the miscreants, as they were powerless to help him. In short, law and order had ceased to exist so long as the invaders cared to remain. Small wonder that respect for the police in my part of the countryside — and I suspect in many others — has slumped.

The country house, with its lush contents, has long been the target of professional burglars but there is now a continuous spate of burglaries in villages and in modest houses on their edges, which was rare in the relatively recent past. The police have a poor record of apprehending these criminals and generally tell the victims that they have little, if any, hope of seeing their valuables again. The same attitude is taken to the widespread thefts from churches, which used to be rare. Recently, in the ancient church next to my house, thieves, who were seen and described by several villagers, stole a medieval funeral helm which was high up on a wall. The police attitude was that it would probably be out of the country within twenty-four hours.

More eloquent of this modern disrespect for churches is the situation in the tiny church of Branxton, in Northumberland, where, in 1513, the bodies of 10,000 Scottish and English soldiers killed in the battle of Flodden Field were collected for burial. Wishing to buy a brief account of the battle on sale there I could not see where to put the 50p as there was no obvious slot. I eventually discovered it on the top of a long, vertical pipe which led to a receptacle below the stone floor. It was a last, desperate way of preventing thieves from rifling the money.

In many country areas motorways and bypasses are now so convenient for a quick get-away that there has been an upsurge in the rustling of cattle, horses and especially of sheep with little hope of their recovery.

While the countryside is fairly free from mugging, compared with cities, it has reached some country towns, especially where there are drug addicts who will do almost anything to get money to sustain their supplies. However, when walking, even in country lanes, I would not go without my blackthorn thumbstick which is a formidable weapon when used to jab. Violent crime in the pursuit of robbery has also hit the elderly living in remote cottages; even women in their eighties and nineties being roughly beaten in a way which the criminal community would have abhorred not long ago.

A new fount of violence is the Animal Liberation movement, whose worst fanatics regard human life as being expendable in their so-called struggle to save animals. All such movements attract boneheads and psychopaths seeking opportunities for violence, including attempted murder. A bomb has been placed under the car of a scientist involved in research with animals. Some of these self-styled do-gooders are among the worst do-badders to the countryside. Activists who have deliberately released hundreds of ranched mink into the countryside are directly responsible for the loss of millions of birds and mammals on which the established population of the mink, a savage killer, feed and will continue to do so, probably in perpetuity.

The activities of others opposed to the ancient country sports — the so-called 'antis' — often involve wanton damage, including serious threats to human life, such as unscrewing wheelnuts on shooting vehicles, in anticipation of an accident, perhaps on a motorway. Most of them do no work and pursue their campaign at the taxpayers' expense. It is mainly people of urban culture who claim to find country sports 'unacceptable', which is the 'in' word widely used by the media to give the impression that a vast majority opposes them. In fact, the right to hunt, shoot and fish, which is a civil liberty thoroughly established in law, is very acceptable to more than four million people who take active part in them and to others who take the reasonable view that, while they would not want to indulge themselves, they have no objection to others doing so. With traditional farming methods and cottage industries virtually extinct, hunting is the last colourful, ancient activity left in the countryside. It is easy to convince people who have no personal interest in any sport to say that they are against it. I greatly dislike pop concerts which invade the countryside because, to me, they are a filthy row but I appreciate that millions enjoy them and should be allowed to do so.

I have little doubt that the main target of those who affect to abhor country sports, including Labour politicians, is the privilege ascribed to those who practise them. This attitude was demonstrated on a Hampshire shoot recently when, shortly before a pheasant drive was to begin, a middle-aged rambler appeared, walking towards a line of guns which included the King of Sweden. Naturally, the King had security bodyguards who politely requested the stranger to make a modest detour. He refused, claiming his rights of passage and insisted on walking through the line.

The extent to which the import of any zealous anti-bloodsporter could cause havoc in a country community was well recognized by Sir Joseph Nickerson, who had the responsibility for choosing the vicar of Rothwell village. When candidates came for interview he ensured that it would be on a shooting day. They were required to come out and watch a shoot, standing at the back, and would then be asked to pick up one or two shot birds. The day I witnessed this exercise the candidate was a rather ethereal young man who, I sensed, was doomed the moment I saw him bringing back a pheasant holding it, rather distastefully by one leg.

While the conduct of those who pursue sports with aspects of cruelty can never be beyond reproach, our best riposte is the robust one that hunting in its various forms, far from being inhuman, is very human indeed and the love of it is an integral part of the nature of many men and quite a few women. It is the 'antis' who are inhuman in this anthropological sense and except for those few who are vegetarians, they are hypocritically inconsistent. The stand of the 100-per-cent vegetarian who objects to the taking of life is understandable. The anti-bloodsporter and the animal rights enthusiast who eat meat and fish are humbugs, as they would quickly appreciate if they visited an abattoir.

It is no exaggeration to describe many of the animal liberationists and 'antis' as rural terrorists. In addition to them, the full-blooded political terrorist has had an impact on the peaceful atmosphere of the countryside. Caches of IRA explosives, guns and ammunition have been dug up in remote areas including in my own county of Berkshire. Shortly before the MP, Ian Gow, was assassinated in 1990 I noticed two young men who had pitched a bivouac tent in a secluded position by the River Kennet and who seemed to spend the whole day in it, however sunny, as though trying to hide themselves. When they disappeared I reported the matter to Scotland Yard's anti-terrorist unit which was pleased to receive the information and questioned me briefly. It may have had no significance but the fact that I thought it might and took some action was a sad reflection on the horrors that can and do happen in the countryside today, though I suppose that country informers were common in the days of the highwaymen, of which our local gibbet is a constant reminder.

Because of the terrorist danger in the countryside, armed protection is now necessary for Royals and senior politicians taking part in country sports. I have attended many shoots where participants have had to be accompanied by two armed detectives at all times. This has sometimes extended even to the close relatives of politicians. A retired general I know found his country house surrounded by dug-outs manned by armed police after his name appeared on an IRA hit-list. A Jewish friend with close links with Israel has been unable to go trout fishing on his own water for many years, unless accompanied by an armed guard, because his name has kept appearing on Palestinian hit-lists intercepted by Scotland Yard.

One of the few figures who shot without one was Lord Mountbatten and when I remonstrated with him for this, while dining at a country house, he replied, 'Who, in his right mind, would bother to blow up an old sod like me?' Not long afterwards he was assassinated by a bomb placed in a small boat containing children and other members of his family while visiting his Irish country home.

The countryside has always has its share of murders, some of them especially infamous in the annals. However, there have been no murders to compare with the 'Hungerford massacre' — the mass-killing in the streets of our country town, two miles away, in 1987. My wife was backing her car out to go shopping there when a neighbour told me, 'Don't let her go! There are seven people shot dead in the street there!' I thought he must have gone mad but, in fact, the number was soon to be seventeen, some, people whom we knew. I had occasionally seen the killer, who eventually shot himself after being cornered in the Hungerford school, when going past Littlecote House to our trout-fishing because he did odd jobs in the theme park there. He was quiet and nondescript which, perhaps, was why he decided to make a name for himself.

While the horror soon faded from the Hungerford streets the impact of the evil on country sports has steadily grown. Mainly to allay public concern, governments have introduced progressively draconian restrictions on the ownership of shotguns and ammunition. Those Chief Constables who would like to outlaw shotguns for all whenever a criminal uses one to commit murder, especially of a policeman, usually hark back to the massacre.

I never imagined that I would be suspected of being a murderer, and a mass-murderer at that, but it did happen — as a result of my love of shooting. In the spring of 1965 I flew to Ireland to fish the Slaney for salmon, leaving my dark blue Jaguar car in the garage at my country home, in Surrey. While we were there, an anonymous caller telephoned Scotland Yard to say that he had seen a man pick up a prostitute in Kensington Road and drive off with her in a navy blue Jaguar of which he gave the number. He claimed to be responding to a police plea for information concerning such a prostitute who had been found murdered after a peculiar sexual assault — the sixth to be killed that way, their naked bodies having been dumped, mainly in the area of Shepherd's Bush. The car was mine and, while I was fishing away contentedly in Ireland, the police took possession of it. As soon as they opened the boot they felt that the solution to a modern version of the Jack the Ripper horrors was in their hands because the plastic lining was heavily stained with recent blood — just what they were looking for. While the forensic scientists went to work in the laboratory the police powdered the car in search of the victim's fingerprints. Had I been at home I could have saved them trouble and expense because the bloodstains were those of several hares which I had brought back from a big shoot in Essex. The car had been returned by the time I reached home and I would never have known of Scotland Yard's suspicion that I was a mass murderer, had not my daughter chanced to mention that the car had been tested by the makers for a brakes problem — the device used by the police to secure it.

Who was the anonymous caller? The police never found out but I suspect was someone with a personal grudge. Fortunately, though Scotland Yard can be a leaky place, no newspaper picked up the story which could have been damaging had it become public. After thinking about the experience I telephoned Scotland Yard to offer a lead to the real killer. A detective inspector was sent round immediately by John

Du Rose, who was in charge of the investigation. The tale I had to tell was a strange one.

Some weeks before I had left for Ireland I had been in the habit of leaving my car in an open car park on a bomb-site near Smithfield Market. A personable young man occasionally in charge of the park had warned me that vandals sometimes damaged the cars there and offered to put it into a lock-up garage nearby in which he kept his motor-bike. I agreed to this and assumed that it was done. One morning when I went round to collect the car I found that it had been washed and that even the chromium plating had been meticulously polished. I was delighted and asked who had done it.

'Oh the girl who works here did it,' the young man replied.

'Give her a tip from me,' I said, putting my hand in my pocket.

'No need for that, Sir. She had nothing else to do.'

I shrugged and drove away, also realizing that the inside of the car had been carefully cleaned.

A few days later, when I called to pick up the car again at night, I noticed that the handbrake lever was broken and asked the Pakistani who was in charge if he knew how it had happened.

'No. But I wouldn't let that young fellow use a car like this if I were you.'

'He doesn't use it,' I replied. 'He just takes it over to a garage across the way where he parks his motorcycle.'

'There's no garage, Sir. And no motorcycle.'

I looked at the speedometer clock. There was more than 100 miles on it since I had last parked the car. The Pakistani confirmed my fears. The young man had been using the car for joy-riding — and God knows what else. I cursed myself for being such an idiot but after the police intervention it occurred to me that the car might well have been used to pick up prostitutes, as someone had reported.

I recalled that the young man told me that he lived in Battersea, which is near the Thames, and the police had already stated that the murderer must be someone who knew the back streets near the river intimately. Further, my suspicion explained why the car had been so scrupulously cleaned and polished, inside and out, after one of these evening excursions. The fact that my car had been at home in the country on the night that the last prostitute had disappeared meant little because the man had access to other cars parked there all night as it was a rule that the keys had to be left at the ticket office.

The police interviewed the young man and when I dined later with John Du Rose and other detectives engaged on the case, they assured me that he had been eliminated from their inquiries. They were not prepared to say why and my inquiries suggested that they had not been as searching as the facts seemed to warrant. By that time, they seemed to be satisfied that the culprit was a policeman who had committed suicide. I was never impressed with that story but there were no more 'Nude Body' murders.

CHAPTER 23

THE REAL CONSERVERS

W hile modern agriculture has inflicted great damage on the British environment through the ripping out of hedgerows, monoculture and the excessive use of fertilizers, pesticides and weedkillers, the countryside is still enormously in debt to farming and particularly to the big estates. The lay-out of the deciduous woods, often on high ground, which gives the British landscape its particular quality, is not natural but the consequence of careful planning, sometimes for aesthetic appeal but, more often for the purposes of game-shooting. Many of the most beautiful woods were planted to act as coverts to harbour pheasants which could then be flushed from the trees in a challenging manner. New plantings still being made are often for the same purpose. Though they may ultimately be felled for timber they would be uneconomic but for the shooting rents which they command and, without that extra advantage, they would be cleared and ploughed to contribute to the prairies which have blighted the countryside.

Though too much arable land has been over-exploited, much remains as it was in the days when old-style husbandry, with crop rotation, was so much more suitable for wildlife that there were hares, partridges and plovers in many fields and corncrakes in the meadows. Without active farming, game and true wildlife would be much thinner on the ground than it is because, contrary to common belief, when land reverts to scrub it is much less capable of sustaining mammals and birds.

This is even more true of moorland which is poorly managed or left entirely to nature. The great areas of purple heather which give such aesthetic enjoyment are not a natural phenomenon. Without regular and expensive intervention by man they would be inexorably invaded by coarse grasses and bracken. Dartmoor offers an example, while Cumbria, the whole of Wales and large areas of Durham have lost most of their heather in the last fifty years. On managed moors the heather is maintained by artificial practices such as controlled burning, draining, the limitation of grazing by sheep and the elimination of bracken and other weeds. This is possible, economically, only if there is extra revenue from the creatures which feed mainly on the heather — the grouse.

A further permanent threat to the heather moorland is the conifers which have been planted there in enormous numbers, especially while that practise was subsidized by tax relief. Not only are such conifers alien to the British scene but the hundreds of square miles of semi-dark environment they create supports little wildlife and no plant undergrowth. The march of the conifers has devastated the habitats of many moorland birds like the curlew, merlin and golden plover.

While most of the ancient rivers still exist, many are in disgracefully dilapidated state for a nation which prides itself on its technology. The opposition to pollution and abstraction has stemmed from angling interests, which continue the endless struggle. Even where pollution does not exist or is minor, the artificial effort needed to keep a river in order is not generally appreciated. Enormous sums are spent over the years by the owners of Scottish salmon rivers to save the banks from erosion and preserve the pools. Without the fishing interest nobody would bother to keep the southern rivers in order by the necessary dredging, weed control and maintenance of the flow through the use of weirs and hatches. One has only to look at a disused canal to see the inevitable results of neglect.

Britain's waters have been substantially augmented over the centuries by man-made lakes to attract water-fowl and provide fishing, many recently being created from worked-out gravel pits. Apart from providing attractive water-scapes, havens for wildlife and recreational facilities, these still waters would seem to be reasonably immune to 'development'.

Clearly, the common factor involved in the confrontation of the countryside and its maintenance is country sport, the urban belief that if hunting, shooting and fishing were prohibited rural Britain would be the same, but without the cruelty, being false. The creative initiative originated mainly with landowners, large and small, and still remains mainly with them in spite of all the activity by environmentalist groups. The landowners are largely supported by the indigenous country dwellers who favour country sports as a factor which binds the community, as well as being sources of additional income. There is, for example, no shortage of beaters and other ancillaries for shoots, an activity which helps to offset the current loneliness of farm labour. It used to be common to see several people at work in fields but, now, though one may see the odd tractor at work, often with no driver visible, the fields are empty. So much is done so quickly by so few that most fields are visited for only a few days a year. So the sociability provided by a shoot is welcome.

As regards the quantity and quality of wildlife, country pursuits are responsible for the very existence of much of it. In Britain, in the 1990s, there are probably more freshwater fish, more pheasants, more mallards, and more deer than at any time since Tudor days. With the exception of the deer, which is a natural population explosion due to escapes from private parks, this surprising situation in a small, over-populated island being progressively built upon, is entirely due to what are commonly castigated as 'blood sports'. If the shooting fraternity did not rear and release millions of game-birds each year, the pheasant, instead of being easily Britain's most numerous bird, could become rare and even extinct. Without moor management and keepering, grouse would go the same way. The partridge owes its substantial revival to shooting. Even with mallards the additions made by sporting interests are now very noticeable. In short, those who run shoots and fisheries and those who subscribe to them, far from being destroyers of wildlife, are net preservers who shoot less than half of the game they feed into the system each year.

Well-keepered estates are conservation areas for mammals of all types, save for a few numerous predators like foxes, mink and rats. By reducing human disturbance they maintain the habitats for many species of wild birds, for the days of the gamekeepers' gibbets are largely gone, with most owners keen to preserve owls, hawks, falcons and other raptors. They have changed their attitude to the killing of such predators, not only because they appreciate they they can be safely tolerated, but because of respect for them. Further, regular exposure to predators may be an important factor in engendering the behaviour that makes a game-bird touchy and likely to fly challengingly high and fast. Some shoot owners have extended their mercy to the woodcock, partly because it is such a delightful and harmless bird, but also because they feel a necessity to get their own house in order. One friend convinced himself that it was inconsistent to condemn Europeans for shooting our small migratory birds and then shoot their migratory woodcock. Several species like the curlew, the redshank and some geese which used to be shot for sport are now protected by law. By the nature of their privacy, shoots and fisheries also preserve the habitats of many plants, butterflies and other invertebrates.

The effects of angling on fish stocks form the most undeniable contribution of country sports to wildlife. Because of its growing popularity, the development and maintenance of fisheries and the permanently established habit of returning catches, there may well be more and bigger coarse fish in Britain than at any time. While greedy commercial interests have made devastating inroads into the stocks of salmon, most sea-fish and many mammals, trout are now more plentiful than they have been for centuries, because of the interests of anglers who pay the costs. Trout farms, which have occasioned much criticism because they cause pollution, make an essential contribution for, while anglers would prefer wild fish, their growing numbers make this a pipe-dream. As truly wild game birds are thin on the ground, trout would be thin in the water if left, entirely, to natural breeding.

There are, of course, some rivers still stocked only with wild trout but the sparsity of their numbers demonstrates the difficulty which wildlife experiences in an industrialized and over-populated country without assistance from sportsmen. The numbers of artificially-bred rainbow trout in rivers, lakes and ponds may already exceed the total of brown trout which fall to the rod each year in Britain. Originally a native of Californian mountain streams, the rainbow grows so rapidly that fish up to the six-pound mark, and even beyond, can be reared and introduced each season. In spite of the excellent sport they provide, some purists agitate for their removal because they are not indigenous. Yet many who do so delight in shooting the pheasant, which is also a foreign introduction.

Rainbows rise readily, often on days when brownies are sulking, and the sight of a great bow-wave moving towards a dry fly adds enormously to the excitement of a day's fishing. Pound for pound they fight harder and tend to leap more than the brownie. A five-pounder can fight as fiercely as a grilse and is likely to take off so that one has to run with it. Often when I have been salmon fishing in Scotland in a virtually empty river, because the grilse have been abstracted by netting, I have wished I had stayed with the rainbows on the Kennet.

While the ranched salmon is reared for the market and is not wanted in rivers, it has probably reduced the poaching of wild fish and the commercial viability of netting them by keeping down the price which they can command.

Though the numbers of some birds have declined under the impact of loss of habitat and chemical farming, others have become more numerous and Britain is one of the few countries where one can look in the sky or on the ground during daylight and, most probably, see a bird. While visiting the open Italian countryside of Umbria, recently, the sky was empty while, around Assisi, a modern St Francis would have difficulty in finding the smallest audience of birds, save for a few jackdaws. An environment without wild birds, however beautiful, is impoverished and nowhere is it richer than on a well-keepered British shoot where great flocks of songbirds thrive on the crops and food intended for the pheasants and partridges, safe from the magpies and jays which kill them elsewhere.

The sad Italian situation is the result of what happens when egalitarian ideals take command. An Italian acquaintance of mine had a large shoot near Turin, originally bought through industrial enterprise, which he kept stocked with pheasants and ducks. The local authority fell under the control of Communists who introduced new legislation making it an offence to shoot more than three gamebirds in a day but enabling anyone to do so on anybody's private land. As a result the land was no longer stocked, the keepers were dismissed and, soon, there was little for anyone to shoot. The pheasants were so quickly eliminated that the local 'sportsmen' turned their attention to the songbirds which had formerly been protected from their ravages. The comparable danger in Britain lies in a socialist government motivated by the concept of a countryside with its woods, fields and rivers open to all for, once granted, such political rights are usually irreversible, even when an opposing government comes to power.

The EEC politicians and bureaucrats in Brussels also seem to be motivated by the politics of envy and the ideology of egalitarianism. Eagerly looking for work and areas of interference, they are examining ways of controlling the pursuit of game by 'tidy' legislation affecting all member countries, and edicts curtailing country sports in Britain, such as a ban on the rearing of gamebirds for shooting, could well emerge. While their excesses have, so far, been stemmed, it is not impossible for a situation to arise where the British government, whatever its complexion, could trade off some control in return for support on some other EEC legislation regarded as being of greater value.

A lifetime of close contact with politicians of all parties has convinced me that their prime motivation, at all times, is the securing of votes to keep themselves in Parliament and, if possible, to keep or put their party in power. The steady spread of rural voters to the towns over this century has, inevitably, reduced the politicians' interest in the countryside. The mechanization of all aspects of agriculture has enormously reduced the numbers employed on the land. Many houses in villages and small market towns are weekend second homes for people who vote in the towns. So the country's political issues take a poor second place to those of industry both in Parliament and the media.

The emergence of 'green' movements, with the possibility of votes, created a surge of interest and the 'environment', a term little heard of before, suddenly became highly political but now that the 'greens' seem to be in decline, the main parties are losing their apparent

226

concern. Labour politicians, in particular, tend to take little interest since most of them represent urban areas and few have any feel for the countryside. When they do intrude into country affairs it is commonly for some reason of socialist ideology. They dislike both tradition and the privilege which they associate with fox-hunters though most of the ardent followers are farmers and other country-dwellers. As with capital punishment, it is the consciences of MPs, or their wishes to pacify vocal minorities which are decisive.

The extraordinary ignorance of Labour politicians about the countryside was unforgettably demonstrated by Harold Wilson in a conversation I had with him about a controversial political book which had appeared in 1978, not long after his resignation as Prime Minister. The book had opened with a description of how one of the authors had gone out into a London surburban garden to see if he could shoot a woodpigeon he had seen there without upsetting the neighbours. When I reminded Wilson of this he corrected me by saying, 'No. It was a partridge.' I pointed out that partridges were scarce then, even in open country, and there was little possibility that one could appear in a surburban garden. Wilson was so ignorant of wildlife that he continued to insist that it had been a partridge. And this was the man who, for purely political ends, promoted the concept of the 'grouse-moor image' — Sir Alec Douglas-Home, then the Prime Minister, and those like him, were decadent and laughable as they strode over a grouse moor, while Wilson sitting in a deck-chair on a beach had the common touch and was, therefore, laudable.

Sadly, in such issues logic may have little place and making Sir Alec an object of derision through his shooting habits, may well have helped Wilson to win the 1964 general election, which he did by only four seats. So historians may conjecture the extent to which shooting, and grouse shooting in particular, might have changed the course of history, though Lady Home told me that it was her husband's unflattering, half-moon spectacles, seen too often on television, which had swung the balance.

Indirectly, it was shooting which initiated my acquaintance with the man who knew exactly why Wilson resigned in 1976, causing such a flurry of speculation. Years earlier, through my shooting relationship with Lord Porchester (now Carnarvon), I had met Bernard Donoughue, a London School of Economics don who was invited by Wilson to head a policy advisory unit in Number 10 Downing Street after Labour's re-election in 1974. When I was researching a book in 1990, Donoughue revealed that Wilson had assured him that he would be needed for only two years because he was determined to resign on his sixtieth birthday, in 1976. When asked why, Wilson had explained that, as his father had become prematurely senile, he might go the same way and he was not going to let that happen while he was in office.

Mrs Thatcher deprived Labour of the 'grouse moor' weapon by gradually excluding most of the shooting politicians from her Cabinets, perhaps to provide a more common touch image. The succeeding Prime Minister, who took even greater pains to identify with the common man concept, continued the trend. However, the absence of country sportsmen from the Tory top ranks is likely to be of little consequence. When keen shots like Harold Macmillan, Alec Douglas-Home and Christopher Soames were in high office I took the opportunity to ask them why they did not actively speak up on behalf of shooting and, invariably, they replied that their positions made that impossible since they would be seen to be plugging their own interests.

The maintenance of the countryside and its sports will continue to depend on countrymen and women themselves, operating through their own organizations. Their causes will be strengthened by getting their own house in better order and in that direction there are some encouraging trends.

Some intensive farmers are making amends for their recent ravages by replacing hedgerows and planting new ones. Thanks to the influence of the Game Conservancy, many are leaving wildlife headlands — narrow strips of unsown land on the edges of arable fields where flowers and insects can prosper and birds and mammals feed and breed. Already totalling more than 1000 miles, the headlands have greatly benefited the wild partridge population and led to the resurgence of many wild flowers and butterflies.

While pollution and the fight against it will never cease, some rivers have already undergone a heartening degree of restoration as a result of clean-up measures, perhaps the most extraordinary being the Thames. Few rivers, if any, were more productive of salmon and other fish than the Thames and its tributaries but, with its growing pollution by sewage as the population in the Thames Valley soared, its capability to support salmon rapidly declined and ended as long ago as 1820. In 1947, when I could still call myself a professional biologist, I wrote a book about fishes in which the final chapter explained that, with the right legislation and resolve, all river pollution could be prevented. It ended with the words, 'We may yet see salmon leaping under Waterloo Bridge.' Reviewers ridiculed the idea but the Thames is now so clean and well oxygenated that salmon are returning to it annually in such numbers that fish passes are being built by the Thames Salmon Trust at the major weirs to allow them to penetrate the upper reaches and tributaries in which they could spawn.

To establish a stock of returning fish, salmon fry are being placed in these streams in large numbers and results have proved that they can pass down over the weirs on their journey to the sea. So it is more than likely that it will be possible to stand on bridges in many towns and villages in the Thames Valley and watch the king of freshwater fish making its way upstream, as must have been commonplace in the past.

A further development of enormous significance for the welfare of all rivers in England and Wales, and for their wildlife, was the Law Lords' decision, in 1991, that the public cannot claim rights of way on waterways where there is no existing right of public navigation. The alternative would have been the invasion of any and every stream by river craft, with regular and massive disturbance and the moorings, camp sites, marinas and other developments which inevitably follow. The decision arose out of a test case which demonstrated the fragility of rural peace and quiet.

I have little doubt that, had the issue been put to a public vote, town dwellers would have ensured a massive majority in favour of right of access and indigenous country-folk need to take serious note of all threatening trends in public opinion, especially when they have the backing of politicians. Fox, deer and hare hunting with hounds, which gives traditional pleasure to a quarter of a million people and contributes, substantially, to the rural economy had a narrow escape from legal ban in 1992 and is unlikely, I would guess, to last beyond the year 2000. There has been a historical trend against unnecessary suffering and killing, as witness the demise of bear-baiting, dog-fighting, cock-fighting and other sports involving animals and it is likely to gather pace. Killing 'wildlife' rouses much more passion in many more breasts than it used to and, with the continuing impact of nature television programmes and widely advertised appeals on behalf of endangered species, this tendency is certain to inflate, as is the grotesqueness of the image of the country sportsman as someone driven by bloodlust.

That it is not the desire to kill things which induces men and women to pursue game is proven by the fact that in the most popular country sport of all — coarse fishing — nothing is killed, as all fish are returned, the challenge being the defeat of a wily adversary in the peace and beauty of the countryside. When I was young the North Yorkshire streams were full of coarse fish, especially chub and dace, as well as trout, and, while there were legal limits on the size of fish one could keep, there were no limits on numbers. Though most of the coarse fish were virtually inedible it was nevertheless the practice to take them home where, after being admired, they were consigned to the dustbin. I remember catching about eighty large dace in one day and killing them all.

Since the war this disgraceful practice has ceased and, except on good trout stretches where they are a nuisance, coarse fish are now all returned alive, as they are caught or at the end of the day, being temporarily retained in keep-nets. Fifty years ago, any angler who put back what he caught would have been regarded as an eccentric figure of fun. Now any angler who kills fish, even specimens, is regarded with scorn and may be expelled from his club. So coarse fishing can no longer be regarded as a 'blood sport'. This change, for which fishermen deserve everlasting credit, is a remarkable example of the relatively recent surge in conservation because it was spontaneous and not the result of any outside pressure, as it was never thought that fishing would come under serious threat. It is not just because their catch is inedible that coarse-fish anglers release it. They do so to conserve stocks and to show respect and gratitude to their quarry though, as I learned, painfully, one should not expect gratitude in return.

Casting into a small pond, which had once been a stew, I hooked and landed a huge cock brown trout. As the pond was very near a fishing hut on the Kennet, I took the trout to the river, left it in my net, and brought the weighing scales to the fish. It was over seven pounds and remains the biggest brownie I have ever caught. At that moment the sun came out and the fish looked so beautiful that I decided to release it into the river, where someone might catch it later in circumstances more worthy of such a splendid creature. I held the fish gently in the water until it was sufficiently recovered and as I released it the trout turned, quite deliberately and bit me severely on the thumb, drawing a lot of blood.

Sadly, the returning of any sizeable trout is uncommon in Britain though in the United States there are long stretches of rivers where trout and salmon may be fished for only with barbless hooks and all must be returned unharmed. Though catch-and-release conserves wildlife, which includes fish artificially reared and stocked into rivers, there are many British trout waters where it is compulsory to kill all landed fish above a minimum size limit. Objectors argue that once a fish has been caught on a fly it is unlikely ever to rise again. This is simply not true, as the long American experience shows and as I, and many others, have demonstrated to ourselves. Fish have such short memories that I have re-caught the same brown trout on several occasions and once did it in consecutive casts with a dry fly. While nymphing for trout I hooked a large rainbow at about 5 p.m. which gave me such a battle that I decided that I would let it go if I managed to net it. I eventually landed a superbly proportioned six-pounder and, while gently removing my fly, I noticed another nymph, tied like a small, pink shrimp, on the other side of the trout's mouth. I removed that too and after holding the fish in the current, watched it swim away, almost cheering as it went. I recognized the little shrimp as a pattern used by a lady who fishes the beat and put it in my fly box. About an hour later she came up the bank and I asked her if she could remember losing a big rainbow in that area. She did and when I told her I had recovered her fly she predicted that there would be about an inch of nylon still attached to it because her cast had broken during a strong fight. I gave her the fly and, sure enough, it was exactly as she had described it. She had lost the fish at about 1.30 p.m. *that same day* — less than four hours before it greedily took my nymph.

It is also argued that many trout which have been released subsequently die. This should not happen if they are handled without blood loss and, if barbless hooks are used, they can often be released without being netted at all. In any case, they will certainly die if knocked on the head. The kill rule is understandable in the case of rainbow trout, which quickly lose condition after reaching a certain size, and are unable to breed in most British waters. In the later summer, rainbows can be seen going through all the motions of courtship, often chasing each other over long stretches of the river but without producing offspring. With brown trout, which can live for twenty years, the kill rule makes no sense. On stocked waters many trout anglers catch far more than they require for the table or the deep-freeze and should be given the option of returning the rest to rise and fight another day. This practice could substantially reduce re-stocking costs and anything is better than a blank space in the water.

Further, even on heavily stocked waters recognizably wild trout are caught and putting these back to breed more wild progeny is sensible. Once a fish has been defeated the objective has been achieved and, when the habit of automatic killing has been set aside, the joy of seeing a good fish which has fought well swim away to its lair far exceeds any satisfaction from applying the 'priest'.

The true objection to permitting the release of trout seems to be the fear that some anglers will go on fishing long after they have caught their prescribed limit and so disturb the water far more than they should. But no rule is likely to stop the angler who is unsporting enough to behave that way. While the occasional culprit may be caught, any fishery has to be run on trust.

Recently a really off-beat objection to catch-and-release has been raised — that unless an angler wants to eat his catch he should not pursue it, because to fish purely for sport is to make the quarry into a toy. This would exclude the millions of anglers, who pursue mainly inedible coarse fish and those who prefer a kipper to salmon or trout. The crackpot argument arose out of the slowly-growing practice of releasing salmon in the interests of preserving stocks and was aimed at the remote possibility that it might become compulsory to do so. It was based on the fear that pursuing fish solely for the pleasure of catching them would give the opponents of 'bloodsports' a dangerous weapon. In my opinion the reverse is true, because when fish are returned there is no blood and the argument that anglers fish for the larder is specious, these days.

My first pangs of remorse about killing a salmon were felt one winter's day many years ago. After I had hooked and landed a fourteen-pound springer on the Upper Blackhall beat of the Dee I noticed a tag on its adipose fin stating that it had been tagged in Greenland and giving the date and the address to which the tag should be returned. While not normally given to such penitent thoughts, I told the ghillie that it seemed a shame to kill the fish when it had battled its way so far, against so many hazards.

'You had better give up fishing, Sir, if you think that way,' the ghillie said as he dispatched the salmon and took it to his hut to weigh it and enter it into his records.

I knew, of course, that returning such a fresh fish would be regarded as highly eccentric and that each fish caught raised the capital value of such a beat by a figure which has now inflated to several thousands of pounds. Indeed, on several beats which I fished then as a guest all the fish caught were immediately sold to help pay the rent and, if possible, even make a small profit.

Happily practices sometimes change for the better. Until a few years ago all salmon were gaffed but now nearly all are netted or beached, the gaff being an emergency tool to be used with sorrow rather than with relish. Better still, hen salmon are being regularly returned in the autumn, this being compulsory on some beats. If it were done in the spring it would help re-establish the early season run which has almost disappeared from some rivers, though the main hope lies with the sportsmen who are backing campaigns aimed at reducing and, hopefully, eradicating netting in the high seas and estuaries. While salmon remain so scarce anglers should set an example by restricting themselves to a daily bag limit of one or two fish, especially in the spring. Any additional fish could be entered in the records provided they have been witnessed by a ghillie. The weight does not matter because it is the number of fish per annum, rather than their size, which determines the capital value of a beat.

As yet, this practice has little appeal for some of those who have bought time-shares in salmon fisheries and are keen to increase their value against the day when they might want to sell them. Some of these are foreigners with no deep-seated reason for conserving British salmon and are keen to kill as many as possible, however poor their condition, during their sojourn on the river.

Nevertheless, the arguments in favour of permitting an option to put any fish back are so potent that those who oppose it are treading water against the tide of conservation as well as common sense. I believe that the catch-and-release principle will gradually be applied to all game fish and, in the process, angling will be much better placed than shooting to withstand the pressure from the 'antis', the politicians who support them and genuine conservationists.

As I have said, most shooting men would be delighted if, at the end of a drive, all the dead pheasants could resurrect and run into the wood for, again, the sport is in the challenge, not the killing. Failing that miracle, there has recently been a spontaneous move in the shooting fraternity to set limits to the numbers of birds being shot because of a revulsion to excessively large bags. The person most responsible for the change in attitude to huge bags was probably Her Majesty the Queen, following a shoot which she attended at Broadlands in the 1960s, when more than 2000 birds were killed in one day. Lord Mountbatten was anxious to put on a memorable day for his guests, including Prince Charles who shot 200 birds at one stand. He had in fact shot 199 when the final whistle was blown but when a high, last bird came over him he asked permission to shoot it and did so. The area looked like a battlefield and the Queen, who was picking up, objected to the carnage, saying, 'It is obscene, Dickie! It's obscene!' It was surprising how quickly and effectively news of her displeasure spread among the owners of big shoots.

I should confess that I have been party to bags of over 1000 birds and felt neither greedy not guilty when the quarry was well presented. I have felt exhausted and, on one occasion, which was grossly excessive, most of the guns were urging the keeper not to send any more. However, I was astonished, rather than shocked, on the first day that I was in a line which accounted for more than 1000 pheasants. I have to confess to having enjoyed it and being surprised how quickly and easily the total was reached. Many people affect to shudder at the thought of such numbers but I have yet to see anyone who, when given the opportunity, did not strive to ensure that he had a fair share of it. Further, those who were not in the thick of the action clearly regretted it. Nor have I ever come across anyone who declined to attend a shoot because too many birds were shot there, though such people may exist.

Some of the most memorable days I have enjoyed at famous shoots have been with the owners and their families, such as the Carnarvons at Highclere, when the bags were under 250 and often far less. Limits of under 500 for eight guns are becoming popular, if only because the bigger days are so expensive.

Except for a few shoots, mainly in Norfolk, the bulk of the pheasants shot have been reared for the purpose and then released some weeks before the season begins. Critics claim that it is horrific for a gamekeeper to be hand-feeding his charges like chickens one day and going to great lengths to have them shot the next but few of them object to the killing of chickens. Yet game-birds are also a crop which would not exist otherwise and they have to be harvested. It seems to be the enjoyment of the harvesting to which the critics object.

There are undoubtedly, some circumstances which are almost indefensible. One such, in my experience, concerns a keeper who, each year, trained a thousand ducks to come to be fed at the sound of a horn. When the day of the first shoot arrived, instead of receiving food when they responded to the horn, they were frightened into the air to be met by a fusillade of shots. Even the most hardened of us, probably including the keeper, felt that there was something obscene about it.

In general, however, when such excesses are avoided, as they usually are, the shooting of reared birds can be amply justified. The crop argument also applies to grouse shooting for, on well-managed moors, the birds are present in artificially large numbers only as a result of intensive keepering.

If the number of birds one shoots in a day should be limited by principle what about the number one shoots in a lifetime? Lord Ripon, the prime shot of the Edwardian era, probably holds the all-time record of more than half a million head of game, which included many rabbits and hares. In a long but much later shooting life Joe Nickerson shot half as many, nearly all game-birds. If any others in recent times have shot more I have never heard of them. These enormous numbers cannot effectively be criticized on conservation grounds, because both men were responsible for putting far more birds into the countryside than they or their guests ever shot. To set a limit on lifetime totals would be to limit the number of days an individual may shoot, which would be a gross interference with private liberty.

An intriguing new development which could affect the animal rights argument against country sports derives from the recent statement by the Pope that animals may possess souls. In the past the dogma maintained that, as the contrary was the case, man could do what he liked with animals without committing sin. If religious zealots were to join with the 'antis' on this score they could be a formidable combination.

Neither the theologians nor the politicians are prepared to give serious thought to the most pressing of all problems — over-population. In recent years the condom has been given publicity and availability beyond anything I ever imagined possible but only in the context of AIDS. The saving of life attracts votes, as do child and single-parent financial benefits which encourage breeding, but any suggestion that having children should be self-limited is seen as dangerously counter-productive in a free society. There is much talk about returning to Nature but not to Nature's first law — the survival of the fittest. On the contrary, everything has to be done at any expense to enable the unfit to survive and the infertile to breed. Yet over-population is manifest, worldwide, with many countries suffering devastating effects. In parts of Africa, communities have out-bred the possible food supply with recurrent famine the inevitable consequence, as over-cultivation degrades the land to desert. Less damaged countries can provide emergency food in stop-gap measures but every year, in spite of the starved children seen on television, there are always more of them. 'Feed the World' fiestas make good television but the West is encouraging the expansion of nations of beggars.

In the tropical countries rain forests are being irrevocably destroyed to provide money and living space with catastrophic global consequences. Even disaster like the millions said to be lost in cyclones in Bangladesh are a consequence of over-population. People should not be living in the affected coastal areas but there is nowhere else for them. Developed countries, everywhere, are already seeing one disruptive result, affecting their economies and traditional life-styles, in the shape of mass immigration with its inevitable conflicts.

The human biomass now totals something like 280 million tons of flesh and, barring major epidemics or a worldwide accession of good sense, is set to double. Discussing the problems it poses with Enoch Powell, I remarked, 'The penis is mightier than the sword,' to which he replied, with force, 'No. It's the uterus, the uterus!'. Whatever predominates, between them they are the environment's worst enemies, through over-creation.

CHAPTER 24

IN RETROSPECT

I cannot call ageing a joy but, if health holds out and one feels little different, it can be enjoyable and even has its compensations which, I believe, are greater in the country than in a large town. After the age of seventy-five, which most men can now expect to reach, each additional day is a bonus and I get positive pleasure out of waking up once more knowing that everything still works. Surviving is an achievement in itself — especially with so many contemporaries gracing the obituary columns — which is why the aged are respected in some other countries, though not much here any more.

Statistics show that country-dwellers not only stand a better chance of survival but tend to enjoy better health in the process — the 'rural factor' being made up of several components, some obvious, like cleaner air, others more subtle. One of the latter is supposed to be the reduced external stress, compared with city life, but I suspect that much of the stress which modern living is alleged to inflict is mythical, circumstances having been more, not less, exacting in the past. The extra stress allegedly endured by men in their bread-winning capacities was supposed to account for the greater longevity enjoyed by women but some rural experiments have denied that. A study of monks and nuns, who lived simply, were free from financial worries and abstained from drinking and smoking showed that the nuns had a five and half year greater expectancy of life. Among my country friends most of the wives outlive their spouses and the recipe for any woman who does not want to become a widow is to marry a man five years younger than herself.

As regards internal stress, country people tend to be more at ease with themselves and with their lot as part of a local environment which has beauty, long continuity and breeds contentment, with less requirement for change. Anyone associated with agriculture, on which country traditions are still based, has to be an optimist because there are so many unpredictables and an optimistic temperament contributes to happiness while the depressive, who tends to view life as a pointless and wearisome march to the knacker's yard, and the pessimist who concentrates on doom, can never be happy for long. Of course, depressives do exist in the country but they seem to be considerably rarer than in the cities where, in my view, the endless vistas of concrete and tar macadam are enough to depress anyone. The increased opportunities for exercise and manual effort offered by rural living should improve life expectancy for, as an aged but agile friend succinctly puts it, the essential items to avoid losing are the muscles and the marbles. At seventy-nine my muscular strength is weaker but remains adequate for my substantial needs, helped, I believe, by managing to remain slim, though, in my youth it was the rosy and plump who were greeted with, 'You do look well!'.

The brain, too, still copes though I confess to an increase in emotional frailty in so far that experiences which I could have ridden without much trauma now knock me back. I first became aware of this at the age of seventy-five when my beloved ridgeback dog, Sheika, died in harrowing circumstances. Until then I had doubted that anyone could die a natural death from grief but my surprisingly excessive reaction suggested that for a very old person the extra stress could be decisive.

To a considerable extent, I attribute my health to being a pharmacophobe, to coin a term, meaning a hater of drugs because my long association with doctors made me wary of many of their medical advances. A drug is usually given to alleviate some symptom affecting a specific organ but it circulates round the rest of the body, producing side effects on other organs and I have seen too many withdrawn for that reason, often after causing appalling damage. Doctors have a name for such tragedies — iatrogenic disease, disease caused by the treatment. Common symptoms have common causes and, with just a few exceptions, the body puts itself right.

I am also wary of any feeling of really exuberant health because it has so often been an early sympton of impending disease. Whenever I am conscious of feeling really fit I go down with a snorting cold or some other infection with forty-eight hours, a paradox for which I offer a simple explanation. The unusual feeling of well-being is caused by the infecting germs during their incubation period. The first toxins produce a slight rise in body temperature which stimulates the general metabolism, it being an accepted fact that a rise in body temperature of about one degree peps up the body chemistry.

The famous diagnostician, Lord Horder, told me that, in his experience, the hazards of health were so capricious that we live by accident. Few would deny that robust health is the greatest manifestation of good luck and it is one of life's worst injustices that some individuals get a miserable share of it. However, one should never begrudge anyone their good luck, however exorbitant it may seem, because one never knows what fate has in store for them.

While doctors are best avoided, so are lawyers. I am indebted to that much-feared libel lawyer, Peter Carter-Ruck, for the excellent advice that going to law is like going to war, the only certainty being the cost. In law, as in life generally, it is unwise to expect justice.

In the 1950s I was involved in the establishment of the new science of gerontology, the study of the ageing syndrome, through my friendship with one of its pioneers, Vladimir Korenchevsky. In the belief that senility, as we know it, is unnecessarily premature, its purpose was to discover ways of adding active years to the human life-span and Lord Beaverbrook was so keen on that advantage, along with the obvious value of such discoveries in selling his newspapers, that I was encouraged to attend every conference and visit any relevant laboratories anywhere in the world. My activities made good copy and stimulated interest in gerontology but, to date, nothing spectacular has materialized, no pills, no potions. Indeed out of all the promising leads and expensive endeavours only four reliable prescriptions for preserving a healthy body and mind — all depressingly prosaic — have emerged — avoid becoming overweight, mainly by cutting down on calories; remain active with regular exercise; do not drink too much and do not smoke at all.

As all civilizations have felt a need for alcohol, or some similar drug, and have discovered their own ways of making it, usually from fermented liquors, it is reasonable to assume that many people find that life is not tolerable without it. But from my earliest days as a biologist, when I used alcohol to harden plant tissues to make them easier to section, I wondered what it might do to mine. So, though needing to drink some wine at lunch or dinner when entertaining journalistic contacts — more to establish an ambience of good fellowship rather than in the hope of loosening tongues — I avoided spirits, unlike many of my colleagues. While enjoying the taste of good wine, I disliked its effects so much that after leaving Fleet Street, I gave up alcohol in any form and have continued to dance my way through life, fairly merrily, without need of that crutch. I may, however, have penalized myself professionally because, in theory, writers should benefit from drink in moderation. Writing is a form of exhibitionism and alcohol lowers inhibitions. Fiction arises out of fantasy which alcohol promotes. Liquor also bolsters self-confidence. So, maybe I should not have given it up though my health and pocket have benefited while my wife, who still enjoys a drink, has a chauffeur who will never fail a breath test.

Becoming a non-drinker has certainly created social difficulties for it makes the cocktail party even more pointless, though I can claim that I am not there just for the booze. At any evening gathering outside the Muslim world anyone without a glass in his hand is regarded as odd and hosts rush up to me as though I might be in some danger. While it is extraordinary that it should be the norm for the earth's most intelligent creature to go through adult life with the brain befuddled to some degree, it is non-drinkers who are regarded as the eccentrics. It is also widely suspected that, whatever they may say, former drinkers must have given up alcohol on doctor's orders.

The trouble with alcohol is that while it can warm the heart it can also set the house on fire. It shortens the fuse on the human temper and, almost invariably, when there has been any unpleasantness in my marriages the drink factor has been present to some degree. It has always been a source of surprise to me how so many people can be really unpleasant when intoxicated yet retain their friends, who always make allowances. When one notoriously nasty Fleet Street drunk died in the 1950s there was a tremendous turn-out for his funeral outside London. The man had insisted on being cremated and, after the ceremony, most of his cronies repaired to the nearest pub. As it was a hot day they took their drinks to tables outside and, as they were drowning their sorrow, one of them saw a cloud of black, oily smoke swirling from the crematorium chimney. 'There he goes!' he shouted. And they all raised their glasses to the departing miasma.

I was most unpopular in the *Daily Express*, and with its advertising agency, when I reported the early Medical Research Council experiments on drink and driving, along with the prediction that legal limits would be set one day. Now, nobody doubts the effects of alcohol on traffic accidents but its impairment of judgement in other ways has consequences, every bit as tragic, by inducing men and women to take risks with their careers and private lives which they would normally spurn. This is especially true regarding sex, as the cases involving public figures regularly testify. People ask, 'How could he have been so stupid?' The answer is that just a few drinks make all the difference.

It is one of life's major injustices that those who begin sexual activity early continue the longest, those who start late tending to finish early. The common belief that each man has a certain number of shots in his locker and that dissipating them in early life will involve the penalty of premature impotence is quite untrue. The simple fact is that both desire and performance depend, primarily, on the level of activity of hormone glands, which may be an inherited feature. Those with a high level will tend to start early and finish late and *vice versa*.

239

The only evidence that medical sexual aids are of any value came to me from Lord Mountbatten. I do not believe it but record if for posterity. Not long before he was assassinated he turned up to shoot for the day with his near neighbour, Sir Thomas Sopwith, and was standing on the steps when I emerged after breakfast one crisp, autumn morning. He looked so fit that I remarked on it to which he replied, 'I look fit because I am fit. And its all due to ginseng. Barbara Cartland put me on to it. I take it every day. It's very good for the balls.'

It would seem more probable that Mountbatten really owed his continuing virility, as I do myself, to the advice, 'Use it or lose it'. I suspect that his general mental attitude to age was more responsible for his apparent fitness and the extent to which this is possible was demonstrated to me in a most dramatic way, in the following spring when I was salmon fishing with the Sopwiths in Scotland. All who remember Phyl Sopwith will recall how, at all times, even into old age, she presented a robust, smiling and upright image, taking enormous care with her make-up and general appearance, being known, affectionately, as the 'Green Dragon' from her green shooting clothes. One evening she came into the hotel dining-room looking radiant then, as she was walking, suddenly bent double in some kind of spasm. In a flash she had become a very decrepit old woman looking half her normal size. As Sir Thomas and I grasped her, I could not help being reminded of the film *Lost Horizon*, in which a beautiful woman suddenly ages when she leaves her native valley, Shangri-la. I do not know how she did it, save through determination, but after leaving with her husband for half an hour, she reappeared for dinner, as elegant as ever. In her late seventies, when she needed a heart pacemaker, she insisted on having it fitted to her left side so that she could get her gun up. I was present when she shot for the last time. Not feeling too well, she said she would join us for one drive, which she duly did. After letting several birds go by she saw two coming high over her, dispatched them cleanly with a right and left and then went home, her enthusiasm undimmed, however limited her physical capability.

Pending further gerontological advances, there are two ways of coping with the ageing syndrome — pack in as much as possible into the remaining years, hoping that the effort will not reduce them by imposing too much strain. Or take things leisurely in the hope of extending your life-span, which, of course, it may not. I have tried to compromise — packing in as much as possible but pacing myself by doing none of it in a tearing hurry or under stress, though I cannot resist the old satisfaction of writing a newspaper article against the clock if suddenly asked to do do. (In my Fleet Street days when I cursed the telephone if the office called me at home, my wife predicted that the time to worry would be when it did not ring. She was right.)

I strongly subscribe to the belief that if you retire out of life, life will retire out of you, so retirement, in the sense that one suddenly ends the habit of a lifetime by ceasing to do any work, can be a killer, boredom being the terminating factor. Old age serves a purpose only if you do something with it. It is ironical that, on retirement, after being ruled by time for so many working years, long-serving employees are traditionally presented with a large clock. I have no doubt that its furtive purpose is to underline the fact that time is up for, having made a speech and staggered out with the clock, it is difficult to return. Nevertheless, some do so because they cannot cut the cord which has sustained them. A former Chief of Staff assured me that one old Army officer who had retired with the usual formalities continued to turn up at the War Office and simply sat in his old room from which nobody had the heart to remove him.

While several journalists I know have found frequent returns to the office to be compulsive, I wanted no more of Fleet Street when I reached the retiring age of sixty-five in 1979. Determined to begin operating as a freelance writer from my country home the next day, I declined any retirement party and stipulated that there should be no present of a clock or anything else, especially as I had always disapproved of the interminable collections of money, often for people I did not know or even disliked. Like old soldiers, old journalists should simply fade away and I did so, as far as the *Express* was concerned, simply walking out of the back door without a goodbye and even avoiding the Last Farewell reunion in the machine room of the old 'glasshouse' building, before it was torn apart. Professionally, I have always been too busy with the future and still am. I still go to the office every day but the journey is ten yards instead of many miles and the joy of not having to travel to London is inestimable. All I miss are the old facilities, the Jaguar, the expense account and the services of my excellent secretary, my definition of retirement being working twice as hard with none of the resources. The country is supposed to be a place for relaxation but, like a pregnant woman, I find it difficult to relax when I'm in labour and I usually am. Work has given me more pleasure and satisfaction than anything else and, while I may not have achieved much, I have made the most of a modest ability and have sold everything I have ever written — thirty books, including nine novels, and items filling thirty-six fat cuttings albums. I have also had fun and excitement.

I knew I would be driven to work on because I have always felt guilty when idle. I find that most working people dislike retirement because to enjoy idleness you need to be born to it and be free from a sense of guilt. Men feel unmanned sitting around in the departure lounge waiting to be called while their wives work harder than ever. A continuing sense of achievement, however modest, is essential. It means that I have no armchair repose but, as Lord Beaverbrook was wont to say 'We will repose long enough in that wooden box'. His sharp response when I told him I was publishing a book called *Sleep and How to Get More of It* was a rasping 'You should write a book called Sleep and How to Do with Less of It!'

No discipline is needed to go to my desk, the discipline to stop being usually exerted by my wife, though I confess to the occasional expletive followed by a dash down to the Kennet for an hour or so. (This gives my wife the chance to tell callers, 'He's down on the river with his nymph'.) With continuing inflation, I have no option but to work, anyway. It is rare for a staff journalist to be able to acquire capital and I had no financial aptitude compared with rich friends to whom a balance sheet sings a song. I attribute this to my mother's insistence, based on her childhood poverty, that to be in debt was dangerous when the way to wealth is to borrow money and use it creatively. There is much in the quip that while Jesus saves, Moses invests, which is why so many of my Jewish friends have been so successful. They had more productive family advice. However, one compensation of being penny-concious was a rooted objection to buying fat cigars for fat bookmakers or of risking money on any form of gambling.

Though my newspaper pension looked adequate on paper, it was obvious that inflation would quickly erode it for, as recently as 1979, few people outside government organizations had pensions which were index-linked. As for the state pension to which I had contributed over so many years it proved to be fraudulent. On my sixty-fifth birthday I received a letter imparting the message, 'Hurray! You've got a pension but you are not getting it. And though your wife is over sixty she is not getting it either. But you will both get it in five years time.' This swindle is based on the actuarial hope that before the age of seventy, when the Treasury can no longer withhold it, you will die, as many do.

My social sin was in keeping myself employed to fight inflation and pay tax in the process. Those who opt for the armchair get the state pension at sixty-five. They include some of the richest men I know. A pension for which one has paid, and been forced to pay, should have nothing to do with need. I console myself in being rich in the comparative smallness of my needs which a country life facilitates.

The most difficult step in coping with future ageing was to decide to give up my old home, with its heavy maintenance costs, and move to a smaller house within a village. We chose on the principle that it should be the last move because, as with a tree, the older one becomes, the more traumatic it is to be uprooted. Experience has underlined the wisdom of being within a community in such violent and criminal times and with the convenience of shops and a post office within easy walking distance.

To continue working effectively anywhere a functioning memory is an essential requirement and I attribute mine to my mother who, as a repertory actress, learned two major parts each week and acted them twice nightly without ever fluffing a line, all incidentally, for £3 a week. A good memory can continue far into physical senility, as it did with Sir Thomas Sopwith who had remarkable recall even at 100. With some, however, memory can suddenly desert them. Not long after the late Lord Clark impressed the world with his superb television series, 'Civilisation', I had reason to contact him and he told me that his memory had suddenly 'quite gone'.

While the human body has the ability to replace most tissues which die or suffer damage it cannot replace brain cells — for an obvious reason. All our knowledge and skills reside in the brain tissue and they would automatically be lost if the brain cells were replaced on a regular basis as blood cells are. So when ageing makes serious inroads into the brain cells memory is bound to suffer. Seeing this happening to so many close friends keeps me constantly aware of the need to make the most of my own memory store while I can. My wife calls me an old man in a hurry but I have always been excessively conscious of the passage of time and the need to waste none of it, especially since I entered the bereavement bracket, with contemporaries disappearing in droves. How quickly I have gone from being the youngest at a shoot to being the oldest! A week may be a long time in politics but, past seventy, it is a sizeable slice of what life remains which, perhaps, is why it seems to fly so quickly.

I can still make some money but I cannot make time so the need to conserve it has generated a few useful rules. When asked to make a speech or take part in any other function I apply the principle — duty, pleasure, cash or credit? If none of these apply to the request I decline it. I never read, watch or listen to anything about actors, actresses, pop stars or 'show biz' of any kind. Nor do I read much about competitive sport or ever go to watch it. The saving in time is significant.

Like all things, a photographic memory has its penalties for it also thrusts into consciousness sins, errors and discreditable events in shameful detail. Fortunately a heavy programme of work, involving constructive thought, keeps them at bay.

For the ageing such a programme has been facilitated to a major degree by the advent of the word processor. As a typical two-finger typist making many errors, I always sat down at a typewriter with some reluctance but I go to my word processor with pleasure. For this boon I am indebted to a former CIA officer, the late Miles Copeland, whose pop-star son had bought him such a machine. When he explained its advantages I remarked that I was too old to learn such new tricks but saw the wisdom of his rejoinder — 'It's because you are old that you need it.' A few weeks later I saw a word processor displayed at the Newbury Agricultural Show. I ordered one and a pretty girl was sent to spend a day and a half instructing me in its use. It has been of value in more ways than one. It has altered my eyesight so that I no longer need glasses to read the smallest print or to tie on a trout fly but, as there is never anything for nothing, it has misted my long sight so that I need them for driving and shooting.

With a word processor, a telephone and a fax machine the country writer is almost self-sufficient but the tendency to be chair-borne for too long needs to be offset by the discipline of physical endeavour. For this the country offers enormous advantages. Walks of every kind abound around my village and a fair-sized dog demanding daily exercise is a spur to taking them, though I always prefer to walk with a purpose — bird-spotting, fishing or shooting. Recently, at seventy-seven it gave me enormous satisfaction to wade the whole length of the difficult New Fawn stream on the Little Blackhall beat of the Dee and to take three salmon on fly in the process. However, following a drowning tragedy that recently befell a fishing friend, and which my wife nearly simulated, I did wear a survival kit — a lightweight canvas neck harness inflating into a float round the head when a cord is pulled in an emergency. Salmon anglers of all ages should wear one.

As regards the practicability of shooting up to the eighties, and beyond, my most impressive evidence concerns a day when Harold Macmillan and Field Marshal Sir Francis Festing were fellow guests of Sir Thomas Sopwith at Compton. After breakfast, the keeper approached me and another guest, also then in his early sixties, to say that, as the old gentlemen could not be expected to deal with the mass of high birds we would see, he was relying on us to fill the bag. Macmillan was then very lame and Festing was bent almost double but, between them, they shot us out of the sky.

244

With shooting requiring quick reactions and meticulous self-control, at what age should one retire from it? Several times in recent years, after shaming exhibitions, I have vowed to call it a day. Though few enjoyed shooting more when I was on form, I would have put my guns away had not my wife and I realized that if I gave it up there would be friends of many years standing and lots of acquaintances whom we would probably never see again. It is not just the shooting that one would miss but all that goes with it. Nevertheless, I had reached the stage of the ageing process when my reaction time was too slow and, still using 12-bores, my muscles were apparently incapable of catching up with a bird fast enough to hit it in the head. Further, being a lifelong bad loser, I was finding it increasingly difficult to pretend that I enjoyed a day when I shot poorly. By changing my technique I was able to continue but the support costs of big-time shooting are prohibitive for those with falling incomes and as old friends give up or die the number of shooting invitations progressively declines, though, occasionally, an unexpected new one cheeringly arrives.

The country sportsman is often asked, 'If you had to give up either fishing or shooting which would it be?' Being unwilling to face such an appalling choice, my evasive response has always been to point out that Nature has so arranged things for the trout and salmon fisher that the question does not arise since most shooting takes place during the closed season for fishing. But if the absurdly mounting costs forced me to give up shooting I could do so with rationality and equanimity, having enjoyed a wonderful run, whereas if I gave up fishing it might well signify that I was tired of life.

Living close to good fishing means that enjoyment of it does not require a whole day's expedition as most shooting does. So a busy writer can more easily find time for fishing, a two- or three-hour session being sufficient. 'He died in his waders' would not be a bad epitaph for me but, with inflation as it is, 'He died at his word processor' is likelier.

With age, increasingly, the quality of the next day's activity and well-being depends on the quality of the previous night's sleep and physical exercise is one way of ensuring it. I have always slept better in the country, partly because of the quiet but mainly, I suspect, because the consciousness that I am there breeds contentment. I developed the habit of snatching twenty minutes sleep after lunch when in my thirties and have continued it ever since, being convinced that it extends the total time I can work productively. The habit of occasional face washing during the day also remains surprisingly effective in combating fatigue.

Lower metabolism is supposed to reduce the amount of sleep one needs as age advances, though I have not noticed it, perhaps because of my habit of taking a long hot bath at the unusual time of 7 p.m. What Rupert Brooke called 'the bension of hot water' washes away niggling cares and, in the process, the bath becomes a literal think tank. With the day's urgency ahead, it is difficult for the mind to wander far in a hasty morning bath but it can in the evening and it is surprising what ideas then intrude into it. For that reason it pays to have a tape recorder handy.

It has been my experience that most ideas arise out of facts and I am often asked how I can cope when 'out in the sticks', cut off from prime contacts, who tend to be in London. A village would not seem a likely area for anyone interested in espionage, treachery and defence secrets but, in fact, several 'spooks' from MI6, MI5 and GCHQ, several former staff chiefs, senior diplomats, defence scientists and politicians had retired nearby. I was already meeting some of them on the river bank, in the shooting field or at the homes of mutual friends, where I recall being asked into the garden, more than once, so that still secret matters could safely be discussed. One surprising new Intelligence contact, whom I first met at a country-house supper, was an unlikely and much underestimated member of the Royal Family who, I discovered, was making a substantial, clandestine contribution to counter the secret Soviet offensive to undermine Western democracy, and the KGB's activities, in particular. The group he had gathered round him had a more realistic appreciation of the danger than the Intelligence authorities.

I was confident that some exciting opportunity would present itself without being sought as it did, shortly afterwards, in the form of the unexpected telephone call from Lord Rothschild leading to the meeting with Peter Wright which made intelligence history. Apart from the Parliamentary and media furores, the legislation bringing both MI5 and MI6 into official existence, with some degree of openness, might never have happened but for the *Spycatcher* affair which sprang from my meeting with Wright.

Following up Wright's disclosures required many surreptitious meetings with various contacts, usually in country locations, none more intriguing than Birch Grove, the home of Harold Macmillan. When my wife and I arrived there by invitation for tea he was alone in his study in the large house and feeling groggy after a fall that morning when he had hit his head on the fender. However, he could not have been more entertaining and my main purpose was to question him about the suspicions held inside MI5 about their former chief, Sir

Roger Hollis, who had kept Macmillan in ignornace about the Profumo Affair.

'Hollis?' he queried. 'He was a Marine, wasn't he?'

'No, that was Sir Leslie Hollis who was no relation,' I replied.

My chance to pursue the Hollis case seemed to have disappeared as the former Prime Minister quickly raised a less embarrassing issue but, much later, I managed to return to my theme. 'Ah, yes, Hollis! He was a Marine wasn't he?' was all I got out of him on that score, then or ever.

A clandestine country lunch which I arranged with the former Secret Service chief, Sir Arthur Franks, was to cause ructions in the Australian court, in Parliament and in the media when Wright ignominiously revealed it. Fortunately, Wright was unaware of even more intriguing trysts.

Opportunity may have knocked again much more recently in the form of a Christmas card from someone unknown to me and containing exciting new information. My meetings with him could end in events as far-reaching as those following my encounters with Wright, providing I live long enough to complete the research. In any event, with the collapse of Communism, which I always felt contained the seeds of its own destruction, it would seem that I was privileged to enjoy operating throughout the truly piping days of the defence, espionage and intelligence era. During that time, among the socialist left, I developed the reputation for being anti-Communist to the point of eccentricity. The exposure of Communism's appalling legacy has left this eccentric feeling vindicated.

Because of the generation gaps and the inability or unwillingness of the elderly to accept the habits of the young there has always been a tendency for the old to be considered as eccentric and my wife insists that many of the villagers think I am. She might be right. I was considered eccentric at school because I would always rather go fishing on my own than play for the school at cricket. When I walk my dog down the canal and ask the fishermen if I can sniff their maggots the locals must think me odd, though the anglers don't because they know how nostalgic than smell can be. Some villagers have also seemed concerned when I have got my nose down on the pavement while walking my chocolate Labrador, Dido, in an attempt to see what life is really like down there at dog-level. I suppose that it looks infra dig but I have never given a fig about dig. The newspaper serialization of Dido's book, in which she reveals some of my secret oddities, has extended suspicion about my sanity. But perhaps the most authoritative evidence is a remark made by that gifted but self-destructive politician, the late George Brown. After I had berated him for some enormity of behaviour he criticized me for my lack of loyalty. 'We eccentrics should stick together,' he said, testily. Anyway, in a world where interesting contrast is in the discard, with towns and their peoples all looking much the same, there is some virtue in just being different.

From birth, we are all like the man falling out of the skyscraper. With some the time-lapse is longer than for others but we all hit the deck eventually. I take much comfort in telling myself that 'I'm, all right so far', but when asked how I am always reply, 'I think I'm all right' because one never really knows what is going on in the deep, dark recesses of the body. Old age does have the last word but from childhood I have always thought that life is marvellous and that the best is yet to come. It has so far and I intend to continue that consolation with eternal gratitude to the countryside for so many blessings, not the least of which is the good fortune that my children and their families live in villages not far away. We should see more of each other but we all have busy lives to lead and I would not presume to try to pass on any of the accumulated wisdom of my experience because it is manifest that every generation is intent on making the same mistakes again. Further, having continued to make so many myself throughout my maturity, I am reluctant to offer advice. The retrospectoscope is the most illuminating of all instruments but its images usually appear too late to be of constructive value.

Still, as regards my prime ambition to live the life of a country squire as closely as practicable, I think that I can truly tell myself, 'Mission accomplished!'

INDEX